AN ALMOST PERFECT MURDER

"Paramedics. Is this an emergency?" George Reade asked.

"Hello. Yes, this is an emergency," the male resident of the house, forty-two-year-old Chaz Higgs, calmly replied.

"What's the address?" Reade asked.

Higgs answered, "It's in the Meadows housing development. Something's wrong with my wife. She's not breathing. I don't know what happened to her."

"She's not breathing at all?"

"No. Not breathing at all. I'm a critical care nurse and I've already started doing CPR, but I need some help," Higgs replied.

Having dealt with thousands of emergency telephone calls in his five years in the business, Reade knew that characteristically there would be breaks or pauses in the telephone communication between the caller and the 911 operator when a caller was actually giving CPR to the stricken person who's awaiting help. The caller typically wouldn't be able to talk with the 911 operator between giving chest compressions and giving breaths, which appeared to be absent in this case. To Reade, it just hadn't sounded like Higgs was administering CPR. Reade also noticed that there seemed to be a lack of urgency in Higgs's voice. He had seemed a bit too calm to have a relative not breathing. Reade also noted that it had not been his experience to have a loved one in an emergency situation taking the time to give specific directions to their house to the 911 operator. In fact, as best ⬚⬚⬚⬚⬚⬚⬚⬚⬚⬚ this was a first in that regard.

Also by Gary C. King:

AN ALMOST PERFECT MURDER

GARY C. KING

PINNACLE BOOKS

Kensington Publishing Corp.

http:/

Some names have been changed to protect the privacy of individuals connected to this story.

PINNACLE BOOKS are published by

Kensington Publishing Corp.
850 Third Avenue
New York, NY 10022

All Kensington Titles, Imprints, and Distributed Lines are available at special quantity discounts for bulk purchases for sales promotions, premiums, fund-raising, and educational or institutional use. Special book excerpts or customized printings can also be created to fit specific needs. For details, write or phone the office of the Kensington Special Sales Manager: Kensington Publishing Corp., 850 Third Avenue, New York, NY 10022, attn: Special Sales Department, Phone: 1-800-221-2647.

Pinnacle and the P logo Reg. U.S. Pat. & TM Off.

ISBN-13: 978-0-7860-1933-5
ISBN-10: 0-7860-1933-6

First printing: September 2008

10 9 8 7 6 5 4 3 2 1

Printed in the United States of America

For my brother, Donald R. Moody

Why, I can smile, and murder whiles I smile.
—William Shakespeare, Henry VI,
Part 3, Act 3, Scene 2

Poison is in everything, and no thing is without poison.
The dosage makes it either a poison or a remedy.
—Paracelsus, 1493–1541

Preface

poi·son (poi´zen), n. 1. a substance with an inherent property that tends to destroy life or impair health.—*The Random House Dictionary of the English Language, Second Edition, Unabridged*

Poison, in one toxic form or another—as well as murder by poisoning—has been around for a very long time. Until the advent of modern toxicological methods of investigation, especially when that investigation's purpose is to determine the means behind the sudden and unexplained death of an otherwise healthy human being, murder by poisoning was once the preferred method to do away with someone, particularly if the murderer felt that he or she could get away with it. After all, in the past, poisoning had been the easiest way to murder someone. It was popular in England in the nineteenth century, because murder by poisoning was so difficult to prove in a court of law. Thanks largely to modern forensic technology, murdering someone by poisoning isn't nearly as popular today as it was one-hundred-fifty years ago. Nonetheless, people occasionally still believe they can get away with such a murder, as the story that you are about to read will show.

The roots of causing the death of another by poisoning date much further back in history, to the time when tribal hunters and gatherers discovered that ingesting certain plants that they had collected for food caused them to die instead of nourishing their bodies. At some point, these early inhabitants of planet Earth realized that poisoning might be an ideal way to get rid of their enemies without, more often than not, arousing too much suspicion. Evidence of murder by poisoning can easily be traced back to the Roman Empire during the time of Christ, but there is also considerable evidence that poisoning was recognized and used as a method to murder by much earlier civilizations, i.e., the Egyptians, Greeks, Indians, Chinese, and Sumerians, which all used poison as a method to kill. In those earlier times, it was often used as a method of suicide as well.

For example, before making the decision to use an asp, which is a small Egyptian cobra, to take her own life, Cleopatra was known to have made the most of her slaves and prisoners to test out a variety of different deadly concoctions, such as belladonna, henbane, and an early form of strychnine, which was known as *Strychnos nux-vomica*. None of them pleased her, however. The first two, while acting fairly fast once ingested, proved to cause a much too painful and agonizing death, and the latter displeased her because it caused the victim to have convulsions that resulted in often hideous facial distortions at the time of death. Of course, that just wouldn't do for the beautiful Cleopatra. It wasn't until she experimented with the asp's bite, the venom of which brought about a swift, if not tranquil, death, that she felt satisfied that she had found a preferred method to bring about death.

Fast-forward several centuries to fifteenth-century Rome, and the Borgias could be found poisoning anyone who had offended them, or merely because they disliked a certain individual. The Borgias, however, weren't alone in practicing what had become somewhat of an art, albeit a deadly one. Many a head of a European royal family utilized poison to kill his enemies, perceived or real. The process was quite simple. Throw a large party, invite the intended victim(s), and place the deadly material in the victim's food or drink, and voila—death followed a short time later, with no one the wiser.

Catherine de Médicis, the homely princess from Italy, was among the worst of the European royalty to rely upon the deadliness of poisons to achieve her goals: getting rid of those who stood in her way. Shortly after she arrived in France to marry Henry Deux, people began falling sick from mysterious illnesses, and they did not recover. Among her more well-known victims was the Dauphin François, who made the mistake of asking for a glass of water following a tennis match. The reason for his death had nothing to do with the tennis game that he had just played. He was killed because he stood in the way of Henry, the second son of King Francis I, being able to ascend to the throne. With poor François out of the way, Henry, along with his dauphine, Catherine, had suddenly become heir to the throne. She was also remembered for poisoning the Cardinal of Lorraine, whom she had considered an enemy. The cardinal mysteriously took ill and died after handling gold coins that may have been treated with nicotine, the source of which had reportedly been Catherine de Médicis. Nicotine had recently been discovered in the New World, and may have made it into Catherine's hands by then.

By the time the Victorian era came into being, poisons

such as arsenic and strychnine were particularly popular, primarily because they were so easy to obtain and could be used with relative ease in secrecy. For a time, murder by poisoning had become so commonplace, particularly with the rise in popularity of life insurance policies, that poisoning someone for financial gain seemed almost fashionable. In France, for example, arsenic was eventually referred to as "inheritance powder." Poisoning soon became the stuff of popular mystery fiction, which undoubtedly contributed, even in some small way, to the use of poison as a means to get rid of someone during that period, and later.

During the Victorian era, when the science of toxicology and its use in forensic investigations was still in its infancy, it was often difficult to obtain a conviction for someone charged with murder by poisoning. Arsenic, clearly a murderer's favorite at that time, was readily available at the local chemist's shop or hardware store. Many people kept it on hand to kill rats, which had long been a problem in jolly old England, making it little wonder that it would be used on unwanted people, too. Toxicology tests at the time were unreliable, and the findings of scientists of that time period were often disputed. As a result, many people often got away with murder.

Seeing the need to be able to detect the presence of arsenic in the human body, chemist James Marsh set out to devise a scientific test that would serve as an investigative tool during a time when murder by arsenic poisoning had become almost an epidemic in England. White arsenic trioxide powder was odorless, and it could easily be mixed with food or drink for the intended victim to ingest and later fall ill with symptoms similar to cholera, plus it was virtually undetectable in the body. It was during the early 1830s, at a time when chemical analysis could easily detect most mineral compounds, but lacked severely in scientific ability to detect organic poisons in the human body, that Marsh's work made its way to the forefront with regard to the budding field of forensic toxicology.

Without going through all of the scientific details here, suffice it to say that Marsh, combining the experimental work of several of his predecessors with his own, devised a standard test to detect arsenic by mixing the suspect fluid with sulfuric acid and passing it through a u-shaped tube. Even if only minute traces of arsenic were present, the procedure would create arsine gas, which, when ignited, would decay into arsenic and hydrogen. By 1836, with the utilization of Marsh's test, it became increasingly more difficult to get away with committing murder using arsenic.

One of the more famous cases that involved arsenic as the suspected poison was that of Dr. Harvey Crippen, a homeopathic doctor who, although married, was having an affair with his secretary, Ethel Le Neve. Dr. Crippen's wife, Cora, mysteriously disappeared around the end of January 1910. Soon afterward, Ethel Le Neve moved into Crippen's house and basically took over Cora's role, including wearing her clothing and jewelry. After suspicion had been aroused among those who knew Crippen, Scotland Yard began an investigation into his wife's disappearance and questioned the good doctor. He explained that his wife had been cheating on him and had actually left with her lover and had gone to America, where, he said, she died. Fearing that he would be charged with his wife's murder, Crippen fled England on a westbound ship with Cora disguised as his son. However, his freedom was short-lived. He was arrested in Canada after being recognized as a wanted man and was brought back to England, where he stood trial for his wife's murder. According to the story, an investigator had discovered a small piece of human tissue buried in the coal cellar. When it was examined, it was found to contain the toxic compound hyoscine, which Crippen claimed he used in making his homeopathic medications. Even though many people to this day believe that Crippen was innocent of his wife's murder, he was nonetheless convicted and hanged late that same year.

As the twentieth century came into being, it brought with it much new industry and many new toxic agents. Poisoning grew, it seemed, exponentially, as new toxic compounds were created, and, perhaps more important, because the populace in general had become more educated. They could now more easily seek out the information they needed through books, primarily, to do away with someone by poisoning them. Poison suddenly gained the interest of the military, both in Europe and the United States, and insidious compounds were developed that could now kill masses of people on the battlefield.

Mustard gas, for example, was first used by the German Army in 1917, during World War I. Nearly odorless, mustard gas, also known as yperite, was placed into high-explosive shells and fired upon the advancing enemy. Its effects were devastating and horrible. Exposure to it caused the skin to blister, vomiting, blindness, and both internal and external bleeding. It also attacked the bronchial tubes of its victims, and literally stripped away the mucous membrane. Soldiers exposed to it died slow, horrible deaths, often taking up to four or five weeks to finally succumb to its effects. Naturally, mustard gas was not a substance to be used on a rich relative for the inheritance, but it is shown here to illustrate how human beings will seemingly stop at nothing in their efforts to refine the art of killing each other by ever-increasing insidious means.

Returning to the more traditional, one-on-one type of poison that a person might consider using to get rid of a spouse, cyanide became somewhat popular toward the middle of the twentieth century. In addition to being used by real-life spies as a form of suicide during World War II, cyanide also became somewhat popular as a poison that, like arsenic, could easily be placed in the intended victim's food or beverage. One documented case involved a father, bent on collecting his child's life insurance money, who placed cyanide in his child's sherbet. And, of course, who can forget the terror that the cyanide-laced Tylenol, which had been purchased from store shelves in Washington State, had caused?

Of course, there have been a number of high-profile murder cases over the last forty or more years in which legitimate pharmaceutical medicines or drugs were used to kill the intended victims by killers who often had been either a medical professional or someone who was closely aligned to the medical profession. The drug in question in these instances is succinylcholine; for all intents and purposes, it is a pharmaceutical grade version of curare. In these instances, succinylcholine, a powerful muscle relaxer and paralytic drug, was used because its effects, when administered to kill, mimics a heart attack. It can be very difficult to detect if the crime lab doesn't know it is looking for it.

In 1967, Dr. Carl Coppolino, a New Jersey anesthesiologist, was convicted of murdering his wife, Carmela, by using succinylcholine. The good doctor, however, was acquitted of murder in another case in which he had been charged with killing another woman using the drug.

In 1984, Genene Jones, the so-called "Killer Nurse," was convicted of murdering a baby in Texas by injecting the infant with succinylcholine. The infant girl had been injected in the thigh and promptly developed apnea and died. At first, the baby's death was attributed to sudden infant death syndrome, or SIDS, and buried. However, as additional evidence surfaced in that case, and the child's family applied more pressure, the baby's body was exhumed. Muscle tissue from the baby's thigh, kidneys, and a portion of her liver were examined. After analysis from newly developed toxicological tests, it was determined that succinylcholine was present in the muscular tissue, as well as the organs that were examined.

In 1991, Dr. William Sybers, who had been a medical examiner in Panama City, Florida, was accused of killing his wife with a lethal injection of the potent drug so that he could be with his mistress. Although convicted, his conviction was reversed and he later pleaded guilty to manslaughter in a deal with prosecutors. And who can forget Dr. Michael Swango, dubbed "Dr. Death"? He was suspected of killing as many as thirty-five to sixty people in various locations during the 1980s and 1990s, using succinylcholine that had been mixed with another drug. Swango ended up pleading guilty to three murders. There was also the case of Efren Saldivar, a California respiratory therapist who dubbed himself the "angel of death," who, after his arrest in 2001, confessed to killing in excess of fifty people using a variety of different drugs, including succinylcholine.

As a testimonial to the difficulty of determining that succinylcholine was used in any given case, as well as the difficulty of obtaining a conviction for those cases that actually go to trial, one can examine the 2002 case of Richard Williams, a former nurse at a veterans hospital, who was charged with ten counts of first-degree murder involving patients at the Truman Memorial Veterans Hospital in Columbia, Missouri, where he worked in 1992. In each of the cases in which Williams had been charged, the prosecution alleged that succinylcholine had been used. However, there were significant questions concerning a relatively new technology that its creators claimed could detect succinylcholine in a suspected victim's tissue samples. These concerns were brought to light and resulted in the dismissal of the charges that had been brought against Williams.

And the list goes on and on, bringing us to the case at hand, that of William Charles "Chaz" Higgs, a critical care nurse who had been accused of murdering his wife, Nevada state controller Kathy Augustine. Like many of Higgs's predecessors in the medical profession who thought that they could get away with murder, Higgs likely thought that he could, too. It's also possible that he has read about some of the aforementioned cases—there have been volumes written on them. Higgs's case was similar to some of the other murder-by-poisoning cases in a few respects. As in some of the other cases in which the intended victim was a spouse, Higgs's chosen victim was also his wife, and a toxic substance was used to bring about her death. However, unlike some of the other victims in the cases mentioned, Chaz Higgs's wife was a strong, powerful woman in a position of authority and influence whose untimely death demanded, along with her family, that justice be served.

Part I

The Investigation

Chapter 1

The city of Reno, Nevada, the seat of Washoe County, is pleasantly situated along the banks of the Truckee River, smack-dab in the middle of where Interstate 80, which runs east and west, and U.S. Highway 395, which runs north and south, intersect. Known as "the Biggest Little City in the World" since 1928, when the two-lane highway that enabled travelers to get across Donner Summit to California was paved, Reno has long been the redheaded stepchild of legalized gambling in the Silver State. Located in the northwestern corner of the state and barely a stone's throw from scenic Lake Tahoe, with all its splendor and idyllic beauty, Reno is less than an hour's drive from the recently relocated *and* reopened world-famous Mustang Ranch. A longtime thorn in the side of at least one state legislator, the brothel is a business that nonetheless captures an attractive share of tourist money from men who enjoy cavorting with prostitutes, some of whom come to Reno for that purpose only. Reno is often viewed as being more peaceful and adorned with greater variations of scenic beauty than its glitzier asphalt jungle cousin, Las Vegas, a day's drive to the south. Sometimes viewed as a miniature version of Las Vegas because it shares many of the same amenities as its cousin, such as resort hotels, casinos, buffets, and wedding chapels, Reno is also a major warehouse and distribution center for the region. Named in honor of Major General Jesse L. Reno, a Union officer who was killed during the Civil War, the city has grown steadily since the arrival of the railroad in 1868—the same year that it was founded—to become the state's third-largest city, behind Las Vegas and Henderson, with a population greater than 210,000.

Situated some 4,400 feet above sea level in a high desert valley, Reno is conveniently located twenty-six miles from the state capital, Carson City, which is also home to the U.S. Mint. Many of the state's legislators and other elected officials, as well as state employees, make their home in Reno and commute to the state capital. Its growing economy in recent years has resulted in considerable new home construction throughout the metro area, and the so-called progress has brought with it a sizeable increase in its real estate prices. Year-round recreational activities, such as fishing, water and snow skiing, swimming, and parasailing, to name a few, abound, and over time, Reno has expanded upon its cultural base in an attempt to provide outlets besides gambling for its residents. There is an art museum there, a pops orchestra, a botanical garden and arboretum, and Reno is home to the Nevada Shakespeare Company. Unfortunately, Reno is also known as the setting for one of the most diabolical and cold-blooded, not to mention cruel, murders the state has ever seen.

A light summer breeze blew gently through the Meadows subdivision, a few miles southeast of Reno, less than an hour after sunrise on Saturday, July 8, 2006. At a pleasant 64 degrees, it was partly cloudy that morning, but there was no chance of rain. With an average of only 4.5 inches of precipitation annually, it doesn't rain much, ever. From the right vantage point, portions of the Sierra Nevada mountain range could be seen jutting above the horizon to the west. Birds had come to life and could be heard chirping their early-morning music throughout this relatively new, somewhat upscale community, where many young and middle-aged professionals and their families made their home. The houses were mostly of the cookie-cutter variety that developers seemed so keen on exporting in recent years from Southern California to their neighbors in nearby states. The original purchase price tag ran about $300,000. The price of the same house in another major West Coast city, such as San Francisco or Los Angeles, would easily cost twice that much. The location was close to the two major freeways that run through Reno, making it an ideal location for those who work in the city or commute to the state capital despite the bumper-to-bumper traffic during rush hour. The houses, typically close to one another, were separated by a mix of well-placed green grass and desert landscaping or, in some cases, an attractive mix of both. The close proximity of the dwellings also made it easier for neighbors to know each other's business, but on the upside, it also made it easier for residents to look out for one another.

Otter Way, located just off South Meadows Parkway and U.S. Highway 395, was a typically quiet street within the Meadows subdivision. Most of the single-family houses on Otter Way were built in 1999, and the community sold out before the houses were even completed, primarily because the location was ideal for those who wanted to enjoy suburban living. Most of the people who live in this community seem to fit into it well; they mesh comfortably with each other, for the most part. One couple who lived on Otter Way, however, didn't quite fit the mold. One neighbor dispassionately characterized them as somewhat of an odd couple, while others chose to keep their thoughts and opinions about their neighbors to themselves. No matter what people thought of that couple, this day in early July would be one that the residents of the Meadows subdivision would not easily forget.

George Reade, a communications supervisor for the Regional Emergency Medical Services Authority (REMSA), was on duty at 6:43 A.M. when the call about a person not breathing was received through Reno's 911 emergency communications system. Reade's job consisted of overseeing the day-to-day operations of the communications center, and one of his duties included taking some of the emergency telephone calls. Reade, who had been in the supervisory role for two years, had also worked as a communications specialist for that company for three years. On any given day, Reade might take a call involving an auto accident, a cardiac arrest, or even an occasional violent crime. It wasn't unusual for him to work through thirty to fifty calls per day. Even though the phone lines had been busy most of the night, none of the morning or previous evening's calls could top the one Reade took at 6:43 A.M.

"Paramedics. Is this an emergency?" Reade asked.

"Hello. Yes, this is an emergency," the male resident of the house, forty-two-year-old Chaz Higgs, calmly replied.

"What's the address?" Reade asked.

Higgs answered, "It's in the Meadows housing development. Something's wrong with my wife. She's not breathing. I don't know what happened to her."

"She's not breathing at all?"

"No. Not breathing at all. I'm a critical care nurse and

I've already started doing CPR, but I need some help," Higgs replied.

"Okay. We're on the way. What's the phone number that you're calling from?"

Higgs gave him the phone number.

"And you're with her right now?"

"Yes."

"And you're currently doing CPR?"

"Yes."

"You're over by Ripple Way?"

"Yeah. There's more than one of the same street name. So, if you come into the housing development, immediately turn right and the road will veer around to the left, and we're on the third court on the right. There's a dark blue Dodge Dakota pickup in the driveway. If I hear you coming, I'll come outside."

Reade instructed Higgs to put the phone down without breaking the connection just in case he needed to provide additional information or to ask for more specific help during the interim before paramedics could get there. Higgs indicated that he would continue administering cardiopulmonary resuscitation (CPR) until the paramedics arrived.

Having dealt with thousands of emergency telephone calls in his five years in the business, Reade knew that characteristically there would be breaks or pauses in the telephone communication between the caller and the 911 operator when a caller was actually giving CPR to the stricken person who's awaiting help. The caller typically wouldn't be able to talk with the 911 operator between giving chest compressions and giving breaths, which would thus account for the characteristic breaks in the conversation, which appeared to be absent in this case. To Reade, it just hadn't sounded like Higgs was administering CPR. Reade also noticed that there seemed to be a lack of urgency in Higgs's voice. He had seemed a bit too calm to have a relative not breathing. Reade also noted that it had not been his experience to have a loved one in an emergency situation taking the time to give specific directions to their house to the 911 operator. In fact, as best as he could recall, this was a first in that regard.

Seven minutes later, at 6:50 A.M., the first shrieks of the REMSA vehicle's siren broke the early-morning stillness on Otter Way. Benjamin Pratt, employed as a firefighter and paramedic for the Tahoe-Douglas Fire Protection District, also worked for REMSA on a part-time basis and was driving unit 310 that morning. His training as a paramedic consisted of nine months of course work at an accredited institution, 180 hours of clinical time in the ambulance, and 280 hours of clinical time in the hospital working with nurses and doctors. Accompanied by his partner, Manny Fuentes, the paramedics knew that they were responding to a lights-and-siren cardiac arrest call, a Code 3. When théy arrived on Otter Way, Pratt radioed Reade with his "310 on scene" message. A man, whom they had seen from a distance of nearly two streets away, was out in front of the house, waving them onto the curb sidewalk area.

The Reno Fire Department (RFD) responded as well and was right behind Pratt and Fuentes when they arrived. Units from the Reno Police Department (RPD) arrived moments later. The first police unit was on the scene at 6:52 A.M. They had by now determined that they were rushing to the home that Kathy Marie Augustine, fifty, Nevada state controller, an elected official, shared with her husband. Neighbors, some of whom were awakened by all of the noise and activity, came outside of their homes to try and see what all the fuss was about.

When Pratt and Fuentes climbed out of their vehicle, they were followed into the house by four firefighters from the other vehicle. The fire department typically comes along on calls of this nature to assist breaking in the door if no one answers, to perform general "housekeeping," like cleaning up after the paramedics, who don't always have the time to clean up because of having to rush the injured or gravely ill person off to a hospital, or to simply help provide manpower in moving the patient when assistance is needed.

Higgs calmly told them that his wife was in the back room. He ushered them through the living area, past the kitchen, and led them through the 1,100-square-foot house to its only bedroom, where Kathy lay motionless on the couple's queen-size bed. The REMSA paramedics immediately initiated efforts to resuscitate the lifeless, middle-aged woman.

Unable to find a pulse, the paramedics carefully removed her from the bed and placed her on the floor, where they continued CPR efforts. For CPR to be most effective, the person needs to be placed on a hard, stable surface; this way, when a paramedic is doing chest compressions, the blood circulates more effectively. The bed, they knew, would be much too soft to attain the results they desired. Next they inserted an oropharyngeal ring, a device that looks like a curved piece of plastic, into Kathy's mouth and underneath her tongue. Its purpose is to pull the tongue out of the way to open up the airway as much as possible before inserting a piece of plastic tubing through the vocal cords, a process known as intubation, to provide a mechanism by which a patient can breathe. As they continued with the CPR, one of the paramedics started an IV and began administering a variety of medications that included epinephrine and atropine because Kathy was still a systole, a flatliner. Their effort, of course, was to get Kathy's heart beating again. Eventually, following a second round of medications, they detected a weak pulse and each suddenly felt a glimmer of hope that she might survive. Forcing Kathy to breathe artificially, the paramedics loaded her into a waiting ambulance. By 7:09 A.M., Pratt and Fuentes, upbeat and excited because they had literally brought someone back from the dead, were rushing Kathy Augustine, who was still unconscious, to the South Meadows branch of the Washoe Medical Center, where she bypassed the hospital's triage system and was admitted almost immediately through the emergency room (ER). They had managed to keep her heart beating while en route to the hospital.

Upon their arrival at Kathy Augustine's home minutes earlier, and amid all of the chaos of the paramedics working feverishly to try and save Kathy's life, RPD officers Steve Mussell and Joe Proffitt had managed to speak to Higgs about the situation. Higgs had been standing outside the front door of the house while paramedics had been working to revive his wife inside the home, which many people who were involved in the case later admitted had been unusual. Normally, the spouse or other close family members remain inside, close to the scene of activity, out of concern for their loved one, where they can see what is going on, and to be available to answer any questions that the emergency workers might need to ask. That hadn't been the case with Higgs, however, but his unusual behavior hadn't been noted until later. Officers Mussell and Proffitt weren't there to make any judgments at that point, but were there to collect information for later assessment as to its value. While it would be difficult to characterize their exchanges with Higgs as a formal interview, they did obtain a few details of the time period that led up to Higgs placing the 911 call. The information that they obtained at this point was sketchy at best.

In response to their questions, Higgs explained to Mussell and Proffitt that he had been alone in the house with his wife since the prior evening. He claimed that he had awakened early that morning and had left Kathy sleeping in their bed. He explained that when he returned to their bedroom a short time later, he discovered that his wife had stopped breathing. He suggested to the two officers that his wife had a heart condition that might have caused her to stop breathing. He didn't go into detail about her condition at that time, but later said that his wife had been complaining recently of a stomachache and heartburn.

Almost immediately upon arrival at the South Meadows hospital, after Pratt and Fuentes removed Kathy's near-lifeless body from the ambulance and wheeled her into the emergency room, Marlene Swanbeck, a nurse and former coworker of Chaz Higgs's, and other medical personnel, including nurse Chris McCabe, obtained blood and urine samples from Kathy to assist in the diagnosis of her medical condition. Both of the samples were retained by the Washoe Medical Center's laboratory—some were preserved just in case they were needed later.

At one point that morning, Swanbeck encountered Higgs at the hospital. She noticed that his demeanor seemed calm. He did not appear excited, and he seemed to be disengaged from the crisis of the situation. She noted that he was not sobbing, that there were no tears, and that he hadn't asked any questions about the condition of his wife. She briefly remembered her past encounters with Higgs, when he often spoke of his intention to leave Kathy. She also remembered how he had referred to her in some very derogatory terms. Her goal at this point, however, was to provide the best treatment possible to Kathy in an effort to save her life and to not sit in judgment of her former coworker.

However, within an hour of their arrival at the medical center, the doctor in charge of the team of nurses and doctors attending to Kathy at South Meadows made the decision that Kathy would have to be moved to Washoe Medical Center's main hospital because of a potential heart problem. As a result of the doctor's decision, Pratt and Fuentes, still at the hospital with Kathy, loaded the patient back into their ambulance and rushed her to the main hospital. Chaz Higgs accompanied them in the ambulance to Washoe Main, riding in the front passenger seat.

The official story released to news media outlets at this point was that Kathy had suffered a massive heart attack and had been admitted to the hospital's intensive care unit (ICU) in critical condition. When asked by reporters what he thought might have brought on the heart attack, Higgs cited pressure over the campaign for state treasurer that she had filed for in May 2006 for the upcoming August 15 Republican primary election. Her final term as state controller was coming to an end, and she had set her sights on bigger and better things.

"Stress," Higgs said. "I think that is probably the factor. She has been complaining about it during the whole campaign."

Higgs stated that although Kathy knew that the campaign for state treasurer would be an "uphill battle to win," she nonetheless had been very determined and had been using her evenings and weekends to win support after putting in full days at the office as state controller.

Responding to questions about whether Kathy's campaign would be able to continue, Higgs told reporters that his wife was in a coma and on life-support systems.

"We won't know the full prognosis until tomorrow,"

Higgs said. "Right now, our primary concern is her health. We aren't thinking about campaigning, or politics, or anything like that."

Her opponents for the late-summer election expressed similar concerns.

"We wish her a full and speedy recovery," said Ryan Erwin, campaign manager for Mark DeStefano, a Nevada businessman who also sought the powerful, coveted position of state treasurer. "However, we know very few specifics about her condition at this time. It would be premature to discuss any campaign-related decisions."

For the next three days, Kathy Augustine remained comatose and lay virtually lifeless in her hospital bed, kept alive by artificial means, as family members from Las Vegas and California traveled to Reno to be with her at her bedside. However, despite the best efforts of everyone involved, Kathy Augustine died at 4:40 P.M., on Tuesday, July 11, 2006, in Washoe Medical Center's ICU without ever regaining consciousness. Her husband, parents, daughter, stepchildren, and other relatives were with her when she died. Her body, along with the blood and urine samples that were obtained upon her admission to the hospital, was promptly turned over to the Washoe County Coroner's Office.

Her cause of death was released to the news media as complications from the massive heart attack that she had suffered over the weekend, even though the definitive autopsy had not yet been performed. Since she had no immediately known history of prior serious medical problems, her sudden death was a shock to nearly everyone who knew her and worked with her. News of her death quickly reverberated throughout state political circles. At a hastily called press conference, many of the state's political leaders expressed their shock and sadness over Kathy's sudden passing.

"We are all deeply saddened by the distressing news of

someone so young and vibrant as Kathy Augustine passing away so unexpectedly," Governor Kenny Guinn said. "On behalf of so many people in our state who knew Kathy and appreciated her dedication and hard work as controller, I offer her family our heartfelt sympathy."

"We are all saddened by Kathy's unexpected death," chimed Senate Majority Leader Bill Raggio, a Republican from Reno. "She should not be remembered for any failings, but for her many years of public service as an assemblyman, a state senator, and two terms as state controller. Even her critics have to recognize she had great talent, humor, and was very dedicated to the state."

Dallas Augustine, Kathy's daughter, made a statement to the media on behalf of her family, shortly after her mother's death was announced.

"She was a great leader, mother, daughter, wife, and friend who will be greatly missed," her daughter tearfully said. "She will always be remembered for her strong commitment to her work, family, friends, and causes. Please remember her that way."

That same day, Detective David Jenkins, a thirty-year veteran of the Reno Police Department, was sitting behind his desk. He was shuffling paperwork and contemplating going home for the day when a note with a woman's name and telephone number was brought to him, along with a message that indicated that the caller possessed information that could be relevant regarding the cause of Kathy Augustine's medical condition. Jenkins knew from experience that suspicious death investigations, even the more simplistic ones, always took considerable time, particularly at a case's outset, as well as a lot of paperwork, to complete. Already tired at the end of what had been a long day, Jenkins knew that he needed to get his second wind, so to speak. In keeping with his reputation of dogged determination at solving crimes, the detective somehow instinctively knew that he would not be going home anytime soon.

Chapter 2

That same afternoon, while the state politicians and Kathy Augustine's family members were busy holding a press conference with reporters from all over the state, Detective David Jenkins picked up the telephone and arranged to see the person who had called in the potential tip earlier that day. As it turned out, the tipster was a traveling nurse, Kim Ramey, an attractive, thirty-something blonde who had worked with Chaz Higgs at his place of employment, Carson-Tahoe Regional Health Care, in Carson City. A critical care nurse since 1999, whose specialty was in open-heart recovery, particularly for patients who had gone through open-heart surgery, such as a heart bypass, Ramey specified that she had worked with Higgs on Friday, July 7, 2006, one day before Kathy was stricken with a "heart attack." Although suspicion about Kathy's untimely death had already been hanging in the air, Ramey's initial telephone call—which had started out simple enough when she had said, "You know, I think you need to know something"—tipped the scales that would eventually open up a full-blown homicide investigation.

"She had some very serious concerns that Ms. Augustine's

medical condition may have been the result of someone having intentionally administered a drug to her," Jenkins recalled as he recounted his first conversation with Ramey when he returned her call about four hours later. Jenkins, who had been assigned to the robbery/homicide unit in the detective division for the past seventeen years, had a gut feeling that this would be quite a challenging case.

When Jenkins met with Ramey, he began by routinely taking down her personal information and how she had come to know Chaz Higgs. She had been working the day shift on July 7, and had arrived for work a few minutes before 7:00 A.M. When she reported to her unit, the open-heart unit, her supervisor told her that she would be "floating" over to the intensive care unit. She explained that as the patient load for the day goes up or down, nurses are often shifted from one unit to another to ensure that the hospital has the correct number of staff assigned to a particular unit. In her case, as a critical care open-heart nurse, she would be able to float to the ICU, but an ICU nurse would not be able to float to the open-heart unit due to the fact that she wouldn't possess the knowledge and skills of that specialty. Ramey had been attending two patients that morning, one of which the doctors and hospital staff were trying to determine whether the patient had viral or bacterial spinal meningitis. She met Higgs, and the circumstances of their speaking came about when she had asked him to assist her, and to bring her supplies and medical equipment that she had needed throughout the day.

She explained that during casual conversation at work that day, she had immediately sized him up as a "player." Going through a divorce herself, she had easily spotted the trait in Higgs and he, at one point, had said that he was going to leave his wife. Sensing that it wouldn't be long before he might try to hit on her, she told Higgs that she had a boyfriend and that the two of them were going to be moving to Richmond, Virginia, in the near future. She felt that if she divulged some of her personal information, such as having a boyfriend, it might serve to put to rest any intentions he might have been considering.

Being a listener, one of the traits of her profession, she had also sensed that Higgs was full of anger. She tried to find out where it was coming from, by listening to him throughout the day. It hadn't taken long for her to discern that the anger she perceived he was harboring appeared to center around his wife, Kathy. Higgs explained who Kathy was—stating that she was a high-profile person who was currently the state controller and was running for the position of state treasurer. Ramey had interrupted him a number of times to explain that none of what he was saying meant anything to her because she wasn't from the Reno-Tahoe-Carson City area; she hadn't been there long and she wasn't planning to stay. She was a self-chosen "traveler" nurse who did not work directly for a particular hospital, but instead moved around a lot and worked as an independent contractor at hospitals in virtually any area for durations lasting only a few weeks to stays as long as several months.

At one point, she said, they had engaged in a brief chat that had begun innocently enough when they had referenced the local case of Darren Roy Mack, forty-five, a pawnshop owner who at that time had become the subject of an international manhunt after being charged with the alleged stabbing death of his thirty-nine-year-old estranged wife, Charla, in their garage. Apparently angry over his divorce settlement, Mack was also sought for the alleged sniper shooting and attempted murder of Washoe County Family Court judge Chuck Weller. Ramey told Jenkins that it was during their brief exchange about this case that Higgs had remarked that Mack had been "stupid" to have killed his wife in the manner that was being alleged. When Ramey had looked at him quizzically, Higgs purportedly told her that there was a much better way to commit murder.

Higgs reportedly told Ramey while he was sitting at the unit's u-shaped nursing station that if he had intended to kill someone, he would have administered "succinylcholine" to the person because the "succs," as it is more commonly referred to among medical professionals, is virtually undetectable in a postmortem examination. Ramey reiterated to Jenkins that Higgs had said that he was undergoing marital problems with his wife, and that he planned on ending his relationship with her. At the time, Ramey had thought that he had meant that he was going to divorce his wife, but now, after Kathy's death, she wasn't so sure what he had meant.

"He said that if you want to kill someone, the way to do it is to hit 'em with a little succs, because they can't trace it postmortem," Ramey recalled. Afterward, she said, he had made a gesture like he was going to administer an injection. "Wow, Chaz, that's too much anger to carry around," she added, explaining that Higgs's comment had made the hair on her arm stand up.

She explained that Higgs had made her feel very uncomfortable, and that it had made her "skin crawl" when he talked to her about how he would kill someone if he wanted to get rid of them. She reiterated that he had frequently talked about leaving his wife that day, and that she had heard him swear at her over the telephone. She claimed that Higgs referred to Kathy as a "fucking bitch." She said that he had referred to her at various times throughout the day as a "fucking stalker," and he seemed intent on painting an unflattering picture of her as a vicious, mean, and hateful person. At one point, he had characterized his wife as "psycho," she said. She claimed to have detected anger and rage as the dominant emotions emanating from Chaz Higgs most of that day.

At another point that day, Ramey said, she had been within earshot of Higgs while he was using the telephone in the middle of the unit, a busy area. She presumed that he had been talking with his wife when she said that she heard him say, "I will fuckin' talk to you when I get home," among other things. Ramey said that she had felt that Higgs's telephone conversation and the language he used was inappropriate, considering the hospital setting. When she asked him about the conversation later, he purportedly told her that Kathy had discovered that he had opened a separate bank account at Wells Fargo and had placed only his name on the account. He was particularly astounded because he had been assured by the bank employee that since the account was only in his name, there would not be any way that she could find out about it.

Since Ramey was leaving town in only a few days, Ramey's coworkers had planned a going-away party for her at a nearby restaurant that evening. Since it was a Friday night, and sensing that perhaps Higgs might benefit from a party atmosphere, Ramey said that she had invited him to attend the party. Besides, although he was new and still on probation at the hospital, Ramey considered him a member of the team. Higgs declined, however, and purportedly said: "I'm just going to fucking go home and tell her." Ramey said that she presumed he meant that he was going to tell his wife that he wanted a divorce.

Even though he had seemed full of anger and rage about wanting to get rid of his wife, Ramey had not initially given much thought to Higgs's remarks until after she had learned that his wife had been found unconscious in her home by him, and had been taken to the hospital in grave condition. She said that after she had become aware of Kathy's situation, she had consulted with a physician, Dr. Richard Seher, who was aware of the circumstances related to Kathy's hospitalization, and that Dr. Seher had encouraged Ramey to contact the police department.

Ramey said that she waited until July 11 to report her encounter with Chaz Higgs because of her plans to leave town in a few days. She was returning to Virginia to finalize a divorce, which she had been going through for more than two years, and she was hoping that the police would just arrest Higgs without any assistance from her. When that hadn't happened, she decided after consulting with others that she needed to come forward with her information.

After taking Ramey's statement, Jenkins, now intensely interested in what had happened to Kathy Augustine, began doing his homework to learn more about the drug succinylcholine. The first thing he did was to go to the Washoe Medical Center in the hope that he could speak with a medical professional to determine whether or not the information he had received from Kim Ramey was even credible or plausible.

Among the many things he learned was that if used correctly by a medical professional, succinylcholine's medical uses include temporarily paralyzing respiratory muscles to allow the easy insertion of breathing tubes. However, if used improperly or with malicious intent, it can be deadly. If injected into the body in larger doses, it can cause organ failure and death. He also learned that it dissipates quickly from a person's bloodstream, leaving behind few traces. The person who dies as a result of succinylcholine being misused goes through horrific and agonizing pain and suffering after the drug begins to take effect, before succumbing to unconsciousness and death—all the while being able to stare helplessly at the person who had administered the injection.

After receiving theoretical explanations from medical personnel regarding the possible link between Kathy's death and succinylcholine, his newly formed suspicions were verified. Succinylcholine could very well have resulted in the medical condition that had led to Kathy's death. Jenkins was also told that the initial medical examinations upon Kathy's admission to the hospital had not revealed any evidence of heart disease, which would typically be associated with a sudden and unexpected heart attack.

The next day, Wednesday, July 12, 2006, pathologist Dr. Ellen Clark performed a definitive autopsy on Kathy's body with Detective Jenkins in attendance. Dr. Clark was a doctor of medicine with specialties in anatomic, clinical, and forensic pathology. She had received her doctorate of medicine degree from Texas Tech University in 1984. Afterward, she participated in accredited residency training in combined anatomic and clinical pathology at the University of Texas, in San Antonio, until 1987, when she transferred to the University of New Mexico, where she continued her studies of combined anatomic and clinical pathology and subspecialized in forensic pathology. She completed her course of study there in 1989. That same year, she obtained the position of forensic and hospital pathologist with Sierra Pathology Associates—her current job in Reno—a private company that performs autopsies for the Washoe County Coroner's Office, where she has been ever since.

The day-to-day duty of a forensic pathologist involves the evaluation of disease and trauma and is characteristically broken down into two major categories: anatomic pathology and clinical pathology. The former involves diagnosis, as well as performing tests on solid tissue that may range from single cells smeared on a slide to intraoperative biopsies and, ultimately, to the autopsy examination. The latter is involved in the designing, performing, and interpretation of tests on body fluids, such as blood and urine. Forensic pathology, it should be noted, is the subspecialty within the area of medicine that attempts to unravel the mystery behind sudden, unexplained, unexpected, and often particularly violent death cases.

At the autopsy's conclusion, Dr. Clark told Jenkins that she had not found any evidence of coronary artery disease or heart disease, which could be attributed to a sudden and unexpected heart attack. Dr. Clark explained to the detective that she did find, however, "two punctate areas of discoloration" that had "an overall configuration in appearance that would be consistent with needle punctures or injection sites." The needle injection sites that she deemed suspicious were located on Kathy's left buttock in the left upper hip region. Dr. Clark also explained that she performed what is known as a "cut-down" of the suspected injection site, which is a straight surgical incision with a scalpel or other similar instrument that allows examination of the skin and tissue beneath the surface injury. She explained that the cut-down revealed a very narrow track of bleeding into the tissue directly beneath the suspected needle puncture wounds. The same procedure was followed for the other wounds present in Kathy's body that were obviously associated with therapeutic or IV tubing, and so forth. She explained that the suspected injection wounds in the buttocks area were significant because of the allegations that were being made that Kathy had been given a drug that had been injected, and because the buttocks injection site did not correspond to any of Kathy's medical records as a therapeutic injury.

Dr. Clark's findings regarding the internal examination showed that Kathy's brain was swollen, which can be associated with decreased blood flow or decreased oxygen to the brain. Although the examination of Kathy's heart, she explained to Jenkins, did not reveal any evidence of the typical hardening of the arteries or blocking of the arteries, which is so often associated with heart attacks, she concluded that there was some evidence of a degenerative change within one of the valves of Kathy's heart, the mitral valve, which allows blood to pass out of the large muscular chamber on the left side of the heart into the main circulatory system. Dr. Clark's determination was that the mitral valve degeneration was minimal, however, and was not likely the cause of Kathy's death.

Dr. Clark did not immediately list a cause of death. She told Jenkins that she would have to wait until all of the toxicology tests had been conducted on Kathy's urine and blood samples to finalize her determination.

When Jenkins followed up with the hospital and examined the medical records that had been generated during Kathy's hospital stay, he found nothing that could account for an injection that had been made by hospital staff on her left buttock, which corroborated the autopsy findings. In other words, no one at either of the hospitals had given Kathy an injection at the site of her left buttock or even in close proximity to it.

Based on what he knew so far, Jenkins had the now-frozen urine samples, which had been collected from Kathy on July 8, 2006, forwarded to the FBI's forensic laboratory in Quantico, Virginia, where it would be carefully and thoroughly analyzed for traces of succinylcholine. Jenkins also took steps to confirm the details of Higgs's employment at the time of Kathy's demise and found that he had access to a variety of drugs, as any nurse would, including succinylcholine, as well as the syringes and needles needed to administer them, during his tenure at Carson-Tahoe Hospital.

As the buzz circulated that Kathy's husband was somehow involved in her death, many people began asking why Chaz Higgs would want her dead. Jenkins later publicly stated that sometimes a murder doesn't make much sense until all of the details have been sorted out.

"Well, if you take the stand that every murder has to be rational," Jenkins told CBS News, "I think you'll be disappointed. All we know for sure is that there was a failing relationship, a lot of acrimony between the two of them, and some allegations of infidelity. That's the ingredients, many times, for violence."

At this point of the investigation, with nothing sufficient enough to rule murder in or out, Jenkins knew that he had to dig deeper. Although his nagging cop's instinct told him that Kathy Augustine had been murdered, officially he was still investigating only a suspicious death. Thus began Jenkins's case of alleged first-degree murder, which would become known as Case Number CR06-2876. He had no idea yet where his investigation would take him. But he would know soon enough.

Chapter 3

Aside from her family and closest friends, Kathy Marie Alfano Augustine was not well-liked by many people, politically or otherwise. She was known to have an abrasive personality, and it was generally known that she frequently yelled at people, particularly the employees in her office at the state capital. She also knew how to play the game of dirty tricks, and many said that she played it well—nearly as well as Richard Nixon, who likely would have been proud of her. She was known around the office as "the bitch," a term that her husband, Chaz, was also known to use when referring to her, according to witnesses. Confident and positive despite the many obstacles that she faced in the political arena, Kathy recognized that she was tough and she was damned proud of it. Her story was one of power, ambition, and enemies. According to RPD investigators, it was also a story of murder—her own. Kathy's murder could have been the perfect crime, had it not been for a single slip of the tongue.

At fifty, Kathy Augustine was tall and attractive, a big-boned blonde with a clear complexion and near-perfect teeth. Although she attempted to smile a lot, as most politicians do, her smile frequently seemed to be forced and, some would say, often did not show in her eyes. No one seemed to know for sure the level or degree of unhappiness that many felt she was endeavoring to mask, but speculation ran high that she was trying to cover up marital issues. Struggling to maintain the façade that her marriage to Chaz Higgs was a solid union, those on the outside looking in could see that trouble was brewing on the horizon; they thought that the marriage wouldn't last. The stresses in her life had begun to show in the lines on her face, and through her growing impatience in dealing with even simple matters. No one, however, even in their wildest dreams, ever imagined that it would be her death that would end it.

Born Kathy Marie Alfano on May 29, 1956, a Tuesday, in Los Angeles, California, to a good, respectable Italian-American family. Kathy, the oldest of three children, was raised in the suburbs of Southern California by loving and caring parents, who taught her and her two brothers strong personal values, such as to always be honest, caring, and giving. Her parents, Phil and Kay Alfano, still reside in northern Orange County.

Tuesday's child is full of grace. If there's one thing that Kathy possessed, at least from an outward, physical perspective, it was grace, and it exhibited itself in the form of poise, refinement, and beauty despite her often bullish character. Her family always seemed very proud of her, and they nearly always supported her in whatever she chose to do. In her youth, she seemed to fulfill all their hopes and dreams, and by the time she finished high school, they firmly believed that she would turn out the way most parents hope and pray their children will. She had given them no reason to believe otherwise. However, somewhere along the path of life, the values that had been encouraged by her family seemed to partially disappear as she became hardened and, some would say, ruthless in her dealings with others. It may have been the failed marriages, or it may have been the taste of political power that had caused her to take the turn at the fork in the road that led her down a different path from where she had started. Whatever it was, something had changed her and turned her into the ruthless, hard-nosed person that she had become at the time of her death.

Kathy's passion for politics began while still in high school. Always pushing herself to her limits, while all the other kids were out having fun, Kathy took her studies seriously. Instead of partying during the weekend nights, Kathy was ambitious and driven. She spent much of her spare time studying and doing her homework, and for a high-school student, she took the word "tenacious" to a new level. She also participated in various aspects of the student body programs, and would graduate salutatorian for all of her hard work.

Prior to graduation from high school, she was awarded the much coveted Lyndon B. Johnson Internship Grant and worked in Washington, D.C., as a congressional intern for the 38th District of California. According to her mother, it was the internship that had cemented her interest in politics, hook, line, and sinker. She had become so engrossed in political affairs and principles that there was no chance of her ever shaking loose, even if she had wanted.

Following graduation from high school and after completing the short internship during her first year in college, Kathy went on to earn a bachelor's degree in political science from Occidental College, a small, no-nonsense private liberal arts institution conveniently tucked away about halfway between Pasadena and West Hollywood. After Occidental, she went on to earn a master's in public administration (an MPA) from California State University at Long Beach.

After receiving her Master of Public Administration, Kathy went to work for Delta Airlines. Her first job there was in crew scheduling, but later she took a position as a flight attendant. This was back in the days when a female flight attendant was still known as a stewardess. She seemed to enjoy flying back and forth across the country, but it soon became clear that her being gone all the time had begun to take its toll on her first marriage, which was short-lived and ended in divorce. According to her brother Phil, Kathy seemed naïve in handling her relationships, particularly when they involved marriage. But she married again and, like with the first marriage, she found herself in divorce court a short time later. Those close to her seemed to think that it was the job that made it difficult for her to hang on to a husband, and while it certainly may have been a contributing factor, the problem lay deeper in reality.

Her brother Phil characterized her as being too trusting of others at times, which often ended up with her dating, and marrying, guys of questionable repute, often on impulse, only to have deep regrets later. She soon became a single mother and found herself raising a daughter, alone. Like all challenges that came her way, she took the responsibility in stride and did the best that she could.

In 1988, when Kathy was thirty-two, the job took her to Las Vegas, where she met Delta Airlines pilot Charles Augustine, sixteen years her senior. The two instantly hit it off, and after a year of dating they decided to get married. Charles, with three children of his own from two previous marriages, legally adopted Kathy's young daughter, Dallas, and they all lived together in a large house in the upscale Huntridge Circle community in Las Vegas.

At first Kathy's marriage to Charles Augustine seemed to be a good fit. For several years they lived the good life in Sin City and seemed truly happy, and as Las Vegas's real estate prices began to escalate, they soon found that their beautiful home had a market value of nearly $1 million. Part of what made her and Charles's relationship work for as long as it did could be attributed to his attitude—he frequently referred to her as "she who must be obeyed."

But Kathy wasn't satisfied at simply being a housewife and mother. She wanted more than that out of life, and her fiery enthusiasm for politics was soon reignited. In no time at all, it had taken center stage in her life once again. Kathy dreamed large, and it was no secret that she knew how to work a crowd, either to her own benefit or to the detriment of an opponent. Her charismatic persona, at least at her career's outset, was difficult, if not impossible, to match.

"She would walk into a room and light it up," said Phil Alfano, her brother, who works as an educator in Modesto, California. "She had that kind of charisma."

Although she knew years earlier that she wanted a political career, it wasn't until 1992 that she really managed to get things under way when she decided to run for a term in the Nevada Assembly, which is the lower house of the Nevada Legislature. It consists of forty-two members, elected to two-year terms without term limits, and each member is from his or her own respective district. Assemblymen and assemblywomen are not paid much, typically only receiving a small per diem fee for the first two months of a particular session. But it is a good place for politicians to begin a political career, particularly for those who want to effect change in their district, and is often considered a stepping-stone of sorts to bigger and better things within the political arena.

It was during Kathy Augustine's 1992 campaign for assemblywoman of her district that she first made waves and used dirty tricks to win her first position to elected office. Trailing in popularity with the voters, she sent out a political advertisement via the mail that depicted a side-by-side comparison of the two candidates. On the left side of the mailer, Kathy appeared in a clear, bright, and well-focused photo, smiling largely, with her clear white skin accentuated. Opposite her photo was a low-quality photo of her opponent, who happened to be African-American. The mailer, in urging people to vote for Kathy, read: *There is a difference.* Kathy won the election by some seven hundred votes. Her tactic drew considerable controversy, particularly among black constituents, and many people called her a bigot.

After completing one term in the Nevada Assembly, Kathy decided that a run for a state senate seat was in order. She got her name on the ballot as a Republican against incumbent Lori Lipman Brown, a Democrat. During that 1994 campaign, she stated in a political advertisement that Brown opposed prayer because Brown had pushed for the senate to begin using a nondenominational approach for the opening prayer instead of having the prayer led by a Christian minister. Instead of participating in the opening prayer, Brown, who maintained that she was an atheist, began stepping outside the senate chambers during the prayer after her request was denied. Kathy also accused Brown, who was a schoolteacher, of being against the Pledge of Allegiance. In reality, Brown was not against prayer in principle, and she did not oppose the Pledge of Allegiance.

"Politics was a game for her," Brown said. "Anything you had to do to win an election was all right."

Brown fired back with a civil defamation lawsuit, which essentially forced Kathy to publicly admit that her campaign ads had been false. Although she had to apologize to Brown for the false ads, Kathy won the election.

Her associates were quick to recognize that she had all the traits of a successful, up-and-coming politician in the state's often highly volatile political arena. Nevada politicians, long known for their "good ole boy" network in which one hand greased gets another's back scratched, were quick to publicly criticize Kathy for her campaign tactics while offering her praise behind closed doors. Kathy became active in all of the Republican women's clubs, serving in various roles and capacities, and generously gave of her time whenever it was needed. She was known to travel out of her way to distant, far-flung areas of the state to attend the various clubs' functions. As a result, she soon became an idol of sorts among Republican women, and served as a high-profile example of what women can do in today's political climate.

In 1998, Kathy made history when she became the first woman elected as the state controller, where she served until her untimely demise. Life suddenly seemed golden for Kathy after being elected controller. She enjoyed a good salary, traveled with most expenses paid, and was able to purchase a second home in Reno so that she would be close to the state capitol building and convenient to her work in Carson City. More accomplished and self-guided than many people in her chosen profession, Kathy moved faster than many of her professional peers. By now, she was all but consumed by her association with the Republican Party, not only locally but nationally as well. She proudly displayed photographs in which she had posed with President George H. W. Bush, and later, his son George W. Bush, First Lady Laura Bush, and Vice President Dick Cheney. It is little wonder that she brimmed with self-confidence, was tough, and possessed a positive attitude, attributes that were immediately detectable by her firm handshake and the fact that she always looked the person to whom she was speaking straight in the eye. She could have been a great poker player because her opponents could never tell when she was bluffing.

Kathy's list of accomplishments was impressive. For

example, according to her official Nevada State biography, she served as a delegate to Russia and the Ukraine with the American Council of Young Political Leaders (ACYPL) in 1993. Two years later, in 1995, she was selected as an executive committee member to the Biennial Assembly of the Atlantic Association of Young Political Leaders (AAYPL) in Paris, France. In addition, she took part in the Council of State Governments Henry Toll Fellowship Program and was also chosen for the Flemming Fellows Leadership Institute's Class of 1996. In 1999, she attended the Governors Center at Duke University Strategic Leadership for State Executives, and she graduated in 2000 from the Greater Reno-Sparks Chamber of Commerce Leadership Program. In 2001, she completed the Harvard University, John F. Kennedy School of Government, Senior Executives in State and Local Government Program.

Among her other accomplishments, Kathy was also a recipient of the American Legion Achievement Medallion, the Community Partners Family Resource Center 1998 Community Service Award of Excellence, the 1998 National Republican Legislators Association, Legislator of the Year, and Nevada Opera Theatre's International Friendship Award, in 2003.

Kathy Augustine formerly had served as chair of the Electrical Industry Restructuring Committee for the Council of State Governments–West (CSG-WEST) and was the past chairperson of the Trade and Transportation Task Force Subcommittee for the American Legislative Exchange Council. She also served on the National Conference of State Legislatures, the Women's NETWORK Board of Directors as representative of the group's western region, from 1996 through 1998, and served as the Nevada State director for Women in Government, from 1997 to 1998.

At the time of her death, Kathy was serving on the Family and Child Treatment Advisory Committee, and was a member of the Government Finance Officers Association. She was also on the State Board of Finance, the Department of Transportation Board of Directors, the Executive Branch Audit Committee, and was the former chair of the National Association of State Auditors, Comptrollers and Treasurers (NASACT) International Committee. She was also serving as a trustee for the Center for Governmental Financial Management and was the NASACT representative for the Electronic Benefits and Services Council, where she chaired the Strategic Expansion and Advanced Technology Committee.

With all of her activities, as admirable as they were, it was little wonder that she had marital problems and found it difficult to keep a husband.

Despite her remarkable achievements and awards, depending upon who was asked, Kathy was characterized as either a brilliant politician or a cold-blooded opportunist who would stop at nothing to get ahead. Because of her penchant for hitting below the belt, many people despised her for the tactics she used in her campaigns. She would do almost anything to win. If she had been a man, she likely would have won praise for being one of the brightest, most adept politicians to have ever held political office. But because she was a woman, she was a "bitch," among other things. But she didn't care—nothing was going to stop her. She wasn't about to let "the turkeys get her down."

It was no secret that Kathy was not well-liked by her employees, who would come and go over the years, sometimes over personality conflicts with her. During an interview, Kathy once admitted to a Reno television reporter at KRNV-TV that she was "tough."

"Yes, I am a tough boss," Kathy had said. "I pride myself in the work that we've been able to accomplish."

As her political aspirations continued to widen, the tension felt at home with Charles continued to grow. He made it clear to her that he did not wish to be a part of her political limelight, and by 2003, after several years of already leading separate lives while sharing the same address, they both realized that their marriage was over. It was time for each of them to move on with their lives.

Before Kathy and Charles could come to terms and finalize their divorce agreement, Charles suffered a major stroke and was hospitalized. Kathy stayed at his bedside at Sunrise Hospital and Medical Center, in Las Vegas, waiting for signs of improvement. She was known to call relatives, crying and sad, and would describe how Charles seemed aware that she was there with him, yet they couldn't communicate with each other. After spending several weeks in the hospital, it seemed to many people that he was getting better. Suddenly, and with little warning, Charles died on August 19, 2003, after several of his vital organs began shutting down. His doctors said that his death was the result of complications from the stroke. Kathy, along with other family members, had been at his bedside when he died. Officially, his death was attributed to the stroke, just like the doctors had said. However, suspicions of foul play would later arise.

At one point during Charles's hospitalization, Kathy had met critical care nurse Chaz Higgs, eight years her junior, and had coffee with him on a few occasions. Higgs had provided care for Charles during a couple of his shifts, which had provided the opportunity for him and Kathy to meet.

Following Charles Augustine's death, Kathy decided that she wanted to give out thank-you cards to all of the nurses that had assisted or provided nursing care for her husband. After handing out all of the cards, she realized that she had forgotten one of the nurses—Chaz Higgs.

When she discovered the oversight, she called Higgs and invited him out to coffee with her so that she could express her gratitude in person for Higgs's efforts on behalf of her husband.

Higgs, a former bodybuilder, quickly saw the opportunity he had with Kathy, and the two began dating in what turned out to be a whirlwind relationship. Attracted by his rugged good looks, Kathy couldn't seem to see enough of Higgs. Three weeks after Charles had died, Kathy and Chaz ran off to Hawaii, and got married in what was termed an unplanned event. There were no family members or friends present at their wedding—just the two of them and the reverend.

No one, not even family members, had known about the marriage until afterward, when Higgs showed up at a social gathering with Kathy in which she was being bestowed the honor of having been selected Italian-American of the Year by the Augustus Society. The award was presented at the Augustus Society's Annual Columbus Day Ball on Saturday, October 11, 2003, at the Venetian Hotel Casino, in Las Vegas. Each year, the organization selects an individual or family to receive the award, and Kathy was selected for her dedication to public service, her history of community involvement, and her contributions to the advancement of Italian-Americans, particularly because she "embodies the spirit of the award and the society by promoting a positive image of Italian-Americans."

"Being selected for this award is a true honor," Kathy told those in attendance. "I have always had strong ties to my heritage and the Italian-American community. Receiving this award provides me with the opportunity to recognize the rich Italian-American culture in this state."

Relatives and friends had simply thought that Higgs had been her date for the evening. However, to the shock and surprise of many people who were present, it was at that time that she had announced their marriage to her family and friends. Both husband and wife were criticized by their friends and relatives for their hastiness, but they didn't care. All that mattered to them was their love for each other—as far as they were concerned, the rest of the world, with regard to their marriage, could go to hell.

The following year, in January 2004, officials at the White House informed Kathy that she had become a finalist for treasurer of the United States. By then, some said, her marriage to Chaz Higgs was already on the rocks.

Chapter 4

When Chaz Higgs married Kathy Augustine, he pur-portedly was not aware of her stature as a politician. He hadn't realized that her job virtually consumed her life and defined who she was, nor had he cared. Kathy made him happy—in fact, he let it be known that during this period in his life, at least at first, was the happiest he had ever been. His happy-go-lucky demeanor and joyous sense of humor, however, would soon change as he began to real-ize just how seriously Kathy had taken her political career.

Kathy's position as Nevada state controller was a power-ful one to be in. Brandishing authority and influence at the uppermost ranks of state administration, Kathy's job al-lowed her to rub elbows with powerful, influential people all over the country. But in reality, when the ingredients of her position were boiled down to the bottom of the pan, she was little more than a glorified bill collector for the state. Her office routinely collected money owed to the state and, in conjunction with the state treasurer, paid the state's bills. Anyone in that post, male or female, could not be soft and would have to shake a big stick in order to be successful at the job, particularly if they hoped to be reelected. There was no doubt that Kathy was good at what she did—she collected millions of dollars in bad debt for the state of Nevada during her first term in office, a regular female "Guido" of sorts who always seemed to be waiting around the next corner to grab money from whomever whenever it was owed.

Her seriousness did not mean, however, that she did not have a sense of humor. When Kathy was in the mood to laugh, she would laugh loudly. A number of state employees recalled that Kathy's laughter could sometimes be heard resounding through the foyers and reception area near her office. At other times, however, her personality could suddenly take an unexpected and rapid turn of 180 degrees, whereby state workers could hear her pounding on her desk and screaming at her employees, scolding them for work that she considered below her standards. Never mind if an employee's quality of work met the state's standards set for any given position—if it didn't meet or exceed Kathy's expectations, people would hear about it. She was known as a perfectionist, and she demanded the best from everyone—not just the best that any given person could give, but what she considered the best that a person could do. Her perfectionism often led to uncomfortable conditions.

One of Kathy's former aides said that Kathy, on one occasion, had instructed her to destroy her cat, which was diabetic.

What had been Kathy's reason for wanting the cat dead? She purportedly had said that the cat had become too much of a diversion at the office, and kept her assistant from doing her work. The office controversy over the unhealthy cat being brought into the office may have spelled the beginning of the end for Kathy's political career, the straw that broke the camel's back. The cat belonged to former executive assistant Jennifer Normington who, along with another state employee, former assistant controller Jeannine Coward, had had enough of Kathy's alleged outrageous tirades. They decided to do something about it. As it turned out, their actions resulted in the first impeachment of a state official in Nevada's 140-year history. Normington and Coward both alleged that Kathy had committed violations of the state's ethics laws.

Specifically, the two women charged that Kathy had created a fearful work environment and in the process demanded that a state employee be used to work on her reelection campaign in 2002, on state time.

"She's a screamer and a yeller and a pounder on the desk," Coward told state ethics investigators. "And, you know, you tried to avoid any unpleasant situations with her."

In a nutshell, Kathy was being accused of misdemeanors or malfeasance in office that pertained to her having her employees "organize campaign fund-raiser events, give campaign speeches, compile and maintain donor lists, format and mail requests for contributions, design fund-raiser invitations, prepare contribution reports for submission to the secretary of state, and maintain a database of Kathy Augustine's campaign contributions," all on state time.

She was also charged with causing computer equipment owned by the state of Nevada to be used for "creating, maintaining, storing, and printing documents" related to her reelection campaign, and for "causing equipment and facilities, provided by the state of Nevada for use by the office of the state controller, to be used for business and purposes related to her 2002 reelection campaign." All three of the alleged infringements were violations of Nevada Revised Statutes 281.481(7), and convictions could result in her removal from office.

In an apparent effort to try and ward off serious legal actions, Kathy promptly admitted to the three counts of "willful" violations. In her admission, she claimed that she had not directed anyone to perform campaign work for her on state time, but stipulated that she should have known that such work was being done. The state ethics commission almost immediately imposed a fine of $15,000 against her, the largest such fine ever levied against a politician in the state's history. However, according to Nevada law, the admission to the violations automatically activated an obligation for the ethics commission to forward the case to the state assembly to decide whether to impeach her or not. After deciding that the charges warranted a trial, the assembly voted for impeachment in September 2004.

Specifically, the Nevada Constitution stipulates: "A public officer or employee, other than a member of the legislature, shall not use government time, property, equipment, or other facilities to benefit his personal or financial interest."

Following the public announcement of impeachment, Kathy was temporarily removed from office by the governor. Although suspended, Kathy's $80,000 annual salary would continue, pending the outcome of her trial. The governor appointed Chief Deputy Controller Kim Huys, who had been in that position for three years, as the interim controller. If found guilty, Kathy could be permanently removed from office and be required to repay the state of Nevada a hefty portion of the money that was spent on her impeachment.

Apparently, Kathy's accusers provided sufficient evidence to prompt Governor Kenny Guinn to call the Nevada Legislature into special session to begin impeachment proceedings against Kathy Augustine. Guinn, as well as several other high-ranking Nevada Republicans, including U.S. senator John Ensign and U.S. representative Jim

Gibbons, had asked Kathy to resign, to spare herself the embarrassment of a trial and to spare the state the expense of calling a special session. However, she refused and vowed to defend herself.

"I think that both sides of the story have to be told," Kathy said in response to the requests that she resign. "Resigning was not an answer."

In October 2004, Kathy sent a letter to the *Las Vegas Review-Journal* in which she stated that she had *always believed in maintaining the public trust,* and insisted that *I will not stand silently and have my integrity dragged through the mud.*

Although it had been suggested that Guinn should wait until the regular legislative session began at the beginning of the coming year, he decided that the special session was more appropriate, because he did not want an impeachment trial to detract from the normal business that needed to be considered during the regular session. He insisted that the regular session was going to be much too busy dealing with more important issues, such as water allocations, property taxes, and general tax increases.

On November 9, 2004, forty-two members of the Nevada Assembly met in committee and listened to the testimonies of a number of witnesses. Afterward, the vote for impeachment was unanimous, and the three alleged violations, referred to as articles of impeachment, were forwarded to the state senate for trial. The senate appropriated $250,000 for the trial expenses, estimating that it would cost at least $15,000 per day. The trial began on November 29, 2004, the Monday after Thanksgiving, and would require a two-thirds majority of the twenty-one members of the senate for conviction.

Kathy publicly maintained her composure and style, but behind the scenes she was, of course, furious over the allegations and the impending impeachment proceedings. Suddenly the issues surrounding her private life, particularly her speedy marriage to Chaz Higgs, took a backseat to the impeachment proceedings. She retained attorneys John Arrascada and Dominic Gentile to defend her. Gentile was quick to caution the lawmakers that Kathy's impeachment, if carried out, might be at their own detriment.

"The assembly and senate are really trying themselves here," Gentile told a reporter for the *Boston Globe*. "Some of them have aspirations for higher political office. All of them have people who work for them who work on their campaigns. If they want to make a sacrificial lamb out of her, fine, but every one of them has disgruntled employees and every one of them will face ethics complaints filed by them if they find that this action is worthy of being expelled from office."

Nevada state senator Dina Titus, Democrat minority leader, shot back at Gentile's suggestion by basically stating that it wasn't a valid argument because of the fact that the legislature only meets for 120 days each year, and therefore most lawmakers do not have full-time staffs to strike back and settle scores.

"If she wants to drag other people through the mud," Titus said, "I suggest they let her do that, because it won't be me or anyone I know."

Titus also made it clear that people were not happy about Kathy's suggestion that her assistant have her diabetic cat killed.

"That was enough for me, 'cause I got a cat," Titus told reporters. "A lot of people who don't like Kathy Augustine think if this (impeachment) is gonna happen, it couldn't happen to a less nice person."

Kathy's lawyer responded by saying that Kathy had only made the suggestion out of compassion for the sick animal, as many people prefer to put their pets out of their misery rather than seeing them suffer. Gentile said that Kathy was the target of spiteful and vindictive state employees.

Titus and a number of other Democrats suddenly saw Kathy's impeachment as an opportunity to settle old scores. Many people began recalling the issue of Kathy's allegedly racist political mailer years earlier, as well as her ascent to the senate by beating Jewish lawmaker Lori Lipman Brown by saying that Brown refused to recite the Pledge of Allegiance. A number of Democrats took the opportunity to renew the scandals. The question of whether Kathy was a bigot, however, remained unanswered despite the fact that she had claimed that she was not.

As the impeachment proceedings continued to heat up, Kathy similarly refused to temper her own feelings about the issue. She offended the governor, who had been an ally of hers for many years, by refusing to meet with him privately at his suggestion. Instead, she told him that she would only meet with him behind closed doors if her attorney was present. She also requested that a special independent prosecutor be selected for her impeachment because she believed that the prosecutor that had been named by the senate, Daniel Greco, the Washoe County chief deputy district attorney, was biased against her. It clearly wasn't the time to be making new enemies—she already had plenty. But Kathy insisted that she would win this battle, just as she had won most of the battles in her career.

If anyone else had been called onto the carpet for Kathy's alleged wrongdoing, especially in Nevada, it would likely have been viewed as simply yet another typical political scandal, one to be added to the state's history of political and/or judicial wrongdoing, alleged or otherwise. However, because Kathy was so disliked by so many people, it became a ripe opportunity for her opponents to try and pull the carpet out from under her.

"I don't expect anybody to embrace Kathy Augustine and say, 'Hey, Kathy, what you did here was good,'" Gentile said to reporters at one of several news conferences. "But they should say, 'Hey, Kathy, the fact that you admitted you should have known about this is good.' This is not the stuff you remove people from office for. It's what we fine them for. If they approach it with an open mind, Kathy Augustine wins."

Chapter 5

As Kathy Augustine's impeachment trial drew nearer, the political mudslinging intensified in Carson City and throughout Nevada. A columnist for the *Las Vegas Review-Journal* had earlier written, when news of the allegations against Kathy had come to the forefront, that *State Controller Kathy Augustine is finally going to get hers*. The columnist Jane Ann Morrison indicated that the two female politicians that Kathy had unseated in two separate elections, using unscrupulous campaign tactics against them, had waited for more than ten years to see Kathy Augustine finally get what was coming to her. Some called it Karma.

"It's hard to wish anyone badly, once you yourself have moved on," said Lori Lipman Brown. "But anytime anyone has done something wrong, you hope justice is done."

Brown admitted that she was gloating over Kathy's legal problems, but not much, except with her husband. Based on those types of comments, it was clear that Kathy had few friends, at least politically, in Nevada.

By the middle of November 2004, although she had already apologized to the people of Nevada for her legal problems, she appeared in an exclusive interview with investigative reporter George Knapp on Las Vegas's CBS News affiliate channel 8. She apologized once again for the mistakes that she had made that led to her impeachment. Knapp's interview with Kathy Augustine was the first television interview that she had granted since her ethics problems began, and it had been granted with the understanding that she would not be asked any direct questions about the impeachment case.

"It's very upsetting as an elected official and a constitutional officer that this would have occurred," she told Knapp. "Yes, it's embarrassing as well."

She was adamant, however, that her mistakes did not justify her being removed from office. She explained how she had admitted that she should have known that more time was being spent on her campaign work than there should have been.

"That's what I admitted to," she said. "But I don't believe that's cause for removal from office. I believe, again, that I will receive a fair trial and will not be convicted in the senate."

As Knapp explained that a number of people had described her as a tough boss and had used the "B" word to describe her character and personality, Kathy explained that in her position it was tough to have many friends, particularly in the workplace. She conceded that she was not well-liked, particularly in Carson City, in part because of the manner in which she ran her office.

"After all, I'm the watchdog for the state's finances and it's my duty," she said. "I won't have a lot of friends when I'm watching how the taxpayer dollars are spent. . . . I'm very independent and I make decisions based on what I believe is best, not only for my office but for the people of the state of Nevada, especially concerning taxpayer dollars. It's another reason this is upsetting to me. I hate that we're spending taxpayer dollars on these proceedings. But I know with due process that you have to go through it."

She explained how she had accepted full responsibility for what had occurred, and that she was paying the $15,000 fine, which had been levied against her, in monthly payments.

"That was a huge fine," she said. "I'm paying it back personally, writing personal checks to the ethics commission. The first of every month, I send them five hundred dollars. That's in the stipulation. It's quite a chunk."

As part of her apology, Kathy agreed that the people of the state were disappointed in her, but she stressed that she wanted to continue as controller. She said that she was "willing and able, and would like to finish the job" that the people elected her to do.

One of Kathy's attorneys, Dominic Gentile, stated that two of the primary witnesses against his client lacked credibility, and suggested that other state politicians might get dragged through the mud if things turned particularly ugly. He said that Kathy's admission that she should have been aware that her employees were working on her campaign during normal work hours was not the same as giving them orders to do the work on state time.

"What she admitted to was that she did not know it was going on," Gentile said. "But it happened on her watch and she should have known, and she accepted the responsibility for it. That does not rise to the level of malfeasance in office."

Gentile said that Kathy has denied that she had ever *ordered* any of her employees to work on her campaign, and suggested to television news reporters that if his client "goes down," she won't be going down by herself.

As Kathy's impeachment trial finally got under way on Wednesday, December 1, 2004, before the twenty-one members of the senate, her attorneys described her as a "mean boss" who was known to throw paper and to have loud outbursts in the office related to her temper. Her lead attorney, John Arrascada, used a PowerPoint presentation to accentuate his point. In one slide, he presented a photo of a painting that depicted an angry mob during the French Revolution congregating around a guillotine, and in another a portrait of Joan of Arc decked out in armor with a halo that encircled her head. Arrascada's argument was that his client's ethics violations really hadn't harmed the citizens of Nevada and did not deserve what he termed the political "death penalty." Such a penalty, he had said, might not only serve to remove her from office, but could serve as the death knell of her political career. He argued that she was a victim of a vengeful grudge being perpetrated by unhappy former employees who had been unable to cope with her often challenging and uncompromising management style. His argument was reminiscent of that presented by President Bill Clinton's lawyers during the opening of his impeachment trial in 1999.

"We know that Kathy Augustine is not a saint," Arrascada said. "We also know that she has not committed offenses that rise up to the level that require removal from office."

It was clear that Arrascada's legal tactics, which he admitted to in later interviews, was to lay strong emphasis on the unfortunate prospect of setting a precedent of removing an elected official from office, while at the same time playing down her unpleasant character traits. He realized from the trial's outset that it would be difficult to conjure up sympathy among Kathy's colleagues—from either party. Despite her often unpleasant personality, though, few could deny the efficiency with which Kathy ran her office.

After taking the senate jury through the list of allegations, he emphasized the historic nature of the impeachment trial and cautioned that the senate would be setting a standard for any future similar actions. At one point, he implied that the ethics commission's unforgiving findings and the $15,000 fine, which they had imposed on her, were sufficient punishment for the violations.

"Impeachment and removal is only for the worst of the worst," Arrascada argued. "What is the harm to the public of letting Kathy Augustine finish her term? Where do we set the bar for what constitutes an impeachable offense in this state?"

On the other hand, Special Prosecutor Dan Greco argued that the "unique and historic constitutional exercise" taking place before the senate was the direct result of the defendant's deliberate abuse of her elected position. Greco stated that she had no campaign staff, nor did she have an office in which to run her campaign, separate from her elected office. He said that she had made the decision to run her campaign out of her office at the state capitol, and had ordered her salaried employees to perform a wide variety of duties related to her political campaign, all on state time and expense in blatant violation of the constitution.

In addition to the two witnesses who had initiated the complaints against Kathy, both of whom testified during the early days of the trial, there was a third witness, who had not been publicly identified previously. Susan Kennedy testified at one point that she had worked for Kathy Augustine for nineteen months, and during that time, she had been asked many times to perform campaign work. During cross-examination, Dominic Gentile was quick to point out that Kennedy's story had changed since she first complained to investigators early in the case. Gentile also pointed out that despite the requests that Kathy had made for her to do campaign work, the investigation had shown that she only spent approximately five hours in those nineteen months working on Kathy's campaign. He also emphasized that Kathy had asked her to do the campaign work after hours.

At another point in the trial, Kathy's chief accountant, James Wells, told the senators that Kathy had, on one occasion, asked him to work on a campaign finance report. He refused, he testified, and after being told by other employees that Kathy would likely fire him for his refusal, he began looking for work in other departments. However, he said that he had not been disciplined by Kathy for not agreeing to her request.

Despite all of the preimpeachment hype and publicity, Kathy Augustine's trial only lasted a week. On Saturday, December 4, 2004, when all was said and done, the Nevada Senate convicted her on only one count: using state equipment for her 2002 reelection campaign. They dismissed the other two counts: Kathy should have known that employees were doing political work for her on state time, and that a state-owned computer had been used for her campaign. The senators instead voted to censure her, which amounted to a reprimand, and allowed the $15,000 fine to stand. It was agreed that she could complete her term in office.

"I'm very happy," Kathy said to reporters, elated and in tears, after the decisions had been made. "I'll be able to return to my official duties on Monday morning."

When asked if she thought there might be some animosity toward her at the capitol when she returned to work, Kathy replied, "After everything I've been through, I certainly, certainly can handle a little animosity."

Due to term limits, Kathy was unable to run for controller for a third term. But shortly after her impeachment proceedings had ended, she announced that, much to the chagrin of her party colleagues, she would likely run for the office of state treasurer, or that of lieutenant governor, in the 2006 election.

Kathy's censure, not to mention her apology, was apparently not enough for some people, particularly for Nevada Republican Party chairman Paul Adams who was quite vocal in his statements by saying that she was an embarrassment to the party. He urged her in a confidential letter not to embarrass the party further by running for another elective office. He wrote that he understood that she had high name recognition among Nevada voters, but added that *your presence on the ballot as a Republican will be an embarrassment to the Nevada Republican Party.* He stated that if she insisted on running, the Nevada GOP *cannot embrace a candidate who has been censured, fined, and impeached for an ethics violation.*

"She admitted to ethics violations and was impeached and censured," Adams said later, after news of his confidential letter to Kathy had been made public. "That would be, in my opinion, an embarrassment to the party and I stand by it. I don't regret sending the letter because I still think that people are looking for ethical candidates."

A short time later, an article ran in a Republican newsletter that criticized Adams's remarks, and took the position that while what Kathy had done as a public servant was unethical, her actions had been no more than what "other elected officials have been doing for years." The article further described Kathy as a political "pit bull," and Adams's suggestion for her not to run again had "assured her candidacy for some race on the ballot next year."

Little did any of her colleagues know at the time, but they wouldn't have to worry about Kathy holding another term in office in Nevada. She would be dead by then.

Chapter 6

Following the definitive autopsy on Kathy Augustine's body, which had been performed by Dr. Ellen Clark on Wednesday, July 12, 2006, the Reno Police Department issued a press release announcing that they were investigating the circumstances surrounding Kathy's death. The news that her death was being investigated by the police had quickly become an unusual story, in part because Kathy had been a significant political player in Nevada, who was well-known throughout the state. It had also quickly become a *big* story for much the same reason. If it turned out that she had in fact been murdered, everyone close to the case agreed that it wouldn't be the typical murder case in which a spouse has killed his partner and has been caught holding the smoking gun. Although Kathy hadn't been a regular feature of the high-society pages of any of the state's newspapers, she was certainly making headlines now. Suspicious death investigations, especially those involving possible murder, made sensational headlines, and sensational headlines sold newspapers. Stories ran in papers throughout the state right after her body had been found and continued for several days afterward, and it hadn't taken long for newspapers across the nation to begin running features about her life and her death.

Investigations such as the one being conducted for Kathy are routine when people Kathy's age suddenly die, with no readily apparent explanation. Although all of the results of the autopsy still wouldn't be known for several weeks, particularly the results of toxicology tests that were being conducted by the FBI, it was clear that Kathy had been in reasonably good health at the time of her death. So far, there had been no evidence of a heart attack—there were no blockages in any of her major arteries, and there had been no evidence of heart muscle damage.

At one point early in the investigation, Detective David Jenkins had learned that Kathy had been diagnosed in 1995 with a heart condition known as mitral valve prolapse, a somewhat common heart valve abnormality in which a valve does not close completely and allows small, but significant, amounts of blood to flow back out of the valve. It typically causes chest pain, fatigue, migraines, palpitations, and anxiety, and appears to be more common in women than in men.

However, Jenkins also learned from Dr. Stanley Thompson, a cardiologist who treated Kathy prior to her death, that Kathy's arteries were clear and that her blood flowed smoothly through her heart. He said that he considered her heart to be generally healthy.

"You can say [her arteries] were one hundred percent normal," Dr. Thompson said. "Everybody . . . would love to have those arteries."

Although Kathy's family had indicated that they were not aware of any history or symptoms of heart problems that Kathy may have had, a well-known Las Vegas cardiologist, Dr. Keith Boman, said that symptoms like stomachache and heartburn, such as those reportedly suffered by Kathy, according to her husband, are often common symptoms of heart problems that are missed or misinterpreted by the patient, as well as the doctor.

According to Dr. Boman, stomach distress, when it exhibits itself as a response to a heart attack, can possibly be attributed to the lack of nerves in the heart, thus causing the pain signals of the heart attack to be sent elsewhere in the body.

"It's very common," Boman said. "And that can occur in men and women. It just appears to be more common in women, again making diagnosis a little more of a challenge."

Boman pointed out that men are more likely to experience the more classic symptoms of a heart attack, such as a dull ache in the arm or the overwhelming discomfort of pressure in the chest. In women, he said, the symptoms are not necessarily as straightforward as they are in men.

"Instead of being pain," he said, "say classically in the chest, substernal, crushing type discomfort, sometimes they will have it in the back, or maybe the arm. Or maybe it will be epigastric, in the stomach."

It was also announced that same day that Reno police had obtained and executed a search warrant at the Reno home Kathy shared with her husband, Chaz Higgs. Because of the information that had come out of Jenkins's interview with Kim Ramey and her comments about succinylcholine, and the fact that the autopsy had found what appeared to be a needle mark on Kathy's left buttock, investigators were, of course, looking for anything that might reveal the presence of the powerful anesthetic or the means to administer it, such as a needle and syringe, inside the house.

Among the items collected from the Otter Way home during the execution of the search warrant were bedding items, including sheets and pillowcases, and the contents of trash containers. A yellow-and-black nylon backpack that Jenkins had found on the floor in the master bedroom, lying next to the bed in an area between the master bedroom and the master bathroom, was noted but not taken at that time. The backpack, along with virtually anything else that seemed pertinent to the investigation, was photographed in the location where it was found before being examined or moved. Later, when the backpack's contents were examined, Jenkins discovered among the items inside it a vial of a controlled drug called etomidate. Etomidate, Jenkins learned, was a short-acting intravenous anesthetic. It is sometimes used for conscious sedation, commonly used in an ER setting. The vial's seal hadn't been broken, and the twenty milligrams inside appeared intact. Little else of significance was found during the search—there weren't any syringes, needles, empty vials of drugs, and so forth.

With the so-called massive heart attack theory that had been initiated by Chaz Higgs virtually ruled out, Jenkins and his colleagues had little choice but to await the FBI's toxicology reports. In the meantime, Jenkins continued studying the facts of the case as he knew them at that time, and began backtracking through the events of the morning of Kathy's death, beginning with the 911 call made by Higgs.

Jenkins reviewed statements that Higgs had made to reporters during press conferences, and made it a point to speak to the paramedics who had responded to Higgs's emergency telephone call. He researched that Higgs had said, "I went in to try and wake her up, I couldn't get her to wake up, and I checked her out. It was like an instinct, because, as I said, I am a critical care nurse, so it's something I've dealt with before. I just checked her out, she wasn't breathing, she had no pulse, so I started CPR." Jenkins made note of how calm Higgs had sounded on the 911 tape recording of his call.

When Jenkins spoke with Benjamin Pratt, the first paramedic to arrive at Kathy's home, Pratt recalled how Higgs had been waiting outside for them, standing on the sidewalk, when they arrived. Pratt told the detective how Higgs had stated that he had found his wife in bed and unresponsive, and that was when he had begun cardiopulmonary resuscitation. However, Pratt and his colleagues told Jenkins that it is necessary to perform CPR on a solid surface, such as a floor, so that sufficient compression on the chest can be maintained to keep blood flowing through the heart. Pratt said that it was common knowledge among paramedics and medical professionals that the person being administered CPR be placed on a hard, flat surface, but when they arrived, Kathy was lying in her bed.

Pratt also told the detective that Higgs did not appear excited or agitated, as most people are during such an emergency, and that he remained out of the bedroom while they worked on Kathy. Although Pratt's information was similar to that which had been written in the report taken by Officers Steve Mussell and Joe Proffitt, the first officers at the scene, the detail that was now being related seemed to have more significance than it had initially.

Manny Fuentes, the paramedic who drove the ambulance to the hospital, told Jenkins how Kathy had been relocated from the medical center's suburban branch to the main hospital later that same morning. According to Fuentes, Higgs rode in the ambulance's passenger seat and remained quiet during the trip. He hadn't asked about his wife's condition, but instead began reading a newspaper that Fuentes earlier had folded and placed on the dashboard. Such indifference toward a supposed loved one in grave condition had seemed strange.

"He grabbed the newspaper and started flipping through the pages," Fuentes said.

With little to go on at this point, the Reno Police Department issued a request for anyone who thought they might have information that could help them find answers to the questions they had about Kathy's death, no matter how insignificant the information might seem, to come forward. Phil Alfano, Kathy's brother, also issued a similar request.

"There have been many rumors and suspicions raised about the circumstances of Kathy's death," Alfano told reporters as he read from a prepared statement. *"While our family hopes and prays that she died of natural causes, we are extremely grateful that an investigation has been launched. Our family requests that anyone with information that could assist investigators with this task, please come forward.*

"In addition," he continued, *"the people of Nevada who did not know Kathy are also hearing and reading about the Kathy Augustine we all knew—the fun-loving, warm, and caring person we were fortunate to share our lives with. . . . Yes, Kathy could be demanding, tough, and outspoken. These are the characteristics of any great leader. But Kathy was not the false caricature created by a handful of disgruntled employees and opportunists during the impeachment trial and the weeks leading up to it."*

He added that their family had been searching for *"some measure of good in all of the senselessness,"* and said that their family had become stronger and more thankful for one another since his sister's death.

At another point during the early stages of the investigation, Jenkins learned that Higgs had called Kathy's mother in California and told her that Kathy had suffered a heart attack. When her mother told him that they would be there right away, Higgs told her that there was no need for her to come up to Reno.

The next day, July 13, 2006, the case took on a new aura of mystery when the Reno Police Department formally asked the Nevada Department of Public Safety to assist them in their investigation. The request raised questions, particularly why the Reno Police Department felt they needed help from the state agency. Had there been a particular investigative reason behind the request? Or had the request been made because Kathy had been a state official and the local police had wanted the big boys from the state involved in case things got too sticky? Reno police wouldn't say and chose to play it close to the vest. They also chose to characterize their investigation, as well as their request to their state counterpart, as routine.

"The police department routinely takes deceased persons reports," said Reno Police Department lieutenant Jon Catalano when reporters started asking questions. "Those all go through our detective division when they come to us. In this case, we definitely wanted to determine what the cause of death was. Because of her high-profile position, that makes it newsworthy. But we actually review every death report that comes through our office."

Catalano made no mention of why the state police had been called in.

Governor Kenny Guinn echoed the Reno Police Department's position that Kathy's death was being investigated routinely. To his knowledge, he said, there was nothing suspicious about Kathy's death.

Had Guinn really believed that? Or had he truly not known the details of the investigation at this point?

"And I truly believe it is what they said," Guinn announced at a press conference. "It is a routine process and many times they do that because they have someone who has no known health history of heart problems for herself or her parents, and that's always an indication. Of course, if you don't [have such medical problems], that sort of says to someone, 'Take a look.' And she was fifty years old. She appeared to be in good health."

Although it would remain a mystery as to why the Nevada Department of Public Safety was called in to help the Reno Police Department in their investigation, it also remained a mystery as to why law enforcement investigating this case practically did an about-face and started characterizing the investigation as "routine."

During one of his many encounters with reporters about his wife's death, Chaz Higgs told the *Las Vegas Review-Journal* that he welcomed the police investigation, but he was troubled by all of the rumors, innuendo, and speculation that foul play had somehow been involved.

"I loved this woman who died," Higgs said. "And now there is all this [nonsense] coming up. It is just crazy for people to assume that I had something to do with it."

In the meantime, it was business as usual at the state capitol. Although Governor Kenny Guinn had expressed his condolences to Kathy Augustine's family, he said that it was necessary that he act quickly to find a replacement for the deceased controller. He announced on July 13, 2006, two days after Kathy's death, that he had selected fifty-eight-year-old Steve Martin, a certified public accountant from Las Vegas, to replace her.

"It was vital to appoint a person with the qualifications and background to complete the duties of state controller as quickly as possible," Guinn said at a news conference in announcing Martin's appointment. "As a certified public accountant with a master's degree in accounting, Steve Martin certainly meets those standards."

Martin, sworn in at Las Vegas's Grant Sawyer State Office Building, was a Republican. He told reporters that he knew what it took to run a business, and to "have good rapport with a staff." He indicated that he would be a candidate for the position in the November election. Some people said that the governor's fast appointment of Martin to the position had been politically motivated, which he, of course, denied. One thing was certain, however: Kathy's memory was quickly swept aside to make way for the new controller.

Chapter 7

As the Reno Police Department continued its probe of Kathy Augustine's sudden and untimely death, the state's Division of Investigations, which falls under the domain of the Nevada Department of Public Safety, began helping them out at their request by conducting inquiries at the state capitol. The fact that they undertook that part of the investigation, which was responsible for interviews within the controller's office, while at the same time looking for any potential evidence there, somewhat explained their requested involvement. It seemed to an outsider looking in that the RPD officials did not want to step on any toes at the state level by appearing to move outside their jurisdictional boundaries. Even though there was some overlap and duplication of efforts, everyone hoped that the involvement of the Division of Investigations might turn up something significant that might otherwise inadvertently get overlooked, due to the implied jurisdictional boundaries, since Kathy's office, as well as those with whom she worked, was located at the state capitol, which was in Carson City, not Reno. According to the governor's spokesman, the state investigators would also be looking into whether anything was missing from Kathy's office.

According to Steve Frady, spokesman for the Reno Police Department, the death investigation was still being looked at as "noncriminal," and that "no one has been identified as a suspect or a person of interest." At least, that's what they were releasing to the public days after Kathy's death. Frady reiterated that the coroner's office had ordered the autopsy on Kathy's body due to the fact that her medical history was not sufficient to explain her sudden death. The police wouldn't say publicly at that time whether Chaz Higgs was a suspect in her death, but spouses usually are at the top of the list of potential suspects in murder cases, until they can be ruled out. But the cops in this case were being careful not to use the term "murder" loosely—at this point, they were officially only investigating a suspicious death. Nonetheless, the fact that the police would not release Higgs's 911 telephone call to the public, because it was being used as part of the investigation, was an indicator that things were heating up as far as Higgs was concerned.

On Friday morning, July 14, 2006, police and paramedics were called to Kathy Augustine's 5,500-square-foot three-bedroom house on the 1400 block of Maria Elena Drive, just off East Charleston and Maryland Parkway. The large two-story house, with three pillars in front, is situated at the end of a quiet cul-de-sac in one of Las Vegas's swankier, older neighborhoods, only a few miles from where the state maintained a second controller's office at the Grant Sawyer building, where Kathy had often performed her duties. Kathy's daughter, Dallas Augustine, met the Las Vegas Metropolitan Police Department (LVMPD) officers and the paramedics when they arrived, and led them to a bedroom inside the house, where they found Chaz Higgs bleeding from wounds on his wrists.

According to Metro Police reports, sometime the previous evening, Higgs had locked himself inside one of the bedrooms of the home, which he had shared with Kathy, by tying the door shut with a necktie. He purportedly drank two bottles of alcohol and had taken some pills, the specifics of which were not publicly released. At approximately ten-thirty the next morning, Dallas went to his bedroom to check on him, but he would not, or could not, respond to Dallas, who had urged him to come out. Concerned about his welfare, Dallas kicked open the bedroom door where she found Higgs, unconscious and bloody. Although Chaz Higgs was dressed in a suit, Dallas could see that he had slit his wrists. She found a suicide note inside the room, and it was later determined that he had used a razor blade to open his veins.

Unconscious, Higgs was bandaged up and rushed to University Medical Center, about two miles away, where he was admitted through the emergency department. When he regained consciousness, he told his nurses that he wanted "to die to be with my wife." Although people who attempt suicide can be held for observation for up to seventy-two hours without a court order, Higgs was patched up and released that same day after being evaluated by the hospital's psychiatric department. Although his note was kept under wraps, Dallas Augustine confirmed to reporters that "it was a suicide note. It wasn't a confession."

In Higgs's suicide note, he began by greeting the media and asked them to "please continue the investigation against Brian Krolicki, Mark DeStefano, and Bob Seale. These are the people that ruined my wife's life. Please don't let this die with me." He addressed his brother-in-law

Phil Alfano and Dallas Augustine in the suicide note, and said good-bye to his young daughter, who lived in Las Vegas with her mother. He signed off by saying, *I'm going to Heaven to be with my wife.*

Higgs later spoke to CBS News reporters and told them that he had tried to kill himself because he was despondent over Kathy's death. He described how he had slashed his wrists.

"I actually did it over and over, because I wanted to make sure," Higgs told CBS. "I laid down and said, 'Good, now I can be with my wife.' And that was the last thing I remember. . . . I was hurting. I just couldn't handle the pain anymore. I loved my wife. And I just couldn't believe that she was taken away from me."

When asked if he thought the police were looking at him as a suspect, he acknowledged that he thought they were, but he indicated that he could not understand how people believed he had something to do with her death.

"I asked for the autopsy," Higgs said at one point. "I want to clear it up. My wife was a healthy fifty-year-old woman who dropped dead. I want to find out what happened. People don't know what went on in our home. She was frazzled and stressed-out."

Higgs indicated that he welcomed the police investigation into his wife's death, but was bothered by all of the foul-play speculation that was being bounced around. Higgs said that he believed that the police were ignoring other potential suspects and were instead focusing on him. He said that because his wife was controversial, she had made a lot of enemies. Higgs claimed that he had nothing to gain financially from Kathy's death, because she had left her entire estate to her daughter, Dallas.

When asked to comment about Chaz Higgs's attempted suicide, Governor Kenny Guinn said, "You never know what goes through another person's mind." He said that he would wait until the investigation into Kathy's death had been completed before making additional statements.

A traditional Catholic funeral for Kathy Augustine was held the following day, Saturday, July 15, 2006, at the Guardian Angel Cathedral located on Cathedral Way and Las Vegas Boulevard, the famed "Strip," where about two hundred mourners showed up to pay their last respects. Besides Kathy's family, among those in attendance were Governor Kenny Guinn, Representative Shelley Berkley, a Democrat, and Secretary of State Dean Heller. Although none of her family members spoke during the service, several people who had known her offered words of praise.

"I never thought in a hundred years I'd be here standing before you for the funeral of Kathy Augustine," said Reverend Mike Keliher. "The sudden and unexpected death of Kathy Augustine confronts us all."

Lonnie Hammargren, former lieutenant governor and retired neurosurgeon, known as a colorful personality around Las Vegas, described Kathy as spunky and feisty, and said that he was still considering voting for her for state treasurer. Her name was still on the ballot, and would not be removed due to the fact that May 22, 2006, had been the last date in which a candidate could have their name removed from the ballot. Hammargren also said that he believed that Higgs was only grieving and was not really suicidal when he slit his wrists.

"Nurses know you can't kill yourself by slashing your wrists," Hammargren said.

One person who was not in attendance at the funeral was Kathy's husband, Chaz Higgs. A private burial followed the funeral. Since it was closed to the public, it was not immediately known whether Higgs was in attendance.

Two days later, Greg Augustine, thirty-six, Kathy's stepson, publicly stated that he believed his stepmother's death was suspicious, and that he had a lot of unanswered questions about the death of his father, Charles Augustine, that would not go away.

"He was getting better," Greg said, "and then suddenly all his organs failed. There never was an autopsy."

He said that depending upon how the toxicology tests being conducted by the FBI turned out, he and his family had begun looking into what it would take to get his father's body exhumed to have similar toxicology tests performed on his remains. He indicated that he was suspicious because Higgs had been his father's critical care nurse at Sunrise Hospital and Medical Center and had married his stepmother three weeks after his father suddenly died. But he was also quick to not rush to any unfounded conclusions.

"A person is innocent until proven guilty," he said. "But I am not surprised that he tried to kill himself. . . . I have complete confidence the truth will be revealed."

However, he said that if it turned out that his stepmother had not died as a result of natural causes, his family was prepared to move forward with their plans to get his father's body exhumed.

Greg Augustine, along with additional family members, urged restraint on the part of the news media and the public in general to avoid speculation, which had been rampant, about Kathy Augustine's death. Similarly, Dallas Augustine asked through an intermediary that inference and speculation should be avoided to give investigators time to do their jobs properly.

"She just lost her mother," said her spokesperson. "All of it is so shocking to her. When the autopsy (toxicology report) is released, she will make comments at an appropriate time."

It is fairly common knowledge among homicide investigators that when one spouse kills another for whatever reason—be it for financial gain or because of an impending threat of divorce, or any number of other reasons—the suspect will often attempt to divert attention or suspicion away from himself by acting the part of the grieving husband or wife. After having planned and carried out the murder, the suspect will often set himself up to play the part of a victim as well in an attempt to make himself appear sympathetic to the family and the cops investigating the murder. Sometimes this is accomplished by attempting suicide.

Was Chaz Higgs's suicide attempt genuine, done because he was grieving over his wife's death? Or had he slit his wrists to divert attention away from himself? Jenkins didn't know at this point, nor did anyone else—except Chaz Higgs.

Chapter 8

After Chaz Higgs's suicide attempt, he appeared to disappear from public view. He had not attended his wife's funeral in Las Vegas, nor had he attended a memorial service for her in Carson City. No one had seen him at the house he had shared with Kathy in Las Vegas, and the vertical blinds on the front side of the house had remained closed. Neighbors had not seen any vehicles coming to or going from the house, and there had not been any cars parked in the driveway in recent days. Higgs had not returned telephone calls to reporters for Las Vegas newspapers, some of whom had left notes at the Las Vegas home, and telephone calls to the home in Reno had also gone unanswered. Similarly, the police in Reno had not had any contact with Higgs for several days. Although it seemed that Higgs had vanished, Reno police did not seem particularly concerned because there was not any evidence that a crime had been committed, and Higgs was officially not a suspect in his wife's death. And if the toxicology tests being conducted by the FBI came back negative, the case would be closed, according to Lieutenant Jon Catalano.

Nonetheless, as Detective David Jenkins continued

looking into Chaz Higgs's background, an interesting picture of the grieving husband began to emerge. Jenkins learned that Higgs had been living inside a small travel trailer in a Boulder Highway trailer park in Las Vegas when he had met Kathy Augustine while he worked as a critical care nurse at Sunrise Hospital and Medical Center. Jenkins also knew that Kathy and Charles Augustine had planned a trip to Hawaii in 2003, but when Charles died and Kathy began seeing Higgs, she had asked him to go with her instead. The detective turned up information indicating that it may have been *after* they had arrived in the islands that Kathy had asked Higgs to marry her—despite the fact that she barely knew him. Of course, he had readily accepted, and they tied the knot while there.

When Charles Augustine died, he left Kathy the Las Vegas home they purchased on Maria Elena Drive in 1990 for approximately $350,000, which had a value of nearly $1 million at the time of his death, along with a $1 million insurance policy on his life. Financially, he had left her in very good shape. For whatever reason, Kathy had not placed her new husband on the deeds to either of her properties.

When Kathy's friends found out about the marriage, they told her that she was crazy. And when some of them met him, they could see that, yes, he was handsome, and he was buff. He didn't talk much, and many of Kathy's friends felt that he was self-centered and totally into himself. None of her friends could understand why Kathy would marry someone like Chaz Higgs, and they certainly hadn't liked him.

"Chaz couldn't even pay his bills," said one of Kathy's friends. "We all wanted her to get a living trust. We didn't want him to drain her of everything she had. . . . She kicked him out once, and then took him back. She talked frequently about divorcing him."

Jenkins also learned that Higgs had three wives prior to Kathy, and each of them characterized Higgs in much the same way that Kathy's friends had sized him up. In addition to appearing to be someone who was always finding himself getting into whirlwind marriages, Higgs was also financially irresponsible. He was known to run up considerable credit card debt, and had filed for bankruptcy twice before meeting Kathy Augustine.

Along with his twin brother, Higgs was born on June 2, 1964, and grew up in Virginia and North Carolina. The two boys were raised by their father, William "Bill" Higgs, who was in the U.S. Marines, and they moved around a lot because of their father's military affiliation. As far as Jenkins had been able to determine, Higgs's childhood had not been particularly remarkable. When he was nineteen, shortly after graduation from high school, Higgs enlisted in the navy, where he remained for the next sixteen years. It was while training as a corpsman at Camp Lejeune, North Carolina, that Higgs met his first wife. The couple was married on September 15, 1984.

His first wife described him as athletic, someone who enjoyed weight lifting and bodybuilding and, like Kathy's friends, said that he was very much into himself. At one point during their short marriage, Higgs's wife caught him in bed with another young woman inside their home. Although she had attempted to make their marriage work despite Higgs's infidelity, he couldn't remain faithful to her. In 1985, shortly after transferring to Jacksonville, Florida, Higgs began an affair with a married woman who had an infant child. After divorcing his first wife, Higgs eventually married the woman with whom he had been having an affair, following her divorce from her husband. It was in

1989, while still living in Florida, that Higgs filed his first bankruptcy. Following his marriage to wife number two, Higgs legally adopted her infant child.

In the autumn of 1990, Higgs had received a transfer to San Diego, California, where he was to report for duty on a medical ship. His second wife had opted to get out of the navy so that she could be a full-time mother to her child. While on their way to San Diego, Higgs left his wife in Las Vegas, a 5½-hour drive to his duty station. She found work as an apartment manager near the Strip, and the two seldom saw each other afterward. They were divorced in the summer of 1992, and Higgs was ordered to pay $400 per month in child support for his adopted child.

For the next few years, Higgs remained single, until he was transferred for duty in Manama, Bahrain, where he remained from July 1993 to February 1997. While stationed in Bahrain, however, Higgs met the woman who would eventually become his third wife. She was the mother of a two-year-old child. While it wasn't clear where the marriage occurred, public records show that Higgs and his third wife filed for bankruptcy on October 29, 1998, in Alexandria, Virginia, a year and a half after returning from overseas.

Higgs was discharged from the navy on March 1, 1999, after sixteen years of service. At the time of his discharge, he was an E-6, the rank of a medical corpsman. After his discharge, Higgs and his third wife relocated to Louisville, Tennessee. They didn't remain there long. That same year, they moved to Las Vegas. Possessing an associate's degree in nursing, Higgs continued his education by taking courses from the University of Phoenix via the Internet, where he reportedly received a bachelor of science and a doctoral degree. Higgs and his third wife divorced at some point during the time that they lived in Las Vegas, where both remained afterward.

Armed with his degrees, Higgs took the examination for his nursing license in Nevada in 2002, passed it, and went to work a short time later at Sunrise Hospital and Medical Center, where he met Kathy Augustine, who would become wife number four.

At some point, Higgs changed his birth name, William Charles Higgs, to Chaz Higgs, because he thought that Chaz was a more fashionable name and sounded trendier. Because there were no public records documenting a legal name change, it could not be determined when or where the name change occurred, or if it had actually been done legally.

In the midst of all of the questions and uncertainties about his past, one thing stood at the forefront: Chaz Higgs was a real piece of work.

Chapter 9

As the aura of mystery surrounding Kathy Augustine's death grew in intensity, the story began to shift gears to quickly become one of political intrigue that served to cast doubt on why the Nevada State Police found it necessary to bring in its investigative arm to assist the Reno Police Department with their investigation. The official story, of course, was that the Reno Police Department had asked for their help with the case, but as the story continued to unfold, it caused many people, including investigative journalists for national television news programs, to begin asking questions. While it is no secret that corruption has always run high at all levels of government in Nevada, it appeared that, just prior to Kathy's death, the Nevada controller was preparing to blow the whistle on alleged significant dishonesty at the state level. Some people believed that it may not have been a coincidence that Kathy had become the target of the state's first impeachment proceeding against one of its elected officials. After all, it was no secret that people in high places at the state level of government wanted her out of the way—most of the state's politicians did not want to sit idly by and see her win yet another position of elected office. What better way was there to get her out of the picture than by disgracing her politically?

According to Barbara Woollen, a Nevada business-woman who was running for lieutenant governor in the 2006 Republican primary election, Kathy Augustine approached her one day, after she had announced her run for state treasurer, and confided in her that she had initiated an investigation into corruption in the state. Woollen explained the situation briefly to CBS News *48 Hours* when reporters for that program came to Nevada to cover Kathy Augustine's suspicious death.

"She told me that she had information that she thought I needed to know about," Woollen said. "It involved political corruption. Misappropriation of funds, slush funds."

Woollen told reporters that Kathy was aware that her politically volatile investigation into political corruption and financial transgressions had placed her life in danger.

"She said that a prominent Republican figure had thrown her against a wall," Woollen recalled, "and said the following to her: 'What are you doing? You're going to "F" it all up. If you know what's good for you, you'll drop out of this race and go away. Otherwise, you better watch your back.'"

According to Las Vegas political analyst Jon Ralston, the Republican leadership in Nevada were staggered and taken aback, not only by her investigation into corruption, but also by her announcement that she was going to run for state treasurer right after being impeached while state controller. They also felt that she had betrayed the party.

"I think they were flabbergasted," Ralston said. "I think they were upset. I think they didn't know exactly what to do because some thought, 'You know what? She might have a chance.'"

Despite the threats and other tactics that were being

used against her, allegedly by her colleagues inside her own political party, Kathy rejected their attempts to get her to quit. At one point, she appeared on Ralston's television show to defend herself, and he had asked her on the air if she had ever thought about resigning.

"When you know that what you did, did not rise to the level of impeachment," she replied, "then it was a matter of staying there and fighting for something you truly believed in."

Ralston recounted some of Kathy's political misdeeds, and made comments about the ruthless politician that lay beneath her on-camera smile.

"I think people really, really despised Kathy Augustine because of the tactics she used," Ralston said to *48 Hours* correspondent Troy Roberts. "She really hit people below the belt. And she really used the most divisive wedge, personal, emotional, inflammatory issues to get ahead."

But was it her political persona that had upset people so much? Or was it the fact that she had launched an investigation that had the potential to not only embarrass some of the state's elected officials but to possibly bring them down as well? Given the mystery surrounding how Kathy had died, the questions really needed answering—but the police did not seem to have an interest.

Some people hinted that Kathy's political problems began after her state colleagues realized that she was being considered for the position of U.S. treasurer. One of her close friends, Nancy Vinnik, had been vocal about it.

"She was being looked at for a position in the U.S. Treasury," Vinnik said. "And I think there were some good ole boys that didn't like that. That's when all the troubles in her life really, really started to happen—politically."

But had it really been the U.S. Treasury position that she was being considered for that had upset people in her party? Or was it fear of her perfectionist ways that bothered them, knowing that someone as thorough as Kathy might actually get to the bottom of the purported political corruption involving slush funds that she was attempting to bring out into the open? Were the alleged wrongdoers really *that* fearful that she might actually expose them?

"Everything in her whole life was organized," Vinnik recalled as she explained how Kathy possessed an emblematic type A character trait. "That was just Kathy. All of her clothes were color coordinated. All of her suits were in order. She was a perfectionist to a T in everything that she did."

Interestingly, according to *48 Hours,* the threat against Kathy was never taken seriously by the police and was not investigated. Neither were a number of other alleged serious threats against Kathy's health and safety—they were all apparently ignored by the police as they investigated her death.

Phil Alfano, Kathy's brother, told *48 Hours* a similar account. He said that Kathy had told him that there were several people who had tried to scare her to keep her from running for state treasurer.

"She did tell me that several people had warned her to be careful," Alfano told CBS correspondent Troy Roberts. "There were threats made to her."

But there was another troubling aspect surrounding the involvement of the Nevada State Police being so active in the investigation of Kathy's death. According to the *Las Vegas Sun,* while the Reno Police Department was still referring to their case as a death investigation and proclaiming that Chaz Higgs was neither a suspect nor a person of interest, the state police were apparently closely monitoring all of the media reports, print and broadcast, that came out about Kathy's death. At one point, the *Sun* had launched its own investigation and had reporters scrambling to try and learn as much about Chaz Higgs as possible. During the course of their efforts, they spoke to each of Higgs's ex-wives in an attempt to develop a profile of the newly widowed man, and at least in one instance that the *Sun* documented, the Nevada Division of Investigation had been there afterward advising the source not to speak with the news media.

The big question on the minds of many people was *"why?"* Since there hadn't been any gag orders issued in the case, what made the state police think that it was their responsibility to advise people not to speak with the news media? And even if a gag order had been issued, it would seem that a violation of such would become an issue for the court and not a police agency. Were there larger issues behind the actions of the state police? Had those in power at the highest levels of state government given orders for the state police to monitor the news media reports and, wherever possible, put a lid on the flow of information? If so, why? If it is the job of the investigative arm of a police agency to determine the truth behind criminal activities, what was there to hide?

When the *Sun* brought the matter up to the Reno Police Department, the response that the newspaper received was that the Reno Police Department had not asked the state police to instruct people not to talk about the case.

"They probably did it thinking they were helping us," Lieutenant Jon Catalano told the *Sun*.

Helping them do what? Find the truth? Or cover up the corruption that Kathy Augustine had purportedly been trying to expose?

Like the circumstances of Kathy's death, their action was a mystery that might never be solved because no one, it seemed, wanted to ask the questions needed to arrive at the answers. After the *Las Vegas Sun* article about Chaz

Higgs came out—with the information buried deep inside about the state police advising people not to speak with the media—no one, it seemed, had been interested in pursuing the issue any further.

According to the *Las Vegas Sun,* Chaz Higgs's name had first shown up in news media accounts as early as March 2005, right after he had filed a complaint with the Nevada Ethics Commission against Senator Steven Horsford, a Democrat who represented north Las Vegas. Higgs alleged in his complaint that there were irregularities that pertained to some of the senator's campaign contributions. According to published reports, Horsford claimed that Higgs's complaint had been filed purely for retribution for criticism he had voiced during Kathy Augustine's impeachment proceedings. Nonetheless, Horsford later filed amendments to some of his campaign reports, and the matter seemed to go away. Questions, such as whether Higgs had filed the complaint at the behest of his wife, or whether he had done it on his own, or whether Horsford had been a part of Kathy's larger corruption investigation, were never adequately answered.

Chapter 10

As the summer of 2006 passed quickly for most people, it seemed to drag on forever for Kathy Augustine's family as they anxiously awaited the results of toxicology tests that were being performed on Kathy's blood and urine by the FBI's crime laboratory. As July came to a close and moved into August, her family and friends recalled her laughter, the fact that she was an accomplished pianist, as well as a swimmer in school, and an upbeat person who was fond of collecting elephant figurines and throwing birthday bashes for members of her staff. Although many people had known her as tough and abrasive, there were just as many people, perhaps more, who had seen and recognized the funny, kind, and caring side of Kathy Augustine. Her brother Phil pointed out that her favorite singer had been Barbra Streisand, a liberal Democrat.

On the other side of the coin, there were those who would always remember the Kathy Augustine who seemed to make waves wherever she went. Nevada Republican Party chairman Paul Adams, who had worked hard to get her ostracized from her party, was one of those people. About two months before her death, Adams had introduced a motion at the state GOP convention that would effectively change the party's bylaws to prevent party support, financial or otherwise, for candidates who had been impeached and found guilty. His motion was approved, and many people, both from within and outside the party, had viewed his actions as an unswerving political assault against Kathy.

Adams had also made the remark after her death, published in the *Las Vegas Review-Journal:* "My goal was for her to live a long and productive life, just not as a Republican candidate." Kathy's family, including her mother, had read Adams's statement and had taken offense to it. Phil Alfano indicated that he was going to "make sure her reputation doesn't get trashed." After taking considerable heat over making the remark, Adams apologized.

"I understand all of it has been difficult for them (Kathy's family)," Adams said. "I would apologize for any difficulty I caused for the family, and from now on, I will have no more comments."

Nonetheless, as cruel and mean-spirited as such comments may be perceived, they do go with the territory of being a politician.

At another point during the summer, Kathy's brother announced that a scholarship fund had been established in Kathy Augustine's name. It was designed for students who wanted careers in public service.

"It is one way for her spirit to live on," Phil Alfano said.

Recounting an episode depicting the marital lives of Kathy and Higgs, Winifred Cindy Baker, a nurse and a witness on behalf of the state, who had been mentored by Higgs at Washoe Medical South, related an incident in which Kathy had brought Higgs into the hospital's emergency room for treatment of what was termed a "severe allergic reaction." Higgs was obviously having a difficult time breathing. While hospital personnel were attempting to obtain information about Higgs and his condition, Kathy was purportedly talking about herself and an unspecified project that she was currently working on. At one point, Baker interjected and explained to Kathy that the hospital staff was not there for her at that time, and that they were there for Chaz, who presently wasn't doing too well. Baker's remarks clearly hadn't won Kathy over as a friend, and Kathy, regardless of Chaz or his condition, hadn't hesitated to let her know it.

"I can have your job by the end of the day," Kathy reportedly said to Baker.

There were other incidents of unpleasant exchanges, usually over the phone when Kathy would call to speak with Higgs.

The next time Baker saw Kathy Augustine was on the morning of July 8, 2006, when paramedics brought her into the emergency room. Although Kathy was being treated by Marlene Swanbeck and Chris McCabe, Baker was on duty that morning. Curiosity took her into the area where Swanbeck and McCabe were working on Kathy, but only for a brief moment. Baker saw Higgs when he showed up at the hospital, and she spoke to him as any employee would to another.

Because it had been determined that Kathy needed a heart catheter, not to mention the fact that she was critically ill due to an as-yet-unknown cause, the decision was made to move her from Washoe Medical South to the ICU at Washoe Medical Main. According to Baker, she made the decision to visit Kathy and Higgs later that day, at about 8:00 P.M., thinking that Higgs might need some help or support from his coworkers. After passing a little time in the ICU waiting room, Baker was allowed to enter the area where Higgs and Kathy were to be found.

While Higgs was talking to a nurse with a chart in her hand, presumably about Kathy's condition, treatment, and prognosis, and going over lab reports, Baker walked up to Kathy's bedside. Kathy appeared to be conscious, but she wasn't. Her eyes twitched uncontrollably, and a nurse later said that the reason her eyes were twitching was because she was having seizures. Baker held Kathy's hand at one point and said, "I'm so sorry" before leaving.

Baker said that her actions in the ICU room with Kathy that evening were the result of compassion due to the fact that Kathy was her coworker's wife—despite the fact that Kathy had shown her unpleasant side by threatening to have Baker fired from her job.

The Nevada primary election, with Kathy's name on the ballot for state treasurer, occurred while everyone waited to find out once and for all whether Kathy had died of natural causes or whether she had been murdered. Not surprisingly, she collected 26,000 posthumous votes. It wasn't enough votes to get past the primary election, but her family took solace in the fact that there were so many people who had voted for her even though she was dead. It was an impressive number of votes for a dead person, made all the more remarkable because state law requires that notices be posted in every polling location in the state explaining that her name was on the ballot even though she was deceased.

Soon the month of August had passed, and Chaz Higgs had retrieved what few personal items he had from the two houses that he had shared with Kathy and left the state. Taking one of the vehicles that had been left to him in

Kathy's will, Higgs moved to South Carolina, where he stayed with relatives. Almost everything had been left to Kathy's daughter, Dallas.

"Not much was left for Chaz," Phil Alfano said.

Whether Higgs knew the details of the will that Kathy had drawn up in 2004 was not clear. He had claimed to know the will's details before Kathy's death, but the possibility that he only found out after her death could not be ruled out. If he had known that everything would be going to Dallas Augustine in the event of Kathy's death, it would serve to diminish motive if it turned out that Higgs would be charged in her death. On the other hand, it could be a different matter entirely if he hadn't had prior knowledge of the will's contents and had presumed that he might get a bigger piece of the pie in the event of his wife's demise. A last will and testament can be a vile thing when aligned with a person who possesses murderous intentions.

Even though Higgs had no criminal record, the Reno Police Department made sure that they knew where he was at all times through communications with law enforcement agencies in South Carolina as they awaited the toxicology reports from the FBI. They also had information that Higgs had a relative in the Hampton, Virginia, area that they factored into the contingency plan they had put together, which would be ready, if needed.

As September rolled around and autumn drew near, the stress levels of Kathy's family naturally rose higher. They all wanted to know what had happened to Kathy and were anxious to get some closure over her death so that they could get on with their lives. But the tests were taking so long. What everyone had been led to believe would take only five or six weeks had by now stretched to eight weeks, and then nine. They began to wonder if they would ever know what had really happened to Kathy.

"It's really tough on my parents," said Phil Alfano. "They lost a daughter. . . . The wait has caused them a lot of stress. It has caused me stress. . . . They can't do just one test if they don't know what they're looking for. If they do not find drug A, then they have to do a test for drug B. The wait has been tough on all of us."

Lieutenant Jon Catalano told family members that he sympathized with them, but said that "three months is not out of line" to receive a toxicology report from the FBI in a case that was not specifically labeled a homicide.

"We were hoping for that quick turnaround," Catalano said. "It hasn't happened. We thought this death would have a high priority. That's why we wanted them to do it instead of our local crime lab. We are a little bit anxious because it is taking a long time."

Meanwhile, Kathy's family began expressing their opinions about Chaz Higgs. They described their initial relationship with him as cordial, "not unfriendly." Although Higgs's family had liked Kathy, many of the Alfanos, particularly Kathy's mother, hadn't liked him. She had kept her feelings to herself for a long time, but when asked, she decided that it was time to express her feelings more honestly.

"I didn't like him," said Kathy's mother, Kay Alfano. "And I told her so. . . . None of us liked him."

She went even further by saying that she believed that Higgs, not any of Kathy's political enemies, had killed her daughter. She said that she had based her opinion on "the way he acted." She said that while Kathy was in a coma in the hospital, Higgs had not shown any emotion. He had not shed any tears when she died after the family decided to remove her from life support.

"When she died, he just sat down," Kay said. "He just sat there. Didn't say a word."

The family, according to Kathy's brother, Phil, hadn't

taken their suspicions to the police because they really hadn't known what had happened. He said that they had nothing to go on except for their feelings, and they were concerned that the police might think that they were over-reacting.

According to her family, Kathy had been confiding in them for quite some time before her death that her relationship with Chaz Higgs had been a troubled one. He was irresponsible with their money, and had significantly over-drawn their bank account because of his spending habits.

"He was always broke," Kay said. "He was always asking her for money."

According to Phil Alfano, Higgs was also verbally abusive toward Kathy. Phil believed that Higgs had been unfaithful to his sister, an insinuation that Higgs would later deny.

As they continued waiting for an answer from the FBI, the question on everyone's mind was, of course: what had happened to Kathy? The case received so much widespread attention that speculation over Kathy's death continued to run rampant, in spite of requests from her family that only the facts should be dealt with. Some of the unwanted spec-ulation continued to center around how Kathy and Higgs had met in the first place, and had decided to marry so quickly after the death of Kathy's husband Charles. Many people chalked it up to Kathy being eccentric, while others seriously considered that there might be more to it because of the unusual connection between her two husbands.

"There are questions," agreed Lieutenant Catalano.

At times, particularly during the first few months after Kathy's death, it had all seemed so much like a television soap opera—the kind the public couldn't get enough of.

Chapter 11

Although everyone connected to the case was growing more impatient by the day to learn the outcome of the tests on Kathy Augustine's blood and urine, they also understood the process that the specimens had to go through for any conclusion to be reached. To compound the tedium at work here, they also realized that the process was a bureaucratic one. First of all, supervisory personnel at the FBI's crime laboratory in Quantico, Virginia, were contacted by authorities in Reno to determine if the FBI's lab could perform testing that could not be accomplished in Reno. When it was agreed that the FBI lab would perform the requested testing, Kathy's blood and urine specimens were sent to the FBI lab via overnight express. When the package containing the specimens arrived, it was received by the evidence control center, where the package was opened. After the contents had been identified and logged in, it was then passed along to the scientist who would perform the work—in this case, Madeline Montgomery, a forensic examiner in the area of chemistry and toxicology. Montgomery held a B.S. degree in chemistry from George Washington University, in Washington, D.C., and had been employed by the FBI lab for eleven years. She had also completed graduate courses from the same university in chemistry, toxicology, and forensic chemistry, in addition to the regularly occurring training provided by the FBI—in-house training that the government believes helps its employees perform their jobs more effectively and efficiently. Also a member of the Society of Forensic Toxicologists and the International Association of Forensic Toxicologists, Montgomery seemed more than adequately qualified to perform the job that she had been asked to do.

When Montgomery received the specimens, one of the first things she did was to make certain that the containers' seals were still intact. Satisfied that they were, she inventoried the contents which would enable her to determine which tests, and how many, she would be able to perform with the amount of specimen she had on hand. In this particular case, she had, of course, been specifically asked to look for one drug, succinylcholine or its breakdown or metabolite product, succinylmonocholine. The drug, she knew, was a paralytic, a form of curare.

According to Montgomery, succinylcholine, being a unique drug, is not routinely tested in every forensic laboratory in the country, which is why it is sometimes sent to the FBI lab. Even at the FBI lab, tests searching for the presence of succinylcholine are not done every day of the week. As such, it required Montgomery to make new reagents and prepare the equipment, to get it ready to go specifically for the succinylcholine testing.

Because the FBI lab has looked for succinylcholine and its breakdown product in the specimens it examines for a number of years, they had placed a procedure online specifically for the breakdown product, succinylmonocholine, as a chemical marker or indicator of the drug's presence in the specimens being examined, before doing anything else.

Not being a very stable chemical, whether it's in a human body or in a test tube in a lab, succinylcholine breaks down fairly quickly through the process of hydrolysis and its reaction to water and enzymes. Enzymes in the human body help break down drugs and other toxins into less toxic materials so that the body can quickly process and expel the material, whatever it is. These same enzymes act on succinylcholine to produce succinylmonocholine in the body. If the breakdown product isn't present, there is no need to go any further with the testing because the succinylcholine wouldn't be there, either.

The test that is used to look for succinylcholine and its breakdown product is called liquid chromatography mass spectrometry.

"It's actually two techniques in one," Montgomery said.

The liquid chromatography (LC) part helps the scientist separate chemicals, such as separating the succinylcholine and its metabolite from other chemicals present in the body.

"It's a separation technique so that we can clean it up or clean up our sample and look at the drug and metabolite away from the other things that may be present," Montgomery said.

The second part of the test is called mass spectrometry (MS), which the FBI likes to call a chemical fingerprinting technique that allows the scientist to look at the chemical and identify its very unique signature pattern so that it can be differentiated or excluded from all other chemicals. The FBI runs the liquid chromatography and mass spectrometry tests twice. The first is called the screening technique, and the second is called the confirmation technique.

Because the LC-MS piece of equipment is utilized on a daily basis to test for a wide range of chemicals that are sent to the lab, including illicit drugs, such as cocaine and heroin, among many others, and prescription medications, it is necessary to ensure that the equipment is always up and running and ready to go for the task at hand. As a result, each day the machine is turned on and a mix of five different chemicals that is known to the scientist is run through it to ensure that it is working properly. The procedure actually tests the range of the machine, and the five chemicals are often referred to as a "known mix." Whenever it came time to look for a particular chemical, such as succinylcholine, the lab technician would run a standard of the chemical through the machine to make sure that it was working properly for the drugs or metabolites that were being looked for on any given day.

There are actually two types of data that are produced by the equipment. Much of the data looks like a graph and has peaks and valleys. The data from the LC separates components based on their size and their chemical nature in time, while data from the MS produces numbers that represent different masses across a mass range and looks like a stick figure graph. Therefore, simplistically put, the LC separates components and the MS provides a chemical fingerprint, thus granting the laboratory investigator the ability to identify the chemical(s) present in any given sample, which is being examined.

To prove that succinylcholine or its metabolite does not naturally occur in a live human being, Montgomery took fifteen different urine samples from volunteers in the FBI's lab and ran them through the processes described to look for the presence of succinylcholine. Finding none in any of the urine samples, she was satisfied that succinylcholine does not show up naturally in the urine of a living human being. To determine what succinylcholine would look like when detected in a urine sample, Montgomery took a sample of her own urine and several samples of the volunteers' urine and added succinylcholine to each. She then ran them through the lab equipment and obtained the "chemical fingerprint." After placing a concentrated sample of Kathy Augustine's urine into the equipment, she placed a "blank," or a negative urine sample, right before or in front of Kathy's sample to verify that there was no contamination throughout the process. It all sounded like overkill to the layman, but it was part of the tedious process of lab work to ensure accurate results.

To Kathy Augustine's family and the Reno Police Department, Wednesday, September 27, 2006, turned out to be the day they had all been waiting for, a day that had seemed like it would never come. But the day had arrived, and that afternoon brought the nervously awaited toxicology report on Kathy's blood and urine. Madeline Montgomery had found traces of succinylcholine in the samples of Kathy Augustine's urine, which had been sent to the FBI for analysis more than two months earlier. She ran the samples of Kathy's urine three times, and each time succinylcholine, as well as its metabolite, was present.

However, Montgomery failed to detect the presence of succinylcholine or its breakdown product in the tissue samples taken from Kathy Augustine's body. Because succinylcholine is such an unstable chemical, as explained earlier, Montgomery really hadn't expected to find the drug's presence in the tissue samples. Because of the body's ability to break down toxins in order to get rid of them, it would have been very unusual to find succinylcholine in the tissue samples, according to Montgomery. Typically, such a drug would be excreted by the body in just a matter of hours. In Kathy's case, she survived— although in a coma—for a few days, until her family decided to have her removed from life support. According to the scientific literature and the findings of the FBI lab, the time period would have been sufficient for the drug to have disappeared from the tissues of Kathy's body.

Similarly, Montgomery had not found succinylcholine or its breakdown product present in Kathy's blood, due to the fact that enzymes in the blood had broken each down further into other chemicals that most people have present in their blood.

After carefully reviewing the report, Detective David Jenkins presented the findings to his supervisor. Afterward, Jenkins spent much of that evening and part of the next day putting together an affidavit for a first-degree murder warrant and presented it to a Washoe County judge. The warrant was quickly approved as a sealed warrant, and Jenkins and his colleagues, knowing that Higgs had been staying with a relative in the Hampton, Virginia, area, notified their counterparts in that jurisdiction and supplied them with a copy of the warrant. Jenkins had asked that the arrest warrant be sealed because Higgs was considered both a flight risk and a suicide risk.

"We believed that Chaz was a flight risk," said Lieutenant Jon Catalano. "Based on what happened in Las Vegas, also a suicide risk."

After completing all of the necessary steps, the Reno detective requested that Hampton police arrest Higgs at their earliest opportunity.

Hampton police quickly organized a plan of action, and began watching the house where Higgs had been staying with a relative. Even though it had taken a little more than a day and a half from the time Reno police received the toxicology report to set up the arrest stakeout on the other side of the nation, the operation went off without a hitch. At a few minutes before 6:00 P.M., on Friday, September 29, 2006, Chaz Higgs, driving the BMW that had been left to him through Kathy's will, pulled into the driveway of the relative's house. Hampton police, in unmarked vehicles and regular police cruisers, converged on the house and surrounded Higgs before he could even step out of the BMW. After explaining to him that he was being arrested on charges that he had murdered his wife, he was handcuffed, placed inside one of the waiting cruisers, and taken to the local jail facility, where he was booked and jailed.

An extradition hearing was scheduled for the following Monday, a necessary legal step before he could be transported back to northern Nevada to stand trial.

Although Kathy's family members had been notified of the information contained in the toxicology report shortly after it had been received, everything had been kept under wraps from the media to ensure a smooth arrest. However, after news of the arrest had been made public, the family began expressing their thoughts and feelings to a variety of media sources, particularly the *Las Vegas Sun* and the *Las Vegas Review-Journal*.

Dallas Augustine told reporters that she'd had no reason to suspect that Higgs had killed her mother until the results of the toxicology tests had come back positive.

"Two months ago, I was faced with my mom's death, and that was completely devastating," Dallas said. "Now I have to deal with the fact that my stepfather is being charged with her murder."

She said that Higgs's arrest had caused the grieving process to begin "all over again."

"I was firm with my believing that everyone is innocent until proven guilty," she added, "and now we have the evidence to go on. . . . Now he can rot."

Following Higgs's arrest, the troubling subject of a

possible motive for him to have killed his wife came up again among family members.

"It is a question that we all are asking," Phil Alfano said. "We can't get inside his head. I am confident it all will come out. . . . You know how it is with a relative. You don't want to say things. But things with him bothered me. . . . Their relationship seemed strange to us from the very beginning. My hope is he does the right thing and owns up to his crime. I hope he spares my family additional grief."

Phil, who was the executor of his sister's estate, reiterated his thoughts about the will, and said that Higgs had only received the couple's vehicles, some sports equipment, and little else. It was hardly enough to kill someone over—if he had known that the bulk of the estate was going to Kathy's daughter.

Kathy's family apparently wasn't alone in thinking that the relationship between Kathy and Higgs had been unusual. An elderly neighbor couple, John and Dotty Tsitouras, who had been longtime friends of Kathy and Charles Augustine, had been suspicious of Higgs long before Kathy had died.

"Everyone who knew Kathy over the years had something negative to say about him," Dotty said.

Approximately a year before Kathy's death, Dotty said, Kathy had confided to her that she had been planning to divorce Higgs because he had spent all of the money in one of Kathy's bank accounts.

Dotty's husband, John, however, was considerably more to the point in his opinion about Chaz Higgs, and said that he had pointed the finger at him as being responsible for Kathy's death shortly after she had died. He said that he had made it a point to stay in touch with Kathy's family following the tragedy.

"I always thought he was a phony," John said to a reporter for the *Sun*. "I think Chaz was a complete con artist, and I think that is going to show up in his dealings with previous ladies. . . . It certainly puzzles us to this day that Kathy was taken in by Chaz. He always seemed to strut and pose. He seemed pretty apolitical. He was a bodybuilder. He had diamonds in both ears. . . . I couldn't figure out what Kathy could have possibly had to do with him. I suppose none of us are quite what we seem, on the surface."

Meanwhile, Greg Augustine made good on an earlier promise that he had made about having his father's body exhumed if the toxicology tests came back and showed that his stepmother had not died from natural causes. He promptly hired Las Vegas attorney Dominic Gentile, who had represented Kathy during her impeachment proceedings, on behalf of the family to ask Las Vegas authorities to investigate his father's death for evidence of foul play. Specifically, he wanted tissue samples from his father's body examined for traces of succinylcholine.

"It would be irresponsible for me not to do this for Dad," Greg said. "He did suffer a stroke, but he was getting better."

Charles Augustine had also been moved into the hospital's rehabilitation ward when he suddenly took a turn for the worse and died.

Dr. Cyril Wecht, the famed forensic pathologist, attorney, and medical-legal consultant, agreed with Greg Augustine's actions about having his father's body exhumed.

"I think they've got to in light of the facts of this case," Wecht told a reporter for the *Las Vegas Review-Journal*. "I would."

Chapter 12

In preparing his case against Chaz Higgs, Detective David Jenkins had learned as much as he could about the potent muscle relaxant known as succinylcholine. A pharmaceutical grade relative of curare, which originated in Central America and the northern part of South America, succinylcholine ranks among the highest in terms of being most potent on toxicity charts of known poisons. Its primary medicinal use, as previously stated, is to temporarily paralyze a patient so that emergency medical personnel can insert a breathing tube into the trachea. Hospital ER personnel like to use it because it is fast-acting and its paralytic effect diminishes rapidly. It only works as it is supposed to do when injected.

After succinylcholine enters the body, there's no turning back as it rapidly begins muscular paralysis, beginning in the area of the face and eyelids. Shortly thereafter, the person injected loses his ability to swallow or to even lift his head. The pulse drops radically as it moves into the area of the diaphragm, and the person becomes unable to breathe on his own as the drug paralyzes the lungs. If the person has been placed on a respirator, as they would be under a controlled medical setting, there are usually not any problems with the drug as it metabolically works its way out of the body and gradually releases the person from its grip of temporary paralysis.

Although there are no antidotes, if artificial respiration is performed during the time that the drug is active, the person generally recovers and suffers no adverse side effects. On the other hand, if the person does not receive artificial respiration, they die a slow, horrible death of suffocation, all the while being able to see and hear the actions of the killer as additional organs become damaged and begin to shut down.

In Kathy Augustine's case, it isn't readily known why she was still alive when the paramedics arrived. Not breathing, and with a pulse so weak as to be only barely detectable, she should have been dead. Perhaps it had all been a matter of timing—had the paramedics been a minute or two later, perhaps they wouldn't have been able to keep her alive through artificial respiration. Her body, however, had apparently been deprived of oxygen long enough to cause sufficient brain damage for her to become comatose.

"You have to breathe for them," said Dr. John Brouwers, a Las Vegas anesthesiologist. "The breathing muscles become paralyzed, and you can't breathe for yourself."

Although succinylcholine hasn't been widely used as a drug for deliberately killing people, it has been chosen by those bent on murder, particularly by those within the medical profession. It appears to be a favorite of such killers because it mimics the symptoms of heart failure.

Succinylcholine was first synthesized in 1906, but its usefulness as a neuromuscular blocking agent was not realized until 1949. Typically, the drug is administered through intravenous injection, and the aforementioned paralysis occurs and ends within about five minutes when the amount being injected is controlled. Reason dictates that a subcutaneous injection of the drug, such as would be the case if injected into the hip or buttocks, would likely take longer for it to act, as well as run its course, and might entail the holding down or some other incapacitation of the victim to prevent her from seeking assistance, or fighting off the killer, before the drug took effect. Before the 1980s and the case of Genene Jones, there had been no definitive method of analysis for succinylcholine in human tissue.

As he learned more about the drug, Jenkins found himself grateful for Nurse Kim Ramey's tip. Even though his gut had told him that Kathy had not died from a heart attack due to stress, as Higgs had claimed, he had sensed foul play. After all, Kathy's own family, including Greg, her stepson, did not believe that she had died from a stress-related heart attack.

"This woman thrived on stress," Greg Augustine said. "She has been through seven or eight elections, and an impeachment. Running for treasurer wouldn't cause her stress. She would have been excited."

One of Kathy's friends had echoed Greg's sentiments, Jenkins noted.

"I don't believe that stress would have caused a heart attack," said the friend. Kathy did not drink alcohol, and she did not take drugs, either, according to the friend. "Even when she was in the roughest times, the toughest times, she was always above it."

Furthermore, nothing that incriminated Higgs in Kathy's death had been found inside the house in Reno that the two had shared. When Jenkins and his colleagues then checked with the Carson-Tahoe Hospital, where Higgs had worked, an inventory of the hospital's supply of succinylcholine did not confirm that any was missing or otherwise unaccounted for. If not for Ramey, Jenkins realized, no one would have thought to look for succinylcholine at the time of autopsy, because it is not normally included in routine toxicology tests. If they hadn't suspected its use because of Higgs's slip of the tongue, Kathy's death would likely have been labeled a heart attack and gone unsolved.

"You have to be thinking of it and looking for it, or it's not going to show," Dr. Cyril Wecht told a reporter for the *Las Vegas Review-Journal.*

When all was said and done, just about everyone at the Reno Police Department and at the Washoe County Coroner's Office were of the opinion that the succinylcholine had been injected into Kathy only a short time before she was admitted to the South Meadows branch of the Washoe Medical Center. There was little, if any, doubt in anyone's mind that Higgs was responsible for his wife's death. Being a critical care nurse, Higgs had the means to obtain the drug that had killed his wife. Being alone with her inside the house also provided him with the opportunity to kill her. What seemed to be lacking was the motive.

A number of people that Jenkins had spoken to during the course of the investigation had described the marriage between Kathy and Chaz as unusual and odd, and some had even said that Kathy was making plans to divorce him at the time of her death. She had even confided to a close friend, whose husband had recently died of cancer, that she had made a mistake in marrying Higgs.

"You know, I made a big mistake," the friend quoted Kathy as saying.

She had reportedly told her friend that she had rushed into her marriage with Higgs after her husband Charles had died, and she cautioned her friend not to make that kind of mistake.

"She said, 'I know you are going to be lonely,'" her friend said. She said that Kathy told her that "it's going to hit you all of a sudden that you are alone. But don't make the same mistakes that I made. Don't listen to someone say they can take care of you."

Jenkins, as well as prosecutors, began to wonder if an impending divorce was a strong enough motive to murder someone. It was, they reasoned, if he stood to lose financially because of a divorce, but had everything to gain if Kathy died. On the other hand, a simple divorce often takes care of a lot of problems—without going to the extreme of killing one's partner. Plus, there was the fact that Higgs had been married, and divorced, multiple times before hooking up with Kathy. That fact served to diminish an impending divorce as a motive for murder. Why should he suddenly change his routine now and resort to murder? It just didn't seem to make much sense.

Having flown to Virginia to participate in the arrest of Chaz Higgs and the search of his car, Jenkins finally took possession of the yellow-and-black backpack that had previously been noted in the Reno house that Higgs and Kathy had shared. Jenkins removed the backpack's contents one item at a time, and carefully documented each item: a can of tuna fish, a can opener, medical literature, Higgs's identification, a belt, and documents and papers associated with employment at a hospital. He also found the *Nurses' Drug Guide,* the *Handbook of Hemodynamic Monitoring,* a pamphlet outlining the *Nevada State Board of Nursing Practice Act, Mosby's Diagnostic and Laboratory Test Reference* book, and a Sudoku puzzle book. There was also a nurses' dictionary that had been bookmarked between pages 214 and 215. Interestingly, the subject matter on those pages concerned intramuscular, subcutaneous, intradermal, and intravenous injections.

Also found during the police search of Higgs's car was a stack of three-by-five index cards that contained information regarding medical treatment, dosage, and therapy procedures. The first card on top of the stack read: *dosing for endotracheal intubation and paralytics* and *intubation medications and succinylcholine.* On the surface, of course, this all seemed like damning evidence against Chaz Higgs considering the circumstances of his wife's death. But Jenkins also knew that these types of publications and notes could likely appear in the possession of nurses anywhere, and that required him to keep an open mind. It was great circumstantial evidence, but it could also be shot down by a good defense attorney.

Chaz Higgs was scheduled to appear in a Hampton, Virginia, courtroom on Monday, October 2, 2006, where a decision would be made on whether to initiate extradition proceedings or not. If Higgs fought extradition, it would likely take about ten days to obtain a governor's warrant. However, Jenkins was grateful that Higgs had decided to waive extradition and had simplified the process of returning him to Nevada. Detective David Jenkins, along with another investigator, brought their prisoner back to Nevada.

Chapter 13

During the course of his investigation, both before and after Chaz Higgs's arrest, Jenkins continued putting the case against Higgs together, bit by bit. Some of the information that he would be going over had already been stated in the press, but being a detective, he naturally wanted to put his casebook together with hard information and one-on-one interviews with everyone involved. Among the things he narrowed his focus on at this stage of the investigation were the events of Saturday morning, July 8, 2006, when Kathy Augustine was rushed into South Meadows' emergency room, only to be transferred to the main hospital a short time later on the orders of Dr. Arun Kolli, Reno Heart Physicians, which is one of the two largest cardiology practices in northern Nevada. According to Dr. Stanley Thompson, a physician and cardiologist who was also with Reno Heart Physicians, Dr. Kolli had been on call to take all of the emergencies for the group when Kathy was brought in that morning. However, because it had been determined that an angiogram was needed, a procedure that Dr. Kolli doesn't perform, Kathy was sent to the main hospital, where Dr. Thompson performed the angiogram, also sometimes referred to as heart catheterization. He was on backup call on that date.

Dr. Thompson's educational background revealed that he studied at the University of Colorado Denver School of Medicine, and at the University of Louisville, in Louisville, Kentucky. He performed his internship and residency while in the navy, and his cardiology fellowship was at the San Diego Naval Hospital. He had been practicing cardiology in Reno since 1979, making him well-qualified in his specialized field.

After the catheter has been inserted through the leg and has reached the heart, pressure measurements from within the heart are taken and X-ray dye is then injected through the tubing to determine whether a blockage exists and has caused a heart attack. Artery blockage, particularly coronary artery blockage, is one of the primary reasons that people suffer heart attacks. When the dye is injected into the main heart chamber, it allows the cardiologist to see how well the heart pumps and functions as the dye makes its way out into the arteries, such as the left and right coronary arteries. In the search to determine if a blockage existed in Kathy's arteries, they were photographed from different angles. If a blockage existed, it would be seen as plaque in the artery, a whitish material that would make the artery appear pinched off in the X-ray. But there wasn't any plaque. Kathy's arteries were normal, and Dr. Thompson determined that she did not have coronary artery disease. Normal arteries are not what anyone would expect in a person who had suffered an actual heart attack. The entire procedure, of course, was recorded and could be replayed at will from a CD or DVD.

While her arteries had appeared normal, Kathy's heart, however, at the time that Dr. Thompson had performed the angiogram, had not been pumping correctly. The angiogram had shown that Kathy's heart was not pumping vigorously, and when contracting, it only pumped 23 percent of the blood out of the heart chamber—a more normal reading would have been in the 70 to 80 percent range. Although he hadn't known why Kathy's heart had been beating so poorly, he knew that it wasn't because of a typical heart attack or atherosclerosis, also known as hardening of the arteries. What he had seen was an almost "dead heart," the cells of which were either dead or dying or had been stunned and hadn't recovered from whatever had stunned them.

Dr. Thompson had met Chaz Higgs that morning when Higgs had accompanied his comatose wife to the cardiac catheterization lab at Washoe Medical Center's main hospital. Dr. Thompson told Higgs that the outlook for his wife did not appear very good, considering the state of her condition at the time. He would later recall that he had been somewhat surprised by the lack of emotion shown by Higgs during the meeting in which they had discussed Kathy's very bleak prospects for survival.

Dr. Paul Katz, medical director for the Institute of Neurosciences at Washoe Medical Center, and his partner, Dr. George Bigley, their specialty being neurology, had both seen Kathy Augustine at various times between July 8 and July 10, 2006. After consultation with Kathy's family, it was decided that a CT scan would be performed on her brain, as would an EEG, also known as an electroencephalogram. The CT scan would allow the neurologists to look at the brain itself, while the EEG would show them the type of brain wave activity that was occurring.

The CT scan, according to Dr. Katz, "showed obliteration of the gray-white differentiation," which means that under normal conditions the two can be easily distinguished from each other. However, when the brain becomes swollen as a result of a lack of oxygen, as Kathy's had, the distinction between the gray and white matter becomes obliterated and difficult to discern. Similarly, the results of an EEG that was performed on July 9, 2006, turned out to be severely abnormal, "showing diffuse, poorly organized swell activity," Katz said. When the EEG was repeated on July 11, 2006, the results were worse than they were two days earlier. It all added up to a condition of severe encephalopathy, meaning, in Kathy's case, a dysfunction of the brain because of lack of oxygen. There was no evidence of a stroke or any other bleeding of the brain, and there was no evidence of trauma to the brain. After presenting their findings to Kathy's family, the decision had been made to remove Kathy's life support.

Later, in hindsight, as far as the two neurologists were concerned, the lack of oxygen to Kathy's brain was consistent with her having been administered succinylcholine without any mechanism for breathing assistance. Their findings, however, were also consistent with sudden cardiac arrest.

Yet another physician, Dr. Steve K. Mashour, whose specialty is pulmonary and critical care medicine, attended Kathy while she was in the ICU at Washoe Medical Center. Jenkins learned that Dr. Mashour had performed a full examination of the patient that included her heart, lungs, abdomen, and neurologic functions. Her pupils, as they had been when some of the other doctors had attended to her, were fixed and dilated. Dr. Mashour ordered a CT scan of Kathy's head, without contrast, to see if there was any reason that her pupils "could be blown, meaning an intercranial bleed or whatnot," he said. Because Kathy had "gone down in a [cardiac] arrest–type fashion," he also ordered a CT scan of her thorax, with contrast, to rule out a pulmonary embolism. He explained that a pulmonary embolism is a "blood clot in the lung that basically blocks off oxygen from being extracted from the environment and into the bloodstream," a condition that could easily be fatal. However, when all was said and done, Dr. Mashour had found no evidence of a pulmonary embolism, nor had he found any evidence of brain bleed.

Interestingly, while Dr. Mashour had been going over the lab work results in Kathy's medical chart, he noticed that her urine drug screen had come back positive for the presence of barbiturates. As a result, he had requested that a serum barbiturate level be sent off for reference testing. To his knowledge, however, the reference testing had not been completed as directed, because he had never received any results for the reference testing. Was it possible that, with Kathy's impending death, the order for the reference testing had somehow slipped through the cracks? Whatever the case had been, the results of a confirming test had come back negative for barbiturates, and the matter appeared to have been dropped.

Because of the manner in which Kathy had been stricken, the first medical conditions that doctors would rule out would be heart attack or cardiac arrest, stroke, and pulmonary embolism, which they, in their professional opinions, had done. After each condition being examined had turned out negative, the next thing that would normally be looked at in a case like Kathy's is the possibility of a drug overdose of some kind. In Kathy's case, however, much of the toxicological testing had been done posthumously.

At one point in his investigation, Detective Jenkins spoke with Jennifer Dado, a registered nurse who worked in the emergency room at South Meadows Hospital since May 2004. She had worked with Chaz Higgs, Jenkins learned, for approximately 1½ years, until he had left for South Carolina and Virginia after Kathy died. She had worked with Higgs somewhat regularly, and, she said, there had been an ongoing joke of sorts that had involved him. According to Dado, anytime the nurses were caught up with their own work, particularly during the slower moments in the ER, they would occasionally ask each other, "Is there anything I can do to help you with any of your patients?" When Dado or another nurse would pose the question to Higgs, his reply would sometimes be "You can get rid of my wife for me." Everyone would just laugh it off and then get on with their work, because it had seemed like it was all in jest, a little dark—or gallows—humor that is so common among those who deal with emergencies on an everyday basis. It's a mechanism that is often used to help offset the high-stress levels that go with the job.

According to Dado, sometimes it would seem like Higgs had made the comments because he was unhappy in his relationship. She and the others realized, of course, that Higgs hadn't meant for any of them to literally get rid of his wife for him, but the implication in their minds was that Higgs simply wasn't happy and didn't want to be with Kathy anymore. Dado said that she once advised Higgs that if he and his wife were that unhappy, they should try marital counseling, or that it might be best to just cut their ties with each other and move on. After all, it wasn't as if Kathy or Higgs were inexperienced in severing spousal relationships. Higgs had responded that he was "working on moving out," but that the timing wasn't good at that point.

On the other hand, when Kathy had been going through the impeachment proceedings, Higgs had seemed very supportive of his wife during that time frame, but as time went on, something had begun to change, according to Dado. He became less supportive of Kathy, and had started making the *joke* about getting rid of her. However, even when Higgs had been supportive of Kathy, Dado said, she had never heard him refer to his wife in an affectionate manner.

Nonetheless, Jenkins asked Dado when she had last heard Higgs make the "get rid of my wife" remark. She said it had been approximately six months prior to July 8, 2006.

According to Dado, on one occasion when Higgs had the day off, the ER was short-staffed and she had called his home to ask if he was available to come in to fill a shift. Kathy had answered the phone, and hadn't seemed too happy about the call.

"Chaz, are you interested in working a shift or part of a shift?" Dado said, recalling her brief conversation with Higgs that day when he got on the phone.

"You know, I can't," he said.

Dado explained that she had sensed that Kathy and Higgs were both a little upset that day, and she said that she had expressed that feeling to Higgs on the day that he had returned to work. She said that she was concerned that she might have caused an argument between them.

"No. She's just a bitch," Higgs had replied, according to Dado.

Dado had also heard rumors that Kathy Augustine had attempted to use her influence to get a couple of nurses at South Meadows Hospital fired, but she was unable to relate anything more specific to help validate or refute the rumors.

Jenkins knew, of course, that just because Higgs had purportedly used derogatory language in describing Kathy, and making dark humor jokes about having someone get rid of her, that didn't mean he had killed her. After all, couples frequently call each other names or make derogatory remarks about one another without ever committing an act of violence against the person. Such could easily be the case in Higgs's situation. But the detective equally knew that such dimly lit glimpses into the frame of mind of an intensely frustrated person could also mean the opposite.

Chapter 14

As the investigation into Kathy Augustine's death continued, Detective Jenkins spoke to Michelle Ene, Kathy Augustine's executive assistant. Michelle explained that she began working for Kathy as a state employee in June 2003. Her duties in that capacity consisted of the coordination of Kathy's events, booking and confirming travel, travel expense reimbursement, and so forth. She did just about anything that Kathy asked her to do in the course of her day-to-day job. As an executive assistant, one tends to become close to the boss, in part because so much time is spent with each other. It's just the nature of the beast. In Kathy and Michelle's situation, the two spoke to each other nearly every day, even when Kathy was out of town or away on business, and the two women eventually became friends. Michelle was working for Kathy when Kathy had married Chaz Higgs, and, as friends, the two women naturally talked to each other about their love interests.

According to Michelle, it seemed clear that Kathy had wanted to be with Higgs, at least at first. They scheduled trips with each other, had gone on cruises together, and Kathy would often take him on her political trips and events because she wanted to spend as much time with him as possible. Despite problems that had arisen barely ten weeks into their marriage, Kathy had wanted her matrimonial union with Higgs to work. Kathy had really loved Higgs, Michelle said, and had tried to make him happy. For example, she had bought Higgs a Volkswagen Beetle, or Bug, to restore because she had known that he had wanted one. If he wanted something, she would either give him the money to buy it or she would purchase it for him, as long as it was something that she could afford.

Michelle explained that she had been working for Kathy in 2004 when the impeachment investigation and subsequent trial proceedings had occurred. It had been a tough year for Kathy and for everyone concerned, particularly those who had been working on her behalf. But they had all managed to struggle through it, and when it was all over, much of the turmoil, at least as far as Kathy's political career was concerned, seemed to just go away.

During the three years that Michelle had worked for Kathy, she seemed to thrive on the stress and excitement of being in the political limelight, particularly after the impeachment proceedings ended and she was allowed to finish out her term in office as state controller. Kathy was rarely sick, and Michelle could only recall five or six times that Kathy had been ill during the three years that she had worked for her. She had never complained to Michelle about any health issues.

Kathy had seemed particularly happy in May 2006, which was when she had filed as a candidate for the state treasurer race. Michelle had been with her in the office when she brought out the check for the filing fee. After the filing had been completed, Kathy took Michelle, Acting Chief Deputy Controller Bill Rhinehart, Assistant Controller Mark Taylor, and Chaz Higgs to Adele's Restaurant, in Carson City, for lunch to celebrate her new candidacy for political office.

During their lunch, Michelle had formed the distinct impression that Higgs was being supportive of her new candidacy. Besides talking about his own new position at Carson-Tahoe Medical Center, Higgs had actually seemed happy regarding Kathy's new venture and not upset over it, like others had characterized him. And in Michelle's opinion, Kathy was not stressed-out about the impending campaign. Because politics was her life and her passion, Kathy thrived on all the running around, coordinating events, and attending political meetings and fundraising. According to Michelle, Kathy was looking forward to showing the people of Nevada, after the impeachment, just what she was made of.

At one point, Michelle's details turned to her boss's last few days alive, specifically to Friday, July 7, 2006. They had both been working that day, and Kathy had left the office sometime between 4:00 and 4:30 P.M., about two minutes before Michelle. Michelle hadn't gone home immediately that day after work and, in fact, didn't get home until 10:10 P.M. As soon as she walked in the door, a family member told her that Kathy had been trying to reach her by telephone that evening and had called for her three or four times. Michelle called her back immediately, within two minutes or so of arriving at home.

Kathy was awake and answered the phone. She was very upset with Chaz after she had discovered that he had opened a separate bank account. She was also upset with him because, she had told Michelle, he had told Kathy that he was going to leave her. Michelle said that Higgs was there with Kathy while she and Kathy were speaking on the phone, and Kathy had asked Chaz if he wanted to speak to Michelle's husband about some car jacks that

Chaz had wanted to borrow. Chaz, however, declined. After saying good night to Kathy that evening, the two never spoke to each other again.

Michelle told Jenkins the next time she heard anything about Kathy Augustine had been on Sunday, July 9, 2006, when Chaz Higgs had called Michelle's home to speak with her. She wasn't home at the time, but Michelle's husband called her and told her that she needed to call Chaz right away, which she did.

Chaz, she said, told her that Kathy was in the hospital, and that she'd had a heart attack.

"Is she okay? What's going on?" Michelle said she had asked Chaz.

Chaz calmly explained to her that he didn't really know what was wrong with Kathy, but said that she was in bad shape.

Later that day, at about 8:00 P.M., Michelle, along with her husband and daughter, drove to the hospital to visit Kathy. It was difficult for her to see Kathy laid out in a bed in the hospital's intensive care unit, and it wasn't long before she began crying and the crying turned to near-hysteria. Chaz Higgs was in the room, and he sat down with Michelle and began a conversation with her while Michelle's husband and daughter stood off to the side. As Michelle held Kathy's hand and cried, Chaz began telling her what had happened early on Saturday morning.

Chaz purportedly told Michelle that he had arisen early on Saturday, July 8, and had gone outside to "tinker" on his Volkswagen Bug. That had been at approximately 5:30 A.M. He went back inside the house about half an hour later and had "crawled" back in bed next to Kathy. It was when he tried to snuggle with her that he realized that she was not breathing and began performing CPR while calling 911.

Michelle said that she asked Chaz how much time had

passed with Kathy not breathing, and he had purportedly told her "about an hour." She said that they then talked about the effect that not breathing has on the brain, and how, Michelle explained, Chaz had gotten somewhat technical in explaining how, after six minutes or so, the lack of oxygen adversely affects brain activity.

Their hospital room discussion eventually turned to the subject of the argument between Kathy and Chaz, two nights earlier, over Chaz opening a separate bank account and wanting to leave Kathy. According to Michelle's account of the conversation, Chaz had said that he and Kathy had worked things out and had made an agreement with each other. He also allegedly said that it was too bad "that this had happened," a reference to Kathy and what had happened to her.

Michelle, however, said that she hadn't believed "for one minute" that they had worked things out. She said that she knew Kathy too well, that what had happened on Friday evening had been a big deal in Kathy's eyes and she would never have just let it go. Michelle said that she had become suspicious of Chaz, and began to think that he may have had something to do with what had happened to Kathy. After all, she said, they had been arguing on Friday night, and the next morning she was rushed to the hospital, not breathing—at least not on her own. She said she knew that Kathy and Chaz had "an explosive relationship," and she believed that Chaz might have decided after the argument to take matters into his own hands. She was nearly sure of it after the four of them left the ICU room and walked down the hospital hallway together, when Chaz stopped and made a comment to Michelle's husband.

"You know, I'll have to get those car jacks another day," Michelle said, quoting Chaz.

Michelle said that she thought Chaz's comment about

the car jacks was bizarre, and wondered how he could even be the least bit concerned about car jacks at a time when his wife was on life support and no one knew whether she would survive her horrible ordeal or not. Michelle said that her husband and daughter shared her feelings about the comment.

In the three years that Michelle had worked for Kathy Augustine, she had gotten to know her boss well enough that she could tell what kind of frame of mind Kathy was in the moment she walked through the door each morning.

"I knew Kathy . . . ," Michelle said. "I knew if something was wrong. I knew what she wanted before she asked me to do it."

Michelle said that Chaz had once told her that Kathy had on one occasion said to him: "I wish you knew what I wanted and were more like Michelle."

When the subject of Kathy's general personality characteristics came up again, Michelle said she knew that Kathy could be confrontational. There were times when Kathy had supposedly had confrontations with nurses at the hospitals where Chaz worked, and there had been talk of people either getting fired or being threatened that they would be fired, but Michelle had not witnessed this. And Kathy, she said, had never talked to her about such things. The only confrontational situation that Kathy had ever talked about with Michelle had been over one or more e-mails between Chaz and another hospital employee. Kathy hadn't gone into specifics of the situation beyond saying that the female employee had been fired from Washoe Medical Center and Chaz had been reprimanded because of the e-mails.

Chapter 15

In his diligence of leaving no stone unturned in uncovering the facts of the case, Detective Jenkins soon learned the identity of the female employee who had been fired from her job at Washoe Medical Center at South Meadows over an exchange of e-mails between herself and Chaz Higgs. The woman's name was Linda Ramirez, and she had been employed at the South Meadows campus as an admissions clerk since February 2004. Her duties had her routinely checking in patients, ordering lab work and X-rays, some telephone work, and various other administrative responsibilities. She had been working there a little more than four months when she first met Chaz Higgs in July 2004.

Ramirez had, of course, seen Chaz at various times around the hospital, but they hadn't actually met in a formal sense. The circumstances of their first meeting, she said, when they exchanged introductions, had centered on her birthday when Chaz showed up at her workstation and gave her a rose. The rose had been accompanied by a simple note that read: *Linda, happy birthday.* At the time, Linda had thought that it was a "sweet" gesture on Chaz's part, but it soon seemed like each of them wanted to get to know each other better. As time went on, they developed a more personal relationship at work, and it eventually became nothing more than a "flirtatious relationship," as Linda described it.

As time allowed, she said, the two of them would spend time talking together at work, often at Linda's desk. Linda explained, in response to questions, that Chaz would sometimes talk about his wife. He complained that Kathy was controlling and manipulating, and referred to her as a "bitch." He never spoke about Kathy, she said, in a loving fashion.

"I hate my wife," Linda quoted Chaz as having said. "She's a controlling, manipulative bitch. Vindictive."

Linda explained that she began writing e-mails that were deemed personal and flirtatious to Chaz on January 14, 2005, and ended on January 23, 2005. She wrote them while at work, using the hospital's computer and e-mail system, and sent them to Chaz at his work e-mail account, as well as his personal e-mail account. She also confirmed that she had e-mailed Chaz from her personal e-mail account. Linda said she believed that Kathy had found out about the e-mails, which had ultimately resulted in Linda being fired from her job in February 2005.

Linda said that she'd had no contact with Chaz Higgs after being terminated from Washoe Medical Center at South Meadows until November 2005, when the two began exchanging e-mails again, and continued until August 28, 2006. The circumstances that led up to the new round of e-mail exchanges came about when a coworker had mentioned to Linda that Chaz had been talking about her. As a result, Linda said, she contacted him at his personal account and he had responded. For reasons that weren't entirely clear, Linda had printed out the e-mails and had filed the hard copies away, a practice that she said she commonly followed. Fortunately, she had found the hard copies that she had kept and turned them over to the state, which Jenkins and others, including the district attorney's office, found to be very interesting.

Chaz asked her to e-mail him at his "secret" address. *"Kumustakana,"* Linda explained, means "how are you?" in Tagalog, the primary language that is spoken in the Philippines. She said that she and Chaz would occasionally speak to each other in Tagalog, because they knew the language "a little bit." He used that Tagalog greeting in his private e-mail address.

In his first e-mail of their cyberspace reunion, dated November 4, 2005, Chaz Higgs wrote to Linda: *Thank you for writing. I have to tell you that I have missed you every day since I last saw you.*

Chaz explained to her that he wanted her to understand that what he was dealing with in his personal life was a nightmare. He said that each day he planned on leaving Kathy, and that he was seeking out a place in which to live: *I did what I did with us to protect you from her. I did not want to. I had to. . . . Miss you.*

Much of that e-mail, Linda believed, had been in reference to Kathy, and the part about him doing what he did "to protect you from her" had been, at least in Linda's mind, a reference to the situation that had ended with Linda's termination.

In another e-mail, dated December 8, 2005, Chaz wrote to Linda that *there are prying eyes here as always, so I will write more soon.* He ended it with, *"Miss na miss kita,"* Tagalog for "I miss you a lot." A few hours later, Chaz followed up the December 8 e-mail with another, which, in part, thanked her for writing back to him. He also told Linda how much he missed her and that he had missed her and thought of her every day. He told her that he wanted to be with her. He explained that he had not given up hope that he could be with her again, and apologized for what had happened regarding Linda being fired. He told Linda that he truly cared for her.

The e-mail continued with Higgs telling Linda that he knew that he was giving her so much information because he had it bottled up inside for nearly a year. He explained that he had made a pact with himself that he would tell her just how he felt about her, that she had caused him to feel things that he had not felt before, and that such true feelings normally only occur once in one's lifetime. He said that he wanted to give her the world.

Chaz also wrote that *the other party in this is very vindictive and has a lot of power,* an obvious reference to Kathy. He went on to write that Kathy wanted to control everything in her life, but that she had lost control of him when Linda appeared in his life. Higgs characterized Kathy as "crazy," and had made his life a "living hell" through threats and manipulation. He said that he had seen such things depicted in the movies, but had never expected that he would be experiencing it in his own life. He explained that in Kathy's position, she held the power to make a person's life hell if she so desired.

A portion of the e-mail, as with some of the others, was reflective of Linda's termination at Washoe Medical Center at South Meadows, and Higgs claimed that he only wanted to protect her from Kathy. He wrote that he was willing to sacrifice himself so that Kathy would not be able to hurt Linda anymore.

Chaz also said in the e-mail that he had made a pact with himself to spend each day with Kathy making her life hell, to pay her back for causing him to lose Linda. He indicated that he lived to manipulate Kathy and to cause her frustration: *I hate this woman, and I will make her break.*

He wrote that he got to that point in his emotions after losing Linda. He wrote that it was his *quest in life to drive this bitch crazy. And it is working. She is losing her mind.*

He wrote that he no longer cared what Kathy might do to him, stating that he was no longer scared of his wife. Previously, he said, she had manipulated him, as well as his friends and employers, but that he could now leave her. He indicated that he had set into motion a plan to leave Kathy, and that he now had a place to go. *I will be free, and I will be with you. That is what I want. You have my heart.* He signed off with *Chaz.*

Chaz's characterization of his wife in the e-mails, Jenkins reflected, seven months before her death, was markedly different from the manner in which he had characterized her immediately after she had died. And so were the emotions that he had expressed. After her death, he had exhibited emotions of the grieving husband, and had told the press and just about anyone else who would listen how much he loved her. But in the e-mail, written a little more than half a year before her demise, Chaz Higgs had clearly indicated that there was no love left in their marriage.

Another e-mail in Linda's packet, this one dated February 15, 2006, read: *Just wanted to say* mahal na mahal kita, which means, "I love you very much."

Linda responded three days later with: *How was your Valentine's Day?* Kalbigan ko kinakanto ko, which is translated as, "I am your friend, and I want to sleep with you." She also asked him how things were going with Kathy.

Chaz didn't respond to Linda until March 10, 2006, when he wrote: *The wife is the wife, but not my life.* He said that his Valentine's Day had not been pleasant, but added that he had gone to Mexico during the first week of March and had thought of Linda the entire time. He signed off by telling her that he missed her and to write to him soon.

Although the occasional e-mail exchanges between Linda and Chaz continued in May and June 2006, they had appeared infrequently, according to the hard copies that Linda had produced, and with which she had come forward. One e-mail from Chaz to Linda, dated May 26, 2006, said that he was working on getting out of his "present situation," and that he had an apartment lined up: *In June it is going to happen. Cannot wait. I miss you.*

It wasn't until July 30, three weeks after Kathy's death, that Linda wrote to Chaz and explained that she had broken up with her boyfriend. Chaz responded that he was single as well, and had moved out of Nevada *due to recent events. My wife had a sudden heart attack and passed away.* He explained that he was working as a traveling nurse, but had plans to eventually relocate to San Diego. He asked Linda if she wanted to go with him, and told her that he had never forgotten about her. That e-mail had been written on August 3, 2006.

In the meantime, Linda explained, she had begun reading news reports, mostly on the Internet, about how Kathy had died, how Chaz was being looked at as a suspect, and how he had made a suicide attempt. She asked him, in a follow-up e-mail, if it was true that he had tried to kill himself.

Chaz wrote Linda that it was *great to hear from you,* and he told her that he missed her and assured her that he was not getting into any relationship unless it was with her. He reminded her how he had expressed his love for her previously: *It does not go away. You only have one true love in your life, and you are it. So whatever it takes, that is what I will do.*

Chaz also explained that he wanted to talk to her about what had happened, but he didn't want to make any statements about the case in an e-mail, and because his lawyer did not want him speaking to anyone about the case just yet. He said that he had been contacted by several media sources, including *People* magazine, Fox News, *48 Hours, Geraldo,* and the *New York Times.* He promised Linda that he would see her again sometime.

Chaz wrote that he missed Linda, and truly loved her. He explained how he could no longer hold back the feelings that were in his heart for her: *I would give you the world if you let me because that is what is in my heart for you, the world.*

He said that he might return to Nevada, and agreed with Linda in her opinion that the state *is a little slow, a little redneck.* He asked Linda to go to Mexico with him, and in the next sentence asked her to go to San Diego with him, instead, so that they could *run to Mexico all the time.* He also suggested Sedona and Santa Fe.

You tell me, he wrote. *I'll take you anywhere. I can make you the happiest woman on this earth.*

He reiterated that he wasn't trying to "freak" her out with the things that he was saying in the e-mail, and expressed the emotions that he claimed he felt for Linda.

I just love you . . . , he wrote. *You are all I've wanted since I first saw you.* He recalled the rose that he had given Linda for her birthday, and said that he had felt like giving her a million roses. He said that he had wanted to run away with her: *I do not want anything else in my life, and it has been this way for two years. I want you with all my heart.*

Knowing Chaz had four marriages, and only God knows how many relationships, Jenkins and everyone else associated with the case could only wonder just how sincere this guy was capable of being.

Chapter 16

In the meantime, as Detective Jenkins continued his investigation into Kathy's suspicious death, Kathy's stepson, Greg Augustine, along with assistance from attorney Dominic Gentile, began pushing for the exhumation of his father's body after considering the circumstances of Kathy's untimely death and the fact that Chaz Higgs had served as his father's critical care nurse at Sunrise Hospital and Medical Center. Greg had previously said that he would ask that his father's body be exhumed if it turned out that his stepmother's body contained traces of succinylcholine. Since that fact had indeed been determined, and in part because of Dr. Cyril Wecht's statement that he would want the exhumation under those circumstances if he were a family member, Greg began consulting with authorities in Las Vegas, including Clark County district attorney (DA) David Roger and Las Vegas police lieutenant Lew Roberts. Before long, the general consensus among all of those involved was that it was something that needed to be done.

David Roger may have been moved so swiftly to action with the exhumation, at least in part, because he recalled that he had seen Chaz Higgs before. It had been in the fall of 2002 when Roger happened to attend the same Republican campaign event as Chaz Higgs and Kathy Augustine. In recounting the event to a *Las Vegas Sun* reporter that he didn't remember the specifics of the gathering, but he absolutely recalled seeing Higgs and Augustine there—several months before either of them had claimed they met.

"It's a blur, the whole campaign was a blur," Roger said. "But I remember his face, and I immediately remembered him when I saw him on the news, and we'll find other people who remember. . . . He wasn't very talkative."

Roger said that Higgs had been sitting by himself and had a scowl on his face much of the evening.

"He seemed somewhat standoffish, and it appeared that he didn't want to be at the function," Roger said.

Although it now seemed that Chaz and Kathy appeared to have known each other in 2002, several months before they claimed to have met, this incident hadn't meant anything to the district attorney at that time. Now, however, it somehow seemed significant. Thinking like a district attorney would, Roger determined that such an inconsistency about when they met could cause suspicion of criminal goings-on. Roger stopped short of being more specific, but it seemed clear what he intended to convey.

According to the *Sun,* Kathy Augustine had told a reporter for that newspaper in September 2003 that she and Chaz Higgs had met in July 2003 at Sunrise Hospital and Medical Center where her then-husband, Charles, had been hospitalized and was recovering from a stroke. Six weeks after they claimed they had met, Charles died—presumably of complications from the stroke—and three weeks later, Kathy and Chaz were married in Hawaii. When all of the circumstances were put together in the same pot, it was enough to make any reasonable person suspicious, even more so when the discrepancy pointed out by Roger was factored in.

"We have a reason to open an investigation and exhume a body," Roger said.

In early October 2006, both Lieutenant Roberts and DA Roger confirmed that plans were under way to exhume Charles Augustine's body from his grave site at Paradise Memorial Gardens, in east Las Vegas. They also confirmed that toxicology tests on tissue samples were planned to determine whether he had died from an act of foul play instead of a stroke, as originally believed. Specifically, they were going to look for the presence of succinylcholine.

On Monday, October 2, 2006, the same day that Chaz Higgs appeared in a Hampton, Virginia, courtroom just prior to his return to Nevada with Detective Jenkins, David Roger consulted with renowned medical examiner Dr. Michael Baden regarding whether toxicology tests on tissue samples from Charles Augustine's body could determine whether succinylcholine traces might still be present, even though three years had elapsed since his death.

"I was told that if the decedent was injected intravenously with the drug, it would be unlikely you would find any remnants of the drug," Roger told reporters for the *Las Vegas Review-Journal*. "However, if the decedent was injected in muscle tissue, there would be a decent chance of finding it."

Dr. Brian Andresen, the scientist who developed the process of detecting succinylcholine in the body, said that succinylcholine might very well be the most difficult drug to detect in a corpse, according to the *Review-Journal*. Andresen was responsible for the creation of the Lawrence Livermore National Laboratory's Forensic Science Center.

"On an exhumation, I would say it is going to be very difficult," Andresen said. "If you run the right controls and run the standards, if you do things in a very controlled, systematic, scientific manner, then you possibly can get a positive result, but it's still very difficult. . . . It is one of the worst drugs to analyze confidently. You have to be so careful, and the testing has to be done at the toxicology labs with the most scientifically advanced equipment."

If a body has been embalmed, as Charles Augustine's was, it becomes an even bigger problem. Embalming, according to experts on exhumations, is a detriment in performing toxicology analysis because embalming fluid can interact with the poisons being looked for and sometimes changes the chemical structure of the toxic substances. Nonetheless, despite the difficulties that lay ahead, everyone concerned knew that the only way to find out was to perform the exhumation and the toxicology tests.

According to Andresen, it would be necessary for the Las Vegas authorities and scientists to collect soil samples from the grave site to be used for controls, and the type of embalming fluid would also need to be determined. He said that it would also be necessary to analyze the materials from which the coffin was constructed.

Neither a search warrant nor a court order is required to exhume a body in Clark County, Nevada. The county coroner's office can make such a decision independently without regard to law enforcement's input or desire to either get involved or not get involved, as the case may be. It just so happened that in the case of the Charles Augustine exhumation, the coroner's office, headed by Michael Murphy, law enforcement, and the district attorney's office were all in agreement that this was something that needed to be done.

A week later, on Tuesday, October 10, 2006, two men wearing black suits and smoking cigarettes supervised the television crews and other media types when they began arriving at Paradise Memorial Gardens, also known as Davis

Funeral Home and Memorial Parks, before five o'clock for the morning broadcasts. The exhumation was planned for 7:00 A.M., and only news media personnel with valid credentials would be allowed to observe the process from an area specifically set up for the media so that others using the cemetery would not be disturbed or have to worry about being photographed or videotaped while they paid respects to their deceased loved ones. One of the black-suited mortuary workers drove a golf cart to the main entrance, where he used it to help block access to curious onlookers who happened along and wanted to know what the predawn fuss in the cemetery was all about. According to Coroner Michael Murphy, every effort to show respect to others and to maintain the dignity of the dead was being made by his office and everyone else involved.

"We don't take this lightly, and I mean that with as much sincerity as I can possibly convey," Murphy said. "We are in a unique situation. The family wants answers, the media wants to cover it, but there are other people who have loved ones in that cemetery, and they may be there, grieving. . . . This is probably one of the biggest things that's going on in the state of Nevada right now. And everybody wants to know."

Murphy told the reporters that were present that morning that his office hoped to answer the questions that centered on the cause of Charles Augustine's death. Up until the decision was made to do the exhumation and the toxicology testing, particularly since an autopsy hadn't been performed on his body, everyone—including Charles Augustine's doctors—had believed that his demise was due to complications of the stroke that he had suffered.

Dr. Robert Middleberg, the director of NMS Labs, in Pennsylvania, agreed with experts that had been interviewed by local media that the only way to definitively show that succinylcholine is present in a body exhumed from a cemetery is to exhume several other bodies from the surrounding area that had been interred at about the same time so that levels could be compared from all of the bodies, since succinylmonocholine tends to appear naturally in dead bodies. Middleberg was quick to point out that sufficient data to show what a normal level might be does not exist, and stated that succinylcholine poisoning is a very bad way for a person to die.

"It's really a very insidious poison," Middleberg said. "If you do manage to give it to somebody, that person knows they are becoming paralyzed, and they can't do anything about it. It's a terrible poison to have administered to you. Is it an insidious murder weapon? You better believe it."

Middleberg said that investigators normally wouldn't expect to find succinylcholine in an exhumed body. However, he added, if it was injected into tissue and an injection site was found, some of the drug would remain in that area.

Although Middleberg had suggested that a number of bodies needed to be dug up for purposes of comparing the levels of succinylcholine to rule out that which might have occurred naturally in the form of succinylmonocholine and to show a higher presence of that which might have been deliberately given to a victim as succinylcholine, Murphy indicated that his office didn't have the wherewithal of going that route. Instead, he said, his office would be concerned with the overall picture and would not only look for the presence of succinylcholine, but he would attempt to determine any other manner of death that might have caused Charles Augustine's demise.

Middleberg also pointed out that if traces of a drug, even succinylcholine, were found in the tissues of the exhumed body, it didn't automatically make the probe a homicide case.

"If they find it in a needle site," Middleberg said, "it's a good inference. Keep in mind, though, toxicology is only a piece of information. There has to be more to a case than toxicology."

Later at the Clark County Coroner's Office, Murphy was pleased at the overall condition that Charles Augustine's body was in, considering that it had been in the ground for more than three years. If succinylcholine had been injected into tissue, which was basically their only hope for detecting the drug's presence, they had good samples from which to work. If it had been administered intravenously, there would be virtually no chance that it could now be detected. It was also possible that they wouldn't find any at all because it hadn't been administered by anyone during Augustine's hospital stay.

"Our initial examination has indicated the body is in remarkable condition," Murphy told reporters. "The casket was contained in a concrete vault to seal it off from the elements. . . . It obviously did its job."

In the meantime, Lieutenant Roberts said that homicide detectives had begun their own inquiry into Charles Augustine's death while working with the coroner's office.

"The whole case obviously hinges on the toxicology from the exhumation," Roberts said, obviously in disparity with Dr. Middleberg's opinion that toxicology doesn't make the case. "In addition, we are gathering up some background facts, some medical information. We'll go from there, after we see what [the coroner's office] comes up with."

Following a daylong autopsy, Murphy said it could be months before anyone obtained the results of the toxicology tests.

* * *

Upon his return to Nevada, Chaz Higgs retained California criminal lawyer Alan Baum, with offices in Woodland Hills, on Ventura Boulevard, along with Reno attorney David Houston, to defend him. Both attorneys believed in their client's innocence, and said so publicly.

"He's a caregiver, not a life taker," Baum said.

Baum told reporters that Chaz had kept the Reno Police Department informed as to his whereabouts since the investigation began, and that his client did not stand to gain anything from his wife's death.

"It's as big a mystery to him as it is everyone else," Baum told reporters. "He was quite surprised when Kathy suffered her heart attack and subsequently died. Although he has medical training, he has no better explanation for her demise than anyone else."

Baum said that his client also denied having anything to do with Charles Augustine's death and had no issue with the exhumation. Baum said that he and Chaz believed that the exhumation and toxicology tests would show that Chaz had nothing to do with Charles Augustine's death. He said that Chaz hadn't killed his wife, either.

"Exhumation is unusual," Baum said. "But if it will help in the pursuit for the truth, we've got no problem with that. Chaz is not responsible in any way for Charles Augustine's death, and we are not afraid of the results. It's morbid, but let's clear the air."

On Friday, October 13, 2006, Chaz Higgs, along with his attorneys, appeared before Reno Justice Court judge Jenny Hubach via a video link from the Washoe County Jail in his first court hearing upon his return to Nevada. Shackled and dressed in an orange jumpsuit issued by the jail, Higgs responded to the judge in the affirmative that he understood that he was being charged with murder. He also agreed to waive the requirement that a preliminary hearing be held within fifteen days, and attorney David Houston entered a not guilty plea for his client. Judge Hubach set Thursday, December 7, 2006, for a preliminary hearing.

"I have not seen anything to tell me that [Kathy Augustine] was murdered," Houston said to reporters after the five-minute hearing. "If anyone murdered her, it certainly wasn't Chaz Higgs."

Houston alleged that the police did not investigate other possible causes of Kathy's death after landing on the possibility that she might have been poisoned. He said that the police found in Higgs "a subject and then designed evidence to fit their conclusion." Houston said that the defense team would hire their own experts and would challenge the state's toxicological tests. Houston reiterated that his client had no criminal record and had cooperated completely with the police prior to his arrest. Houston said that he would seek bail for Higgs, who, he insisted, had demonstrated that he was not a flight risk through his cooperation with the police, who, he said, always knew where they could find him at any given time after his departure from Nevada.

"There is no motive in this case," Houston said. "He stood to get nothing. He had no hope of getting anything. . . . Did they really find it (succinylcholine) in her system? I don't know. But I do know if you are looking for something, you can find a derivative of it in the body."

Chapter 17

In October 2006, one of Chaz Higgs's ex-wives, who resides in Las Vegas, talked to reporters for the *Las Vegas Review-Journal* and provided additional background and insight into her ex-husband's life, as well as fodder for local and national news media of all types. The ex-wife, who was married to Chaz only briefly, told of how Chaz used to give her vitamin B injections on a near-weekly basis to boost her energy. The injection site, she said, was always in the buttocks.

In the autumn of 1990, Chaz came home and told his wife that he had been accepted for training as a Navy SEAL. It required a move to the West Coast, and she moved with him. Chaz, his wife, and a female friend of his wife's began their journey westward in a rented recreational vehicle (RV). His ex-wife told a reporter that she suspected him of having an affair with her friend, and he had denied the accusations.

During the trip, they began having problems with the RV's sewage system. It finally failed, and all three of them fell ill. By the time they hit Las Vegas, Chaz became concerned that his wife might be getting dehydrated and was adamant that she needed an IV.

"Instead of taking me to the (military) base, he decided to plug me up with an IV in the living room," she said. "That was not the first time he had stuck a needle in my arm."

She claimed that Chaz brought home medicine that he obtained through his job.

"I can tell you in my house," she said, "I had a pharmacy. And it wasn't stuff prescribed to him."

During her marriage to Higgs, she said, she knew him as "Chuck," not Chaz. She characterized him as being manipulative and obsessed over his appearance, and he had used steroids—presumably as part of his bodybuilding regimen. He had admitted it to her, she said, and it had seemed like he hadn't cared whether she knew or not. Chaz also liked to make promises, she said, in which he vowed to take care of her at a time when she was going through a divorce and needed the emotional support.

"'You can have me,'" she quoted Chaz as saying. "'I'm going to be there for you. I'm going to make things okay. . . .' He knew exactly what to tell me, exactly what to say. He was out there to basically take me away from everything happening in my life. Why did I have to put up with that (from the husband she was divorcing)? Why did I have to stand for those things that my ex-husband was doing to me? Chuck was better than that. He could help me better myself."

She said that he had done a good job of sweeping her off her feet, as well as brainwashing her. She didn't believe that he was faithful to her, however—in part because she had found a letter from a woman among his personal things.

She said that Chaz had spent of lot of time bodybuilding. He also liked to maintain a dark tan, and shaved the hair from his body regularly. He was always concerned over his hair, she said, and wasn't satisfied unless his appearance, to him, was flawless.

"It took him longer to get ready than it did me," said the ex-wife. "Every curl in his hair had to be perfect. His clothing had to be perfect. It was very strange. He was metrosexual before 'metrosexual' was a term."

The ex-wife claimed that she regretted her marriage to Chaz right away, and only a few months into the marriage, she kicked him out of their apartment. She always took him back, though, hoping that he would change and repair their broken relationship. But he never wanted to change, and he was often out all night after saying that he was going to work out at the gym.

"He was at the gym all night," his ex-wife said. "Sometimes he wouldn't even come home. I didn't think you could work out all night long."

She said that her parents hadn't liked Chaz. They had warned her that the relationship was moving too quickly, and her father's opinion of him was that he was "slick." Nonetheless, she said, she ignored everyone's warnings and decided to marry Chaz anyway. The day of the wedding, she said, he had gotten so drunk that someone had to revive him so that he could get married.

"They basically had to wake him up," she said, "to get married. It was rainy outside, and he'd even been outside in the rain, lying down in the rain because he had passed out."

In addition to regretting her marriage to Chaz Higgs, the ex-wife said that she also regretted allowing him to legally adopt her child from her prior marriage. But, she said, he had a way of manipulating people into getting what he wanted. He had brainwashed her to the point that her taste in music, clothing, and the decoration of her apartment changed to suit his wishes, and had convinced her to allow him to legally adopt her child.

"Brainwashing," she said. "If I had to put my finger on one thing, I would say brainwashing. This person knows how to get into someone's head, rearrange the thought processes, and get you to think exactly what he wants you to think."

Looking back, she said, she could not figure out why Chaz Higgs had wanted to establish a relationship with a woman with a child who was in the middle of a divorce.

"The only answer I could come up with," she said, "was that I had property, I had items in my house, I had stability, and those were things that he craved. He had no personal property, he had no real estate, and he had absolutely no stability whatsoever."

Remarried and with a new life, the ex-wife said that she rarely thought about Higgs after getting past the divorce until seeing him on the news one night as a suspect in Kathy Augustine's death. She said that she nearly fell out of her chair when she realized that she was looking at her ex-husband, and the thought of him previously administering injections to her made chills run up and down her spine. She said that she had never suspected that he had tried to poison *her* at any time, but the allegations he was facing with regard to Kathy Augustine had given her pause to wonder.

"I would have never thought about that at all until this came up with Kathy," she told the reporter. "But now that Kathy's dead, I've got to tell you, you start thinking about stuff like that."

When news of Higgs's ex-wife's characterization of Chaz reached Higgs's lawyer Alan Baum, the portrayal was quickly disputed.

"There are some people who are so angry and vindictive that they will take the opportunity to kick someone when they are down," Baum declared. "There was never any indication of any of this sort of thing until Chaz is in the newspaper, and now she is looking for her fifteen minutes of fame."

Meanwhile, amid the flurry of speculation surrounding Chaz Higgs's character due to his ex-wife talking to a reporter for the *Review-Journal,* the subject of why there would be an unopened bottle of etomidate inside the house that Chaz had occupied with Kathy surged to the forefront of "breaking news." Although the subject of the etomidate had arisen before, it now seemed more newsworthy after the ex-wife's comments and the fact that court records had been released that showed the items found during the police search of Kathy's house. The bottle of etomidate seemed significant in this case because of its relationship to succinylcholine. Etomidate is a hypnotic drug that is used to put patients to sleep and, according to Dr. Cyril Wecht, is rarely found outside of a hospital or pharmacy setting. When used in conjunction with succinylcholine, etomidate would be administered first to render the patient unconscious.

"What is it doing there (inside the house)?" Wecht asked when approached by reporters. "It's not something you use to keep away insects or polish your nails. It has a very, very specific purpose, so what the hell is it doing there?"

Wecht indicated that a killer bent on using succinylcholine to murder someone could fully incapacitate the intended victim by first putting them to sleep with the etomidate.

"They are not conscious," Wecht said. "There is no awareness of the adverse effects of the succinylcholine, so there would then be no likelihood of them calling attention to themselves by movement or verbalizing."

Lieutenant Jon Catalano was quick to point out that etomidate was not found in Kathy's body, and the bottle of the drug found inside Chaz and Kathy's home hadn't been opened. Catalano said that investigators were attempting to "determine what the parameters are on this substance and . . . what it does."

Two anesthesiologists, Dr. Anthony Frasca and Dr. Edson Parker, agreed that finding etomidate inside a nurse's residence was "strange." They commented that if someone had been injected with etomidate first, they would be rendered unconscious and would theoretically suffer less when the succinylcholine was administered.

"To kill someone with succinylcholine . . . is particularly cruel," Frasca said. "It could be someone was intending to use etomidate to lower the cruelty factor or to supplement the succinylcholine."

"At face value," Lieutenant Catalano said, "the fact that he did have it shows he was taking what we believe to be controlled substances home from the hospitals (where he worked)."

When the Clark County Coroner's Office had finished with its examination and selective tissue removal from Charles Augustine's body for a variety of toxicological tests, it was taken back to Paradise Memorial Gardens on Saturday, October 21, 2006, and reinterred in the original grave site in a straightforward process, without any type of ceremony being performed, according to Coroner Murphy.

"We are taking a very broad approach to this exam," Murphy said. "The goal of the Clark County Coroner's Office and the reason for the exhumation is to determine, if possible, whether or not the original cause and manner of death was appropriate and factual."

Murphy said that the process of the exhumation and reburial had gone off as planned.

* * *

As preparations for Chaz Higgs's trial moved into November 2006, his attorney David Houston began questioning whether authorities properly carried out the forensic testing on which they had based much of their case against Higgs. Houston complained that he did not know whether tissue samples had been taken from the suspected injection site on Kathy's body, which would have been the proper procedure to follow. All of the information that he had so far received had not shown that proper procedure had been followed, and he was suspicious that the police and the district attorney's office had built their case based primarily on the statements that nurse Kim Ramey had made to police.

"We have not been provided the detailed toxicology or a detailed autopsy report," Houston said. "They said they've given us everything. . . . The case seems to have been built based on a witness statement from a single person as opposed to building the case on science."

"We have an excellent workup on the toxicology," Washoe County assistant district attorney (ADA) John Helzer said in countering Houston's remarks. "We weren't in a hurry, we took our time, and we filed these charges because we believe they are supported by the evidence."

Helzer said that the evidence clearly pointed to Higgs as the person responsible for Kathy's death, and charged that Houston "loves to try his case in the press. That's what he loves to do."

Chapter 18

As the investigation into Kathy's death continued with Chaz Higgs being looked at as the only suspect in the case, Detective David Jenkins and the Washoe County District Attorney's Office considered it of paramount importance that everyone concerned with the prosecution be as well versed as possible on the subject of succinylcholine. In order to make headway in that regard, it was decided that they would have to bring in their own group of experts. One of the experts they talked to was Dr. Pamela K. Russell, a board-certified anesthesiologist from Reno. Russell had been an anesthesiologist for seventeen years, and proved to be quite knowledgeable about the characteristics of succinylcholine. She said that the drug showed up on the board examinations for anesthesiologists because of its complex nature and the complications that can arise from its use. She described it as the "purview of anesthesia and critical care medicine," and indicated that its characteristics are unique.

Russell described succinylcholine as a depolarizing muscle relaxant that was developed from the "(curare) poison of arrow darts of South American Indians." When introduced into the bloodstream of an animal or a human, either through muscle tissue or intravenously, the drug "causes the neurotransmitter at the receptor to release.

"And what happens then," Russell continued, "is that all this neurotransmitter goes to every single muscle, and those muscles go into massive taut spasm. We have no other drug in our armamentarium that does that."

It should be noted that neurotransmitters are defined as chemicals that are used to "communicate, intensify, and modulate signals between neurons and other cells." In other words, neurotransmitters communicate information between the body's neurons by causing the information to pass across the synapses from one nerve to the next. Succinylcholine, therefore, causes the subject to which it was administered to go into "big spasms that look like probably the worst seizure that you would ever see," Russell said.

"And it lasts approximately thirty to sixty seconds," she continued, "at which time, all those receptors then have been loaded, and then the muscles are paralyzed. . . . That's the main characteristic of how that drug works. It tends to be very quick as far as onset. And of most of our paralytic drugs, it tends to wear off about fifteen to seventeen minutes after given."

When asked how long after succinylcholine is administered to a person that the taut spasms begin, Russell said that several seconds are needed "for those receptors to start releasing the neurotransmitter" that causes the spasm to occur. She said that what occurs when the drug is put into the body goes beyond the rigid spasm and includes shaking as a result of muscle vesiculation. In order to avoid the vesiculation and shaking when, for example, a person goes to the hospital for elective surgery but requires a breathing tube, most often the patient is first sedated, then given a different type of muscle relaxer, and then the succinylcholine. In that manner of using the drug, the patient often doesn't remember the experience. What makes the experience so painful are the severe muscle contractions.

"So if succinylcholine is just given alone," Russell continued, "you will sit and be suffocating, unable to move, knowing what's going on around you, your surroundings, and you will continue to feel that until your brain starts to die at six to ten minutes. Then when the brain cells start to die, you'll probably go comatose. Could resuscitate you at the end of that time and probably get [the person] breathing, although by that time enough brain cells would have died that the brain will swell up, and your chances for recovering and being a normal human being are very, very limited. . . . The patients who have told me about that say it's pure terror, worse than any Stephen King novel you could imagine."

As the case moved forward into December 2006 and the preliminary hearing to determine whether Chaz Higgs would be bound over for trial for the murder of his wife approached, attorney David Houston argued that there was no evidence of murder and contended that the FBI crime laboratory had not found succinylcholine in Kathy Augustine's urine and body tissues. He claimed that the FBI lab only found succinylmonocholine, which, he argued, can occur naturally. He presented his arguments before Reno Justice Court judge Barbara Finley in an attempt to seek a delay for his client's preliminary hearing, by then only two days away.

"I'm not sure this is a homicide," Houston said. "I don't know if we are dealing with a crime at all."

Washoe County chief deputy district attorney Thomas

"Tom" Barb, however, argued that the preliminary hearing should be held as planned.

"He can claim whatever he likes," Barb said, referring to Houston's contentions. "I am going forward based on the toxicology report that says there was succinylcholine and succinylmonocholine in her urine."

Barb asserted that toxicology testing to determine the presence of succinylcholine in urine and body tissues had improved considerably over the past few years, and that his office felt comfortable basing their case, at least in part, on the toxicology tests performed by the FBI crime laboratory. Although there have been a number of murder cases in which succinylcholine had been used to kill the intended victim, the case that involved Chaz Higgs and Kathy Augustine appeared to be the first of its type in Nevada.

"I don't see an inconvenience by a continuance of thirty days," Houston argued, claiming that he needed the additional time so that a scientist he had hired would be able to examine the evidence against Higgs. "It is not such an ominous burden for the state that it overrides the interests of justice."

Houston also planned to question the validity of the various findings that Kathy had not died as a result of a heart attack.

"A lot of people die of heart attacks who have no signs of having heart disease," Houston said.

Houston also indicated that he needed more time to obtain the notes written by Dr. Madeline Montgomery, the chemist at the FBI crime laboratory who said that she had determined the presence of succinylcholine in Kathy's urine.

Barb argued that a delay would not help the defense team accomplish anything. The justice court system, where Higgs's case currently was, could not force the FBI to turn over its records as they pertained to Kathy Augustine because the federal government does not have to comply with such lower-court requests. Instead, he said, a district court judge, after Higgs had been bound over for trial and was officially in the district court system, could request such records from the federal government, which could in all likelihood be compelled to comply with such a request.

"He's in the wrong court," Barb said.

Judge Finley apparently agreed and said that the defense team had already had five weeks to get ready for the preliminary hearing. She denied Houston's request for a continuance, leaving intact the date of Thursday, December 7, 2006, for the murder suspect's preliminary hearing.

The preliminary hearing took five hours, spread across two days, and was held before Judge Finley. The judge heard testimony from nurse Kim Ramey, who recounted what she told police about Higgs stating to her, "If you want to get rid of someone, hit them with a little succs." Ramey had also said that Higgs had told her that he was planning to divorce Kathy, but that it would be a "short divorce."

Houston discounted Ramey's statements by saying that it was absurd to believe that anyone would tell someone whom they barely knew that succinylcholine was the perfect means to murder a wife or husband. He also said that after Ramey had spoken to the police, the investigators took the position that Chaz had killed Kathy and failed, along with the FBI crime lab, to search for other feasible reasons for Kathy's demise.

"The science to support this to some is bad science," Houston argued. "It is seeking the results based on the conclusion you have reached. When you approach it, seeking those results, that is the results you get."

The judge also heard testimony from nurse Marlene Swanbeck, who described Higgs's indifference at the emergency room the morning Kathy had been rushed in by paramedics; Dr. Ellen Clark, who had performed the autopsy on Kathy's body and had found two small puncture marks in the upper portion of Kathy's left buttock that she believed had been the result of an injection that had appeared to be recent; and Madeline Montgomery testified briefly regarding the results of the toxicology tests she had conducted. The judge ordered Montgomery to provide copies of her notes to the defense team.

At the end of the hearing, Judge Finley found that there was probable cause to bind Higgs over for trial on the murder charges in district court.

"The evidence is sufficient to bind him over for trial," Finley said. "It is not a determination of his innocence or guilt. A crime was committed, and the defendant was implicated."

Chaz Higgs was present at the hearing; he sat emotionless as the judge rendered her decision. Kathy Augustine's mother, brother, and daughter were present as well, as were several family friends. Kathy's daughter, Dallas, expressed relief over the judge's decision, as did Kathy's mother. Her brother, however, was a bit more vocal.

"We are convinced Chaz Higgs murdered our sister and our parents' daughter," Phil Alfano said. "I am sure a jury will come to the same conclusion. The past five months have been sad. This is another sad day, but we at least are on the path to getting justice for Kathy."

Two weeks later on Friday, December 22, 2006, Chaz Higgs and his defense team appeared before Washoe County District Court judge Steven Kosach, who had caught the assignment to hear the case, where Higgs pleaded not guilty to the charges against him. Kosach set a tentative trial date of July 16, 2007, and noted that everyone would have to remain flexible with regard to the trial date so that they could work around the schedules of the expert witnesses that would be called.

Following the brief arraignment, Houston indicated that he would challenge the determination of the justice court that the state had shown sufficient evidence for Higgs to be tried for murder.

"Neither money nor property was at issue," Houston said. "That, to me, is not a recipe for murder. . . . Chaz Higgs loved his wife."

Houston also indicated that he would challenge the conclusions of Dr. Ellen Clark, which, he contended, were based on the FBI laboratory analysis that he termed "suspect."

The defense counsel said, "With all due respect to the FBI lab, I think we can all agree they've had their difficulties in the past."

Chapter 19

As 2006 came to a close, Washoe Medical Center, which had changed its name to Renown Regional Medical Center, adopted new protocol for medical personnel to gain access to succinylcholine. The new procedures were put into place in part because of all the controversy surrounding Kathy Augustine's death, in which it was generally believed that Chaz Higgs had left the hospital with some of the controlled substance in his possession. In the past, the drug had simply been stored in a refrigerator for which nurses and other medical personnel only needed to enter a password to gain access to it. Following the Kathy Augustine fiasco, it was decided that more accountability was needed for those who had access to the drug. Detective Jenkins learned that Chaz, having only recently been hired at Washoe Medical Center at the time of Kathy's ordeal, had only worked five shifts at the hospital and had not been left unaccompanied because he was still on probation. The fact that he always had someone with him during his period of probation certainly decreased his opportunities to access the refrigerator that contained the succinylcholine, but did it eliminate such opportunities entirely? Finding out with any degree of certainty that Chaz Higgs was *never* left alone—not even for a few minutes—during his shifts would likely prove to be a difficult, if not impossible, task.

On February 14, 2007, Jenkins made it a point of his inquiry to contact Kathryn Almaraz, a registered nurse at the South Meadows Medical Center, where Higgs had previously been employed. Kathryn had been his supervisor for about a year and a half and had gotten to know not only Chaz's nursing abilities, professionally while on the job, but had gotten to know him somewhat personally as well.

Kathryn described Chaz as an excellent critical care nurse with exceptional skills. He was very good with patients, and she had always considered him a good employee. She noticed, however, that during his last six months of employment at South Meadows, his demeanor had changed, and it began to seem like he was under stress much of the time. She said that he had, on occasion, told her that his stress was caused by Kathy. She explained that Chaz often made negative comments about his wife, and called her a bitch often. Some days he didn't want to go home because he didn't want to be around her. One day, she said, Chaz made a disturbing comment about wanting to get rid of his wife.

"He said to me—I actually remember it because it was so vivid—that 'If I didn't have a daughter in Las Vegas, I would kill my wife and throw her down a mine shaft,'" Kathryn quoted Chaz as having said.

Jenkins wanted to know the approximate date that Chaz had made that statement to her, and Kathryn, to the best of her recollection, said that it had been about a year ago, likely in February 2006. That would have been about five months prior to Kathy's death, Jenkins noted. Even though she had described Chaz's statement as "vivid," Almaraz hadn't contacted the police or anyone else because she had

Kathy Augustine, Nevada State Controller, at work at the Nevada State Capitol in Carson City. *(Photo courtesy of Zuma Press)*

Kathy Augustine. *(Photo courtesy of Zuma Press)*

Kathy Augustine, about seven months before her death. (Photo courtesy of Zuma Press)

Kathy Augustine in a happier moment. (Photo courtesy of Zuma Press)

The state capitol building in Carson City, Nevada, where Kathy Augustine worked. *(Photo courtesy of the author)*

The Grant Sawyer state office building in Las Vegas, Nevada, where the Nevada State Controller maintained a second office.
(Photo courtesy of the author)

Charles and Kathy Augustine. *(Photo courtesy of Zuma Press)*

Kathy Augustine's home in Las Vegas, Nevada.
(Photo courtesy of the author)

Charles F. Augustine.
(Photo courtesy of Zuma Press)

Chaz Higgs and Kathy Augustine met at this hospital where Higgs served as one of Charles Augustine's nurses following Charles's stroke in 2003.
(Photo courtesy of the author)

St. Viator Catholic Church, Las Vegas, Nevada, where Charles Augustine's memorial service was held. He was a long-time supporter of the church and was buried in the cemetery area where some of the church's clerics were interred. *(Photo courtesy of the author)*

Entrance to the cemetery where Charles Augustine was buried.
(Photo courtesy of the author)

Charles Augustine's gravesite. *(Photo courtesy of the author)*

Dr. Cyril Wecht, nationally renowned forensic pathologist, publicly recommended that Charles Augustine's body be exhumed and tested for poisoning after it was determined that Chaz Higgs had been one of his nurses at Sunrise Hospital. *(Photo courtesy of Reuters Photo Archive)*

Clark County Coroner's Office, where Charles Augustine's body was brought for toxicological testing. *(Photo courtesy of the author)*

Kathy Augustine and one of her attorneys, Dominic Gentile, listening to testimony at Augustine's impeachment trial in December, 2004. *(Photo courtesy of AP Images)*

Guardian Angel Cathedral, site of Kathy Augustine's memorial service, just off the Las Vegas Strip. *(Photo courtesy of the author)*

Michelle Ene, Kathy Augustine's former executive assistant, pays homage to her boss at the memorial service. *(Photo courtesy of AP Images)*

Family and friends of Kathy Augustine carry the casket and load it into a waiting hearse following the memorial service. *(Photo courtesy of AP Images)*

Chaz Higgs's mug shot after his arrest in Hampton, Virginia, for his wife's murder. *(Photo courtesy of Zuma Press)*

University Medical Center in Las Vegas where Chaz Higgs was hospitalized following a suicide attempt. *(Photo courtesy of the author)*

Chaz Higgs at his preliminary hearing with his attorney, Alan Baum. *(Photo courtesy of Zuma Press)*

Paramedic Benjamin Pratt testifying how he and his partner attempted to resuscitate Kathy Augustine after being called to her home by her husband, Chaz Higgs. *(Photo courtesy of AP Images)*

Forensic pathologist Dr. Ellen Clark as she tells the jury that Kathy Augustine died as a result of being injected with succinylcholine. *(Photo courtesy of AP Images)*

Nurse Kim Ramey telling the jury that she went to the police after Chaz Higgs suggested to her that the best way to kill someone was to "hit them with a little succs." *(Photo courtesy of AP Images)*

Reno Police Detective David Jenkins shows the jury a photo of medical treatment reference cards allegedly found in Higgs's possession at the time of his arrest. *(Photo courtesy of AP Images)*

Washoe County District Judge Steven Kosach listening as Chaz Higgs's attorney tells him that Higgs is ready to return to court following a second suicide attempt. *(Photo courtesy of AP Images)*

Nurse Tina Carbone worked with Chaz Higgs at South Meadows Washoe Medical Center. She testified that she and her husband offered Higgs a place to live when he made it known that he was leaving his wife.

(Photo courtesy of AP Images)

Phil Alfano, Kathy Augustine's brother, and their mother, Katherine Alfano, attend the preliminary hearing on December 7, 2006. Kathy Augustine's family was enraged over bail being set for Chaz Higgs.

(Photo courtesy of Zuma Press)

Chaz Higgs conferring with his attorney at his trial.
(*Photo courtesy of Zuma Press*)

Dallas Augustine, Kathy Augustine's daughter, as she delivers a statement to the news media outside her Las Vegas home following the arrest of Chaz Higgs for her mother's murder. (*Photo courtesy of AP Images*)

no way of knowing whether Chaz was just blowing off steam or whether he really meant to do something like that. Kathryn Almaraz said that she and their manager, Tina Carbone, had talked to Chaz on several occasions about the problems he said he was having at home.

"Both of us had talked to him . . . offering employee assistance programs, encouraging him to get counseling because he was so unhappy with his marriage," Kathryn said.

She said that she had no reason to disbelieve the problems Chaz claimed that he was having with his marriage.

"She was very disruptive," Kathryn said. "She threatened staff. She would threaten him. She would show up unannounced in the emergency room demanding for his paycheck. There were . . . verbal discussions [that] I did not hear, but I could see through the window in the parking lot. Very disruptive of his work."

She said that even though she had not been able to hear them talking to each other, Chaz would be "pretty angry" when he came back into the department to resume his job duties. The disruptiveness of Kathy showing up unannounced regardless of her reason made it necessary for others to cover for Chaz, particularly with patient care, so that he could deal with his wife. Kathryn Almaraz said that in the marital relationship between Chaz and Kathy it had been Chaz, in her opinion, who had been the abused spouse.

"I felt that he needed help," she said. "He needed to get in with a counselor or some type of marriage help . . . to try and figure it out."

Recalling the details provided by Dr. Steve Mashour regarding the drug screening of Kathy's urine having come back positive for the presence of barbiturates, Jenkins broadened his inquiry regarding the tests that had been performed on Kathy upon her arrival at the hospital on the morning of July 8, 2006. Among the people who were included in the scope of his inquiry was Lilian Casquejo, a clinical laboratory specialist at South Meadows whose position entailed clinical laboratory testing.

Lilian confirmed that she was working on the morning in question. She explained that the specimens, packaged in bags that are marked BIOHAZARDS, were typically dropped off at the lab after which they would be taken to a lab employee's workstation, where they would be analyzed. On that particular morning, ER personnel had brought urine samples from a patient named Sarah Lambert, whose initial screening had come back positive for barbiturates. "Sarah Lambert," it turned out, had been a pseudonym or an alias that had been assigned to patient Kathy Augustine by the hospital upon her arrival to help protect her anonymity, presumably because she was a public figure.

The positive results for the urinalysis test for the presence of barbiturates in Kathy's body could have been one of several possible explanations of how someone could have injected her with succinylcholine without her putting up a struggle. After all, if she had been asleep after taking a barbiturate, she might not have felt the injection, depending upon how deeply she had been sleeping, or any struggle that she might have put up could have been reduced to a minimal one. However, subsequent tests that had come back negative, suggestive of an initial false positive, quickly shot down the viability of such a scenario.

Nonetheless, because of the suspicious nature surrounding the symptoms observed at the time of Kathy's hospitalization, portions of Kathy Augustine's specimens had been split off and packaged with identifiers, and then placed inside a freezer to preserve the integrity of the specimens in the event that additional testing needed to be completed later. They were later picked up by someone from the coroner's office.

Tina Carbone, Jenkins learned, like Kathryn Almaraz, had viewed Chaz Higgs as the victim in an abusive relationship with his wife. Tina had been a registered nurse for fourteen years and had been employed at Washoe Medical Center for the past thirteen years. As a nurse manager with fifty-four nurses under her supervision, she was the person who had hired Chaz at South Meadows for the emergency department, just prior to that facility's opening in February 2004. Although Chaz and Tina had occasionally talked about his personal life, he had not talked about his wife much during his first year of employment, Tina said. It wasn't until he had been placed on probation by the hospital's human resources department, at the time that Linda Ramirez had been fired over the e-mail exchanges between her and Chaz, that Chaz and Tina began having conversations about his wife.

Chaz was unhappy at that time because Kathy, he had said, was being very controlling and was very possessive. It had gotten to the point where Chaz began talking about moving out of their house, and had begun looking for a place to stay because their relationship was progressively getting worse. Although he had not frequently used derogatory language about Kathy in Tina's presence, she recalled one occasion in which he had referred to her as a "bitch." She said that because he was often at the triage desk and because her office was behind it, they'd had most of their conversations inside her office because her door was always open. His visits to her office became more and more frequent, to the point where his conversations with Tina had become "problematic," where Tina began to feel that her job was in jeopardy—not because of Chaz Higgs but because of his wife and the power that she wielded.

Tina confirmed that although she had never used succinylcholine and etomidate together on a patient, the two drugs were kept stored inside a rapid-sequence intubation kit, basically a tray of medications and associated supplies, within the emergency department for easy access when it was needed. The kit had an orange tab or seal that had to be broken to get inside it. Succinylcholine, she said, was also stored in what was known as the "Med Select," a storage refrigerator that the nursing staff could open by entering their password. She claimed that it would not be difficult to take a vial of succinylcholine out of the facility undetected.

At one point, Tina told investigators, Chaz's wife, Kathy, had begun harassing her. Tina, a married woman, had offered to rent Chaz an extra room at her and her husband's house if he decided to leave Kathy. As best as she could recall, the harassment had started around the time that she and her husband had made the offer to Chaz, or at about the time e-mails were being passed back and forth between Chaz and Linda Ramirez. Even though Chaz hadn't moved out of the house he shared with Kathy, and had not taken Tina and her husband up on their offer, the harassment continued.

The harassment consisted of letters that Kathy had written to Tina's administrator, and she began coming onto the hospital campus. Sometimes Kathy would wait in the parking lot for her, and she would make telephone calls to Tina, and others, at the hospital. When Tina had had enough and, in part, because she feared that Kathy would cause her to lose her job, Tina took her concerns about the harassment to the State Ethics Board and other outlets available to her, but nothing was done to make Kathy stop. It was then that she and Chaz went to human resources and had a conversation about how they might be able to make Kathy stop.

Although she had indicated that it would be easy for a nurse to walk away from the hospital with a bottle of succinylcholine or some other medicine, the controls in place at the time that Chaz Higgs had worked at South Meadows hadn't turned up any discrepancies regarding missing or otherwise unaccounted-for medications in the emergency department.

Chapter 20

Nancy Vinnik and Kathy Augustine were best friends, and had known each other since 1988. They had met through the Junior League of Las Vegas, an organization of women committed to promoting volunteerism and whose mission is dedicated to helping women develop their potential. They had been friends for the next eighteen years. Nancy told Jenkins and other investigators that Kathy had spoken to her frequently regarding her relationship and marital problems involving Chaz Higgs.

"I talked to her probably at least twice a month," Nancy said. "She came down to Las Vegas from Reno frequently, and I would meet with her for lunch."

Kathy also came to her house for dinner somewhat regularly, affording the two friends plenty of opportunities to spend time together throughout the course of Chaz and Kathy's marriage. Nancy often gave Kathy marital advice, which had a continuing theme.

"It frequently was to (tell her to) 'tell him to leave,' or for her to get out, because I felt that she had made a bad decision (in marrying Chaz)," Nancy said.

Nearly every time Nancy spoke to Kathy to give her

advice to get away from Chaz, Kathy always told her that she loved him. It had seemed to Nancy that Kathy wanted to make Chaz happy.

"Truthfully, it was that she . . . loved him," Nancy said. "He would sometimes apologize to her after he had done . . . very terrible things to her. . . . I would frequently describe him to her as a Dr. Jekyll and a Mr. Hyde."

Around the time of Kathy's funeral, Nancy said, she had traveled to Las Vegas at the request of Kathy's family. Because it was difficult for Kathy's family to dispose of her things at the office she kept at the Grant Sawyer building in Las Vegas, they had asked Nancy to clean it out for them. With the help of Kathy's secretary, Nancy boxed up everything and took it over to Kathy's house on Maria Elena Drive. It was about 4:30 P.M. when she arrived at the house.

Several of Kathy's relatives were there when Nancy showed up, including Kathy's brother Phil. They had come to Las Vegas for Kathy's funeral. Approximately twenty minutes later, Chaz Higgs and Dallas Augustine, Kathy's daughter, showed up "very inebriated," according to Nancy. Phil had calmly approached Chaz and asked him to stay elsewhere. According to Nancy, Phil explained that they had a very large family and that they had already arrived. Several other relatives were on their way.

Higgs, she explained, was not at all happy at that point, and became very upset—to the point of yelling and screaming, "saying that it was his house and nobody was going to tell him that he couldn't stay at that house." He became very volatile, she said, "when all hell broke loose in the house." Chaz had started punching things, including the walls and doorjambs, "and was yelling, swearing, cursing." At one point, there was a very loud noise that came from another part of the house where Chaz had gone. Everyone had initially thought that it had been a gunshot, and Nancy had been frightened to the point that she called 911.

When they investigated the source of the loud noise, they found that Chaz had ripped out the front door. Everyone surmised that what they had heard had been Chaz "pounding and ripping out the front door," Nancy said. He had even damaged the door frame, but had not fired a gun. Just prior to Chaz breaking the door, Nancy had seen him on the phone to someone and had overheard at least part of the conversation.

"I know he was talking to Kathy's mother," Nancy said, "because he said, 'Your daughter is nothing but a fucking whore and a cunt.' And when I heard that, it really . . . was awful to hear that because . . . it was hard just losing a friend, and I couldn't believe that he could call her mother and say something so disgusting and so despicable. . . . I had a feeling that she hung up on him. . . ."

Later, after Chaz had already left the house, Dallas asked everyone to leave. Nancy said that she was so nervous and distraught over all of the commotion at the house that she was unable to drive and it had become necessary for her husband to come and pick her up from a neighbor's house nearby. She said that the entire ordeal had gone on for more than an hour. She said that she had seen Chaz return to the house about twenty minutes later, after everyone else, except Dallas, had left.

The next day, which had been the day before Kathy's funeral, Chaz had slashed his wrists and had to be rushed to University Medical Center's emergency department for treatment.

As winter passed and spring approached, Chaz Higgs languished in jail in Reno, waiting and hoping for an opportunity to be released on bail while waiting for his trial to begin. He had originally been held without bail, but his lawyers persisted in their attempts to get the judge to change his mind. When he was finally granted bail, both of his parents, who were divorced, each put up their respective homes as collateral to cover Chaz's $250,000 bail. Washoe County District Court judge Steven Kosach had set bail on March 1, 2007, with a requirement that he remain in the state of Nevada and stay in daily contact with his attorneys, but it had taken until Monday, March 26, 2007, for his mother and father to make the financial arrangements. When he walked out of jail, escorted by several deputies and one of his attorneys, to a waiting car, he was dressed in jeans and a sweatshirt.

"He's very happy to be free," his attorney David Houston said.

When they arrived at Houston's office, Chaz met with his mother, who was making plans to temporarily relocate to Reno from North Carolina to help provide support for Chaz pending the outcome of his trial, which was set to begin on Monday, June 18, 2007.

"Upon arriving, we walked in and the first thing he did was hug his mom," Houston said.

His mother, Shirley Higgs, had believed from the very beginning that her son had not killed Kathy Augustine.

"He is innocent," she said. "That is all I will believe. I know him better than anyone. I am his mother."

Kathy's family, however, were very angry that Judge Kosach had decided to release Chaz on bail. They prepared a statement that Phil Alfano provided to the news media.

"My parents, my brother and I are angry that a psychopath like Chaz Higgs will be allowed to walk free for the next few months, especially given the evidence already presented and his bizarre behavior immediately follow-

ing Kathy's death," Phil said in the statement. *"No amount of posturing or showmanship by Chaz's attorneys will change the facts of this case or alter the outcome. When a jury knows what we already know, he will be convicted and spend the rest of his life behind bars."*

On Tuesday, May 2, 2007, the Clark County Coroner's Office released a statement that Charles Augustine had died as a result of natural causes and had not been killed by a lethal injection of succinylcholine or any other type of toxic material. Coroner Michael Murphy said that Charles Augustine had died of a stroke, as originally believed. Murphy's examination showed that he also suffered from heart disease and bronchopneumonia.

"There was nothing in our investigation that would lead us to believe Mr. Augustine died of anything other than natural causes," Murphy said at a press conference.

One of Chaz's attorneys, David Houston, believed that the inference that Chaz had anything to do with Charles Augustine's death had been created and suggested to police merely to taint his client's image. Houston said that there were a lot of people "willing to believe Mr. Higgs was a monster responsible for two deaths. And, clearly, it just isn't true."

"They now know that Charles died of natural causes and not at the hands of the criminal," Dallas Augustine said in a statement released to the media. "Charles was a good man. I hope this brings some measure of peace to the family."

"We're relieved to learn that Chaz did not murder Chuck the way he murdered my sister," Phil Alfano said. "Thankfully, Chuck didn't suffer the same fate."

As a result of the findings, there was no reason for Las Vegas homicide detectives to pursue the issue any further.

Similarly, the matter of the purported discrepancy regarding the time frame when Chaz and Kathy supposedly had met each other had not been brought up again. The innuendo and finger-pointing that had been going on suggesting that Chaz and Kathy had plotted Charles Augustine's death appeared to have no substance.

Due in part to the evidence that had been collected and the witness statements that had been obtained during Jenkins's investigation, it also did not appear that Kathy had died as a result of any kind of political intrigue perpetrated by anyone that she had been going after to expose for political corruption, despite a *48 Hours Mystery* episode that had been televised on CBS that had hinted at a murder conspiracy concocted by her Republican rivals.

"My immediate reaction (following Kathy's death) was 'They killed her,'" Barbara Woollen, a former candidate for lieutenant governor, stated. Woollen recalled that she'd had multiple conversations with Kathy in which death threats against her had been alleged because of her inquiries into political corruption that had involved the misappropriation of funds at a time when she had decided to run for the office of state treasurer. Woollen quoted Kathy as saying at one point: "They will do anything to keep me from getting into that office."

The investigation just didn't seem to support that kind of inquiry, however, and the purported political corruption had been left to other entities to deal with; in keeping with political tradition, the issues that involved allegedly corrupt politicians that she had been looking into all but disappeared.

Three weeks before his trial was set to begin, Chaz Higgs's attorney David Houston filed a request to postpone his client's trial. Houston claimed that the FBI laboratory had not provided its complete report to the defense team showing that Kathy Augustine had been poisoned with succinylcholine. Because so much of the state's case against Chaz was science dependent, Houston said the complete report was needed by a defense expert. Prosecutor Tom Barb, however, argued that the initial report had been provided to the defense team in December 2006, and that they should not have waited until such a late date to decide that they needed more information for one of the expert witnesses that they planned to call.

"There's overwhelming evidence Kathy Augustine was murdered and Mr. Higgs was the murderer," coprosecutor Christopher Hicks said.

"There is no evidence Chaz Higgs killed Kathy Augustine," attorney Alan Baum asserted.

"I hate to say this," Judge Kosach said to the defendant. "But the comments you made to Ms. Ramey, if someone heard that, they would say, 'Oh, wow.' It's almost like television."

The judge sided with the state and denied the request.

"I don't want this to get out of hand," Kosach said. "I do not believe the interest of justice will be furthered by a continuance."

Kosach said that the comments Chaz had made to Kim Ramey were "damning in my mind."

Kathy's brother Phil agreed with the judge's ruling.

"It's time for this to move forward," he said.

The defense team filed last-minute pretrial motions in an attempt to keep the state's findings on succinylcholine out of the trial. Houston and Baum argued that they had not been provided the opportunity for their own experts to conduct testing of Kathy's blood and urine samples, and had only recently been told that there was not a sufficient amount of blood remaining for them to conduct their own tests and that the urine samples had "been allowed to deteriorate." They also argued that their experts had not been allowed to observe the testing of the blood and urine samples, either. The defense lawyers maintained that succinylcholine can occur in the body naturally and might "be found even where it has not been intentionally administered."

As a result, read Baum and Houston's motion, *the methods used to test the presence of intentionally administered doses of succinylcholine are hotly contested, and have not been generally accepted by the scientific or legal community as reliable and trustworthy.*

Deputy District Attorney Tom Barb indicated that he would respond to the motions in writing, and Judge Kosach said that some time would be set aside to hear the motions in detail prior to the start of the trial.

Part II

The Trial

Chapter 21

On Monday, June 18, 2007, the trial for Chaz Higgs finally got under way in the Department Number 8 courtroom of Washoe County District Court judge Steven R. Kosach. It was about 9:30 A.M. when all of the lawyers, defense, and prosecution, along with Chaz Higgs, met with Kosach to address the pretrial motions that had been filed. Jury selection had been scheduled for 1:30 P.M., and discussions were under way to allow a defense witness to testify out of order, due to the witness's scheduling conflicts, while the state presented its case. Case Number CR06-2876 was one that was not to be missed—in part because of who Kathy Augustine had been, and because of the anticipated strong and often creative defense that had been put together over the past several months. The usual media trucks with their satellite dishes surrounded the historic courthouse, which sometimes can be found draped in large American flags, especially around Flag Day, which had been four days earlier.

Judge Kosach referred to a motion *in limine* regarding scientific evidence and expert witnesses. A "motion *in limine*" is a legal tool that asks the court to render a decision on whether certain evidence may or may not be presented to a jury during trial. As the prosecutor Tom Barb prepared to call a witness in reference to the aforementioned motion, defense attorney Alan Baum addressed the court.

"Your Honor," Baum said, "it is our belief that it is the state's burden to establish the necessary requirements for the admission of this particular type of evidence . . . therefore I would defer to the state to meet its burden by presenting any witnesses that it wishes to. It's not the defendant's burden when we've raised an objection to the admissibility of scientific evidence. The authority is clear that it's the state's burden, that is, the proponent of the evidence burden, to establish the basic foundation for admissibility."

"We accept that, Judge," Barb responded.

After establishing that it was the state's burden to establish the necessary requirements for the admission of the particular type of evidence that would be presented in this case, particularly that which is centered on the scientific evidence that everyone knew was coming, Barb called Dr. William H. Anderson, chief toxicologist for the Washoe County Sheriff's Office (WCSO) Division of Forensic Science.

Barb elicited testimony from Anderson demonstrating that he had reviewed the analytical data of the toxicological testing done at the FBI laboratory by Madeline Montgomery. Anderson had also reviewed the validation data, which had become an issue of sorts, for the methods and protocols that were used by the FBI, and confirmed that he had discussed the case with an expert witness on toxicology for the defense, H. Chip Walls. Walls, he said, needed additional information about sample availability, among other things, and they had gotten on a three-way conference call with Madeline Montgomery to address Walls's questions. Anderson said that he had no questions for Montgomery, but was there as an interested third party.

"So, Walls, Montgomery, and you were on a three-way call, and questions were asked and answered, and then other documents were provided?" Barb asked.

"That is correct," Anderson replied.

"Have you seen those other documents?"

"I had—one of the primary concerns was an illegible document that Mr. Walls had," Anderson explained. "And I could read my copy. So I received a list and acknowledgment from Mr. Walls that he had received that material, but I did not receive another copy. . . . I did subsequently receive some validation data."

"Based on your review of the documents that have been provided, all of them, do you have an opinion as to the trustworthiness of the FBI testing procedure?"

"In my opinion, the procedures were standard procedures that are used in forensic toxicology to make identifications. They ran appropriate negative and positive controls. And, in my opinion, there's no problem with the identification of either succinylmonocholine or succinylcholine itself."

When Barb had finished, defense attorney David Houston cross-examined the witness.

"Doctor, what's the standard operating procedure as adopted by the FBI for the test of succinylcholine?" Houston asked.

"It's kind of lengthy," Anderson responded.

"Well, let me ask you this. Are you aware there isn't one?"

"I'm sorry. What was that question?"

"Are you aware there is not a standard operating procedure as adopted by the FBI for the testing of succinylcholine? Not succinylmonocholine."

"I see. Yes. It's the same extraction, the same LCC parameters, with a slide gradient."

"I guess the question was—are you aware there isn't a standard operating procedure for the testing of succinylcholine?"

"I didn't see one specifically for succinylcholine."

"All right. The standard operating procedure for succinylmonocholine that was apparently utilized in this case was adopted or created in 2001?"

"I'm not sure if it was 2001 or 2002," Anderson replied.

"It was subsequently amended in 2006, was it not?"

"I'm not absolutely certain."

"Do you recall any amendments going on, possibly even to your lab, that indicated succinylmonocholine can be produced naturally—so, as a consequence, report results of the same with great care?" Houston asked.

"That's published in the literature for decomposing tissues."

"And in this case, essentially what happened is Ms. Montgomery, the chemist, on the fly, converted the succinylmonocholine standard operating procedure to test for succinylcholine, correct?"

"Essentially, that's correct."

"And 'on the fly' means she sort of made it up as she went."

"I don't know what Ms. Montgomery had done, and I don't know what her previous experience with that drug was, but it was just a simple extension of a validated procedure."

Houston pointed out that Montgomery had testified at the preliminary hearing that she had never tested for succinylcholine for the purposes of testifying at trial. He asked Anderson if he was aware of any specific articles or journals that indicate that it is acceptable to modify the standard operating procedure utilized to test for succinylmonocholine for the testing of succinylcholine.

"I don't know that I've seen that . . . no."

Prompted by Houston's questions, Anderson explained that "method validation" means that it can be shown that the method of testing is reliable, that false positives aren't present, and that it can be shown that the testing is reproducible and not subject to interference. He stated that he believed the FBI lab had followed standard operating procedure regarding the testing of Kathy's urine.

During the course of questioning the state's witness, Houston managed to go on record with regard to his concerns about the controls placed on Kathy's urine while it was in one of the FBI lab's refrigerators; how succinylcholine had been added to "John Doe" urine and then attempted to use a liquid chromatograph mass spectrometer to detect its presence; how a power failure had occurred at the FBI lab while Montgomery had been in the middle of repeating the testing procedure after finding evidence of succinylmonocholine in the initial screening of Kathy's urine; how there was no evidence that a technician came in after the power failure to certify that the liquid chromatograph mass spectrometer was operating properly; and how a bag of succinylcholine used in the controls had sat on the shelf in the FBI lab since 1998.

Houston's efforts obviously had been to cast doubt on the FBI lab's methods involved in determining the presence of succinylcholine in Kathy's urine, and to get it into the record in the process—it might be grounds he could use for appeal in the event that Chaz was convicted. Houston also brought out the fact that a drug screen had been done on Kathy's urine prior to sending it to the FBI lab in which no evidence of drugs, such as epinephrine, heparin, or atropine, had been found, and drove home his inferences that some of the toxicology results may have been assumed.

"Doctor, you understand the problems in the science of forensic toxicology of assuming a result, true?"

"Certainly."

"And we've seen that demonstrated in the Sybers case, correct?"

Dr. William Sybers was the Panama City, Florida, medical examiner who had been accused of killing his wife with a lethal injection of succinylcholine in 1991, and whose conviction was later reversed based on problems with the scientific evidence.

"Yes."

"And we've seen that demonstrated in the Sybers case, correct?"

"Yes."

"And you're very familiar with the notion that in the Sybers case it was stated unequivocally that succinyl-monocholine cannot exist in the system endogenously (originating within), correct?" Houston asked.

"I think . . . something to that effect," Anderson replied.

"Sybers was convicted and served a great period of time before that scientific theory was corrected, did he not?"

"Yes."

"So the better thing to do prior to the time of assuming what a certain test may give us is to actually do the test."

"Well, I think you have to temper that with reason, Mr. Houston. There are thousands of drugs that are available. No one can test them all . . . and in this case, for scientific reasons that are straightforward, the drugs you mentioned, for example, couldn't possibly interfere . . . with succinyl-choline. The succinylmonocholine issue was one of interpretation of those results, not one of contradiction of the analytical results."

"Doctor, the short answer is—whatever Ms. Augustine may have had in her urine was not duplicated in the

FBI laboratory in the normal 'John Doe' urine for control samples, correct?"

"I guess I really don't know the answer to that, because I don't know where the control samples were," Anderson responded.

"Well, wouldn't it be important since you're here discussing the method of validation, and how you approve of that, to know something of the control samples that were utilized in order to achieve the result?"

"Well, they were just negative control urines. I mean—"

"How do you know, Doctor?"

"That is all I can tell you. I can only go by what was in the FBI documentation. I have no firsthand knowledge of where those specimens came from."

"Right. Or in what condition they were in."

"No."

"Or in what condition they may have degraded to after they had been stored in a refrigerator for three days after the succinylcholine had been introduced to the urine. Were you aware of that?"

"I thought we were talking about the negative control urines."

"We are talking about the urines in general. I think we have three sets of urine. We've got Kathy Augustine's sample urine, allegedly Kathy Augustine's, correct? Then we've got the urine that was created, I am assuming the 'John Doe' urine to be positive. And then we've got the urine that's created, 'John Doe' urine again, for the purposes of negative control sampling."

"Yes."

"All right. Were you aware all of that urine was placed in a refrigerator for three days after the power outage where the liquid blah, blah, blah machine would not work?"

"I was not aware of that specifically."

"What would the studies or journals that tell us that the urine degradation with succinylcholine already added wouldn't somehow impact or affect the testing mechanism that was utilized?"

"I don't think that particular experiment has ever been reported."

"Doctor, when we consider what we refer to as standard operating procedure, do you have a standard operating procedure to produce the safeguards that the test will be appropriately done?"

"Normally, yes."

"And do you know by looking at the records, the data package, in this particular case, whether Ms. Montgomery sought any sort of assistance or peer review of her methodology referencing the modification of the succinylmonocholine standard operating procedure adopted in 2001?"

"The only documentation . . . I could possibly see was that it was reviewed by the chief of the FBI section, Dr. Marc LeBeau. So he obviously looked at it and approved it. And there's a quality control person signature on it. Frankly, I don't know whether that person would know or not. I do know Dr. LeBeau's knowledge."

Houston pointed out that from information included in the data package that the testing was done solely by Montgomery. He also asked questions regarding the alleged injection site on Kathy's left buttock, and confirmed that the suspicious site had been tested and that test had been negative for any residue of succinylcholine or succinylmonocholine. He pointed out that tests had also been performed on Kathy's blood plasma that had been obtained from two separate draws nearly two hours apart the morning Kathy had been rushed to the hospital, and those tests, too, had turned out negative.

"And all other testing that was done was actually negative

for the presence of succinylcholine or succinylmonocholine, correct?"

"That's right."

"And the only test that resulted in a positive was the test performed solely by Ms. Montgomery on the urine."

"Yes. That's correct."

"Doctor, have you ever tested for succinylcholine?"

"I have not."

"Thank you."

On redirect, Tom Barb questioned his witness about the alleged injection site and confirmed that the fact that the tissue sample from that site had turned out negative for succinylcholine and succinylmonocholine had been the result that Anderson had expected, and was therefore not shocking or surprising to the chief toxicologist.

"And you expected that because succinylcholine would go away in a live body fairly rapidly, is that correct?"

"That is correct."

"Same result for the blood testing?"

"The blood was a little bit more surprising," Anderson responded. "I have since found an article that says after a few minutes you may find it in the urine and not in the blood. But that was a bit more surprising. I thought, if we had any possibility (of finding the drug's presence), that would be in the plasma. The urine was the most likely. . . ."

"How fast does this drug get out . . . of a live system?"

"Succinylcholine itself has a half-life of less than one minute," Anderson said.

"So, if you inject me, and half the drug is gone in less than a minute, then I'm down to a quarter in less than two minutes . . . an eighth in less than three minutes. It goes away pretty fast."

"Succinylcholine does, yes."

"You said this process the FBI used was a simple extension," Barb said. "What does that mean?"

"Succinylcholine—the drug—and succinylmonocholine are very similar," Anderson explained. "They have a chemical called succinic acid. One has got two choline molecules attached to it, and the other has one. Obviously, succinylmonocholine has one. Both are what we would call a quaternary ammonium compound, so they . . . can be extracted by the same procedure. . . ."

"Mr. Houston also spoke to you about the Sybers case. . . . Are you familiar with that case?" Barb asked.

"I'm not intimately familiar with it, but I . . . have some knowledge of it, yes."

"The difference between that case and this case is that in Sybers the samples had been embalmed for nine years, and then they were tested. Is that your recollection?"

"I don't remember exactly how long it was, but it was some period of time."

"Nobody could say what embalming fluid would do to anything in the body as related to succinylmonocholine."

"Right."

"And succinylmonocholine was the only evidence found in the Sybers case, is that correct?"

"To my knowledge."

"In this case, we also have, for lack of a better term, the parent drug, succinylcholine."

"Yes."

"Do you have any doubt that this evidence is—I understand the jury gets to decide whether they believe it or don't—whether this evidence is trustworthy and reliable enough to tell the jury about?"

"I have no problem with this data indicating that succinylmonocholine and succinylcholine were present."

"Thank you," Barb said, finishing his redirect of the witness. Judge Kosach, however, interjected a comment.

"And I would add a question," Kosach said. "To a reasonable degree of medical probability, would your answer be the same?"

"Yes, sir," Anderson replied.

Dr. Anderson was excused to make room for the defense's expert witness as the issues surrounding the motion *in limine* continued.

Chapter 22

H. Chip Walls, a forensic toxicologist who has been qualified as a toxicology expert in federal, state, county, and city courts, in both criminal and civil cases, took the witness stand on behalf of the defense during the pretrial motions. David Houston began the questioning, taking Walls through the information regarding the data pack from the FBI laboratory, including method validation to substantiate or refute the process as it was used by the FBI lab. He explained that in this case the method was designed to detect succinylmonocholine in biological samples, and in performing method validation, the scientist does things to prove that the test being performed can distinguish a positive from a negative, that there is no residual carryover from one set of tests to another, and that no false positives or false negatives have occurred.

Walls said that he was not aware of any standard operating procedure methodology in the FBI laboratory for the detection of succinylcholine, and he confirmed that the FBI had not sent him a procedure for that—he said that they had basically modified the procedure for the detection of succinylcholine in the samples.

Walls testified that the fact that the source(s) of the negative control samples, as mentioned earlier as having come from volunteers in the lab, were problematic for him in that typically such samples are tested to show that the sample does not contain the analyte or target compound of interest. Most of the time, he said, such samples come from healthy individuals "giving a negative urine sample that proves that type of sample is not going to be positive." In this case, he would have liked to have seen samples coming from patients in hospitals that may have been given medications, such as the atropine, epinephrine, and heparin that were administered to Kathy in an attempt to save her life, to verify that they did not interfere with the testing process. When asked whether succinylmono-choline was produced as part of the decomposition process, Walls stated, "Not that we know of."

"What is the definition of 'false positive' and 'false negative'?" Houston asked.

"A false positive is where you find the drug in a sample, whatever target analyte you're looking at, and it's really not there," Walls replied. "Something else has caused an interference that produced a positive result when the drug itself was not there. A false negative is when you have a negative when the drug should be there, but you do not detect it."

When asked about the importance of keeping the urine frozen for the purpose of the testing, Walls said that suc-cinylmonocholine and succinylcholine can degrade as the samples become warmer—the warmer the sample, the more decomposed the sample might get. It had already been shown in the description of the FBI lab's chain of custody that the urine had been shipped frozen from Washoe County and had likely still been frozen upon arrival at Quantico, Virginia. However, due to the procedures in place at the FBI lab, it was also shown that the urine had thawed, been refrigerated, and refrozen at various steps along the way of that agency's bureaucratic staircase. Walls said that the succinylcholine, the parent compound, would decompose very rapidly, but that the succinylmonocholine would degrade at a slower rate and would produce a false negative. In Walls's opinion, the FBI lab had done a "limited validation study" that he would like to have seen performed differently, particularly with regard to the controls.

Walls indicated that he would have liked to have seen a more complete validation as opposed to the limited validation study that occurred. In fairness to the FBI lab, he said, they had done a positive-negative control, which is typical in a forensic laboratory, to identify a compound and to be able to say that a positive can be identified from a negative sample.

Upon cross-examination by Tom Barb, Walls went through a lengthy question-and-answer session that basically resulted in him saying that the colder the samples to be tested are during storage, the better the chances are that the integrity of the samples would be preserved for testing purposes. There would be less degradation of both the urine and any drugs that it might contain.

"Urine samples are different than tissue samples, as far as your expectation of finding anything in it, is that correct?" Barb asked.

"Yes," Walls replied. "Urine is somewhat protected from enzymes that normally break drugs down, so once it's filtered out of the blood into the urine and is stored in the bladder, it may be detectable for longer periods of time."

"So just take this as an example," Barb continued. "A call came in at six forty-five . . . 'Come help me with my wife.' Medics arrive, do their treatment and resuscitate her, and get her to the hospital at about seven-o-five, seven-ten. So that's twenty minutes. First urine sample is taken at seven thirty-five. So we're forty-five, fifty minutes out. Would you expect the urine sample, given that amount of time—we don't know the injection time, but given that amount of time, forty-five or fifty minutes, would you expect the urine sample to contain that drug if it had been injected?"

"Yes."

At the end of the at-times-complicated process of presenting the scientific information, Judge Kosach stated that the law in Nevada on the admissibility of expert testimony is very clear, and he quoted part of it: "The threshold for admissibility of expert testimony turns on whether the expert's specialized knowledge will assist the trier of fact in understanding the evidence or an issue in dispute." He denied the defense's motion *in limine,* and said that he would allow Montgomery, Anderson, and Walls to testify at trial.

The remaining pretrial motions filed by the defense included whether to allow testimony about statements that Chaz Higgs had made to his coworkers about getting rid of his wife, whether testimony about the e-mails between Chaz Higgs and Linda Ramirez should be allowed, whether probable cause had been adequately shown in the affidavits for search and arrest warrants that were filed by Detective Jenkins, whether Jenkins knowingly and intentionally misrepresented what Kim Ramey had told him regarding the conversation that Chaz Higgs had with her about using succinylcholine to kill someone, a motion to dismiss the charges against the defendant, and so forth. Both sides argued the merits of their respective positions on the issues, but Judge Kosach ultimately sided with the prosecution and denied most of the defense motions.

Following a lunch break, jury selection began at 2:10 P.M. in the courtroom next door to Kosach's. Although there were ninety-nine potential jurors in the jury pool, the selection of twelve jurors and three alternates did not take as long as it could have despite the lengthy questioning. Jury selection was completed by early that evening, and the jurors were sent home for the day so that they could get a good night's sleep. They were instructed to report to Judge Kosach's courtroom the following morning, prior to nine o'clock for the beginning of what was expected to be a three-week trial.

Opening statements began on Tuesday, June 19, 2007, at 9:05 A.M. After the jury was seated in the jury box and everyone was accounted for, Deputy District Attorney Christopher Hicks greeted the jury and then began.

"Succinylcholine, or succs as it's commonly called in the medical setting, is a paralytic drug that has devastating effects," Hicks said. "It's commonly used in emergency situations when a person needs to be intubated—they need to have a tube run down their throat so that a machine can breathe for them. It is administered both intravenously and intramuscularly. And when it is administered, it renders a patient totally paralyzed. They cannot move, they cannot breathe, they can't even blink their eyes, and yet they are totally awake. Without the assistance of another person in helping that person to breathe, they will suffocate, their heart will stop, and their brain will likely suffer irreversible damage due to oxygen deprivation."

Hicks described how Chaz Higgs had spoken about that drug on July 7, 2006, while referring to a high-profile murder case in which a Reno man, Darren Mack, had allegedly stabbed his wife to death.

"Mr. Higgs said, 'That guy did it all wrong. If you want to get rid of somebody, you just hit them with a little succs.' The very next morning, his wife, Kathy Augustine, a woman who he admittedly hated, who he commonly referred to in real nasty terms, and who he desperately wanted to leave, was found in their home, with Mr. Higgs, not breathing and without a heartbeat."

Hicks described how treating physicians at the hospital had found no evidence of a heart attack, no evidence of a pulmonary disorder, and no evidence of a brain dysfunction that would explain Kathy's condition that morning.

"However, what was found in her system was succinylcholine," Hicks said.

Hicks explained that Higgs, as a critical care nurse, was commonly around the drug, and the two hospitals where he had worked had very few controls in place that would prevent a person from taking succinylcholine home with them if they so desired. He also described how an autopsy had been performed on Kathy's body and it had revealed that she had not succumbed to death as a result of natural causes—she had died from succinylcholine poisoning. He pointed out that when Higgs had been arrested in Virginia, he had a piece of paper in his car that explained the appropriate dosage for the administration of succinylcholine.

"Ladies and gentlemen, you're going to hear from numerous witnesses during this trial," Hicks said. "I want to go over just a few of them this morning."

Hicks told the jury that the first witness they would hear from would be Kim Ramey, and explained that she was a nurse who had worked at the Carson-Tahoe Hospital, where she had met Chaz Higgs, a new hire, on July 7, 2006.

"You see," Hicks said, "he had been hired as a nurse at that location, and as part of his orientation, he was following around Miss Ramey that day."

Hicks explained that personal conversations had developed between Ramey and Higgs, and Higgs began telling Ramey about the contempt he had for his wife, the fact that he was planning on leaving her, and all the while had referred to her in derogatory terms.

"At one point during that day," Hicks said, "he made a statement to Miss Ramey that literally made the hairs stand up on her arm. He made the statement that 'that guy did it all wrong. If you want to kill—if you want to get rid of somebody, you hit them with a little succinylcholine.'"

Two days later, he said, Ramey experienced that same sensation of the hair raising up on her arm when she saw in the media that Higgs's wife, Kathy Augustine, was in the hospital in a coma. Ramey, he pointed out, had later contacted a detective at the Reno Police Department.

Hicks told the jury that they would hear testimony from the REMSA paramedics who were involved in trying to resuscitate Kathy Augustine at her home early on the morning of July 8, 2006. Benjamin Pratt, he said, would provide details of what had occurred upon his arrival at Kathy's house.

"[Pratt] will further tell you that when he went into the house, he found Kathy laying in their bed," Hicks said. "She was not breathing. She had no heartbeat. Mr. Pratt and his fellow paramedics removed Kathy from the bed, placed her on the floor, on a hard, flat surface, and began to administer CPR. Through their efforts, they were able to get her heart beating again. Mr. Pratt will tell you that during that time Mr. Higgs was not even in the room and that it appeared that he could care less as to what was going on with his wife."

He told the jury that they would also hear from Marlene Swanbeck, who had formerly worked with Higgs, and how she and another nurse withdrew a urine sample from Kathy as they tried to determine what was wrong with Kathy Augustine. Swanbeck, he said, would describe how Higgs had seemed totally disengaged that morning at the hospital, and how, in the past, he had often talked about his intent to leave his wife, how he had referred to Kathy in very derogatory terms, and so forth.

Hicks basically went through the state's witness list as he told the jury who would be testifying and what they would be testifying about, including physicians who had treated Kathy in one capacity or another.

"First you'll hear from Dr. Stanley Thompson," Hicks said. "He's a cardiologist here in town. He will tell you Kathy did not suffer a heart attack. Her arteries were clean. She had no blockage. He will also tell you that he was amazed at the lack of emotion exhibited by Mr. Higgs when he explained to him the condition of his wife."

Dr. Steve Mashour, a Reno pulmonary physician, would testify that there was nothing wrong with Kathy's lungs that would explain her condition the morning she was brought to the hospital. Neurologist Dr. Paul Katz would explain how he had not found any external injuries to Kathy's head, no bleeding inside her brain, or anything else that would explain her condition; he would also explain how she had suffered brain damage that was consistent with oxygen deprivation.

"All three of those doctors will tell you that their observations during their diagnosis of Kathy is consistent with succinylcholine poisoning," Hicks said.

And on it went until he had gone through the entire list,

providing a glimpse of what jurors should expect from each witness's testimony: Dr. Ellen Clark, Dr. Jerry L. Jones, Madeline Montgomery, several of Higgs's former coworkers, Kathryn Almaraz, and Detective David Jenkins, among others.

"In a nutshell, ladies and gentlemen," Hicks concluded, "that's the evidence that we will present to you. And that evidence will show that Chaz Higgs is a calculated murderer who used his trade to accomplish his goal—getting rid of his wife."

David Houston provided the opening statement for the defense and talked to them about evaluating the evidence in the proper context and to not "snatch bits and pieces, as has been done a moment ago" with the prosecution's opening statement. He led the jury through Chaz and Kathy's history together, how he had been happy-go-lucky at first in their relationship, but had changed when he realized that he couldn't live a political lifestyle. Despite having wanted a divorce, Chaz stood by Kathy during her impeachment proceedings.

"And Mr. Higgs stuck it out," Houston said. "He didn't leave. In fact, you will hear from one of the nurses when they asked, 'Well, why don't you just leave?' 'I can't leave her right now,'" Houston quoted Higgs as saying. "And that would be during the course of time that the impeachment was occurring."

Houston drove home the point about context being so important in this case, and asked the jury not to be misled by the "cherry-picking" of statements, ideas, or occasions. He urged that the entire picture be evaluated prior to making a decision in the case, and explained the importance of the medical testimony that they would hear.

"The state's case will not survive beyond the defense pathologist, as well as the other information and facts that will be provided you throughout," Houston said. "Ladies and gentlemen, the idea of looking for justice is such an easy phrase. It's a catchphrase to some. But, truly, it is not because this is a murder case or because it's a high-profile case that we apply that rule in this room. This room has been here . . . way longer than most of us. The idea of it is it's truly meaningful. And I can only ask you on behalf of Mr. Higgs to do everything within your power and honor your promise and to realize the importance of every word you said when you became a juror. Thank you very much."

Chapter 23

Following a brief recess after the opening statements were given, Kim Ramey was called as the state's first witness. After being sworn in, Ramey explained her position as a traveling critical care nurse, an open-heart surgery recovery position that she had held since 1999. She explained that she had made the decision to be a "traveler," a nurse who does not work on staff for a hospital. Due to her specialty in open-heart recovery and the overall nursing shortage in the United States, Ramey said, she had always been able to choose the geographical regions where she wanted to work. Because of poor acoustics inside Judge Kosach's courtroom, Ramey was asked several times to speak up as she testified so that jurors on the far end of the jury box could hear her.

Ramey told of how she and her boyfriend had arrived in Carson City to work at the new Carson-Tahoe Hospital's open-heart center in January 2006. Since the hospital did not yet do open-heart surgery at that time, Ramey and her boyfriend, because of their specialties, had been invited to help the medical center open such a unit and to help them train their nurses in that medical area. In response to

Christopher Hicks's questioning for the state, Ramey acknowledged that she had been working the day shift at the Carson-Tahoe Hospital on July 7, 2006. Just as she had told Detective Jenkins, she explained to the jury how she had met Chaz Higgs that day due to the fact that she had been asked to help out in the hospital's intensive care unit, where Chaz had recently been hired. Because she was required to wear gloves and a gown when attending a patient in the ICU, and didn't want to take the time to change each and every time the need to enter or exit the ICU arose, she asked Chaz to assist her by bringing her the things she needed from other areas in the hospital. That, she said, was how they had become acquainted and began talking that day. One of her patients had bacterial spinal meningitis, and the other had "all kinds of bugs" and was on a ventilator, and having Chaz there to get the things she needed helped her remain as sterile as possible for her patients and saved time by eliminating the need for her to frequently change in and out of a gown.

Because she had immediately perceived Chaz as a "player," Ramey said, she had decided to engage him in conversation by telling him that she had a boyfriend and that the two of them were relocating soon to Virginia. She wanted to make it crystal clear to Chaz that she was not available. She also perceived that "he had this . . . aura . . . of anger," she testified. She said that the anger came out mostly when he was talking about his wife and the fact that he wanted to divorce her.

"Now, did he tell you who his wife was?" Hicks asked.

"Yes," Ramey responded.

"And who did he say that was?"

"High-profile, Kathy Augustine," Ramey said. "I said, 'Chaz, I'm not from around here. That means nothing to me.' 'Yeah, but you know high-profile. She's the state controller,'" she quoted Chaz as having said. "I said, 'I don't live around here. That means nothing to me.' 'Well, she's running for treasurer.' I said, 'It still doesn't mean anything to me.'"

"Now, you had indicated that he referred to her in some other unpleasant terms," Hicks said. "I'm going to ask you. I know it's embarrassing on the stand, but please just tell the jury how he referred to his wife."

"'She's a fucking stalker,'" Ramey responded. "'I'm looking for an apartment 'cause she's a fucking stalker. She's a bitch. She's psycho.'"

Ramey explained that the derogatory remarks that Chaz had made about Kathy hadn't been said all at the same time, but that Chaz had said these things to her at different times throughout the day.

"Aside from the obviously unpleasant terms, did he ever indicate that he loved his wife in any way?" Hicks asked.

"Not at all. There weren't any terms of endearment at all."

"Were there any terms of hatred?"

"That's the only emotion I saw. Anger . . . rage."

In response to questioning, she described how Chaz had been on the telephone in her presence and she had heard part of a heated conversation that he was engaged in.

"What did you hear him saying into the phone?" Hicks asked.

"'I will fuckin' talk to you when I get home. . . . I said I will fuckin' talk to you when I get home,'" Ramey responded. "And this is in the middle of a unit, which . . . to me . . . was inappropriate. Especially with an employee that had just started. He wasn't even off orientation."

She explained that she hadn't known who Chaz had been talking to at first, but she figured that it must have been his wife. She later asked him point-blank what the telephone conversation had been all about, and she said that he told her that his wife had found out that he had opened a separate bank account.

As the questions continued, Ramey's testimony eventually turned toward the talk that she and Chaz had engaged in about the Darren Mack case in Reno. It had been the discussion of the Mack case that had led up to Chaz telling Ramey that Mack should have used succinylcholine.

"He said, 'That guy did it wrong,'" Ramey testified, quoting Chaz. "'If you want to get rid of someone, you just hit them with a little succs because they can't trace it postmortem.'"

That statement, she said, had been the one that had made her "skin crawl" and had caused her hair to raise up. It had also been the statement that had interested Detective Jenkins at the probe's outset.

"Now, you say your hair raised up," Hicks said. "What do you mean by that?"

"I don't know if you guys ever get a physical response to something horrible," Ramey replied. "That's what I get, that physical response. Like goose bumps . . ."

Ramey described how she had felt two days later when she had seen the newspaper headline that had read: KATHY AUGUSTINE FOUND DOWN. Although she said that she couldn't believe it, her gut feeling was that Chaz had done something to his wife. She immediately thought that he had killed her. She said that she waited until July 11 to call the police.

"Now, ma'am, I've got to ask you this," Hicks said. "It seems a little odd that you had this reaction, and you didn't call the police right away. Can you please explain to the jury why that is."

"I had four shifts left," Ramey explained, "and I was going back to Richmond, Virginia, to settle a two-and-a-half-year divorce. I had lawyers up to here. I had everything physically taken away from me. I'm not a millionaire, but I worked very hard over twenty-one-and-a-half years. I—you have no idea how much I despised lawyers. And I didn't want . . . to deal with any more lawyers. I was praying I would watch the TV and watch the newspaper, that they would just arrest him and . . . I would be off the hook."

She said that her boyfriend and a coworker had urged her to go to the police about Chaz's statement. At one point, one of her coworkers had spoken to Dr. Richard Seher, a cardiologist, about the situation. Seher, in turn, had come to Ramey to talk about it. She had become acquainted with Seher due to his specialty and hers having some overlap. They had conversed in the past, sometimes about personal issues, and she had felt comfortable talking with him. After she had explained to him what had been said, Seher told her that she needed to call the police. That was when she phoned Detective Jenkins.

Ramey also provided some basic information about succinylcholine for the jury, basically what it was, what it is used for, when to use it, its immediate effect when administered intravenously, and how it affects a patient. She also said that it was readily available in the hospital for medical personnel to use. She pointed out a bottle of the drug in a photo that was shown to her of the interior of a rapid-intubation kit. She also pointed out a bottle of the drug, etomidate, in one of the photos of the inside of a rapid-intubation kit. She described where the kit was kept, who had access to it, and how it could only be accessed by someone who knew the code of the key padlock that secured the door of the refrigerator where it was kept. Everyone, she said, used the same code.

"Are you familiar with the drug etomidate?" Hicks asked.

"Yes."

"As a critical care nurse with your experience, would there ever be a reason to have a vial of etomidate at your house?"

"No," Ramey responded. "That would be grounds for losing your license."

Following Alan Baum's cross-examination of Kim Ramey, which had amounted to little more than clarifying a few small details about her testimony, and had not brought any new and significant information for the jury to consider, the state called Dr. Richard Seher.

Seher, board-certified in internal medicine, general cardiology, and interventional cardiology, had been practicing in the Reno–Lake Tahoe area for more than twenty-one years. He had been working at Carson-Tahoe Hospital for about nine months, and had come to know Ramey by having worked with her. He described her as a "great" nurse who was "really on the ball," and said that he would "be happy to have her take care of me or any of my family members."

On the morning that he had spoken to Ramey about the comment that Chaz Higgs had purportedly made, Seher had been making rounds in the cardiovascular intensive care unit. Ramey, he said, appeared upset and visibly shaken. He said that he took her to a "side room" that is used for dictation and they, along with another doctor, sat down and talked.

"Dr. Seher, when Miss Ramey approached you, visibly upset as you've stated, what was it that she told you?" Hicks asked.

Hicks's question generated a near-automatic objection from Baum on the grounds that the response would be hearsay. The issue was argued out of the jury's presence, after which Judge Kosach overruled the objection and allowed the question to stand.

"She said, 'I know—I know that Chaz Higgs killed her. I know what he did,'" Seher testified.

"And what did you say when she said that?"

"I said, 'What was it?' And she recounted that . . . when they worked together, she had heard him arguing with his wife on the phone, and he said something to the effect of 'I'm going to leave my wife, take the money out of the account.' Then he said, 'You know, Darren Mack was stupid. He should never have been caught. He should have used succinylcholine. He wouldn't have been caught.'"

"And did you know what she meant when she said 'succinylcholine'? What is succinylcholine to you?"

"Oh, absolutely," Seher responded. "Succinylcholine is a paralytic drug. It's a type of curare. There are several drugs in that category that we use in the hospital as a paralytic agent."

Seher said that when he indicated to her that she needed to call the police, Ramey had been reluctant to do so at first. Seher recounted what Ramey had testified to about not wanting to go to the police because "she had just gone through a divorce, and I think she sort of had it with the legal system." He said that he continued to urge her to contact the police.

"I said, 'You know, this isn't like a traffic violation. . . . This is a real crime. You have to report it. You have to call.'"

"Did you take any steps yourself once you heard what she had spoken with Mr. Higgs about and then after she had told you everything?" Hicks asked. "What did you do?"

"I called my partner, Dr. Richard Ganchan," Seher said. "And there's two large cardiology groups in town, and we take care of the sickest of the sick people. So, if somebody is ill, there's a fifty-fifty chance we're taking care of them. So I called my partner . . . and I said, 'Are we taking care of Kathy Augustine?'"

"And did you find out if you were, in fact, taking care of her?"

"He confirmed the fact that we were indeed physicians consulting on her case."

"Did you give any specific instructions to . . . Dr. Ganchan?"

"We had a very brief conversation," Seher responded. "I said, 'Get a succinylcholine level now.' And he said—after a pause—'Got it,' and hung up the phone."

Chapter 24

"The state calls Dr. Paul Mailander," Washoe County Deputy District Attorney Christopher Hicks said.

After being sworn in, Dr. Mailander took the witness stand and attempted to get comfortable. In response to questions from Hicks, Mailander explained that he worked as an anesthesiologist for Sierra Anesthesia in Reno and nearby Sparks, where he performed surgical anesthesiology.

"If you could please explain for the jury what schooling you had that led you to where you are today," Hicks asked.

Mailander explained that he earned a bachelor's degree in medical engineering from the University of California at Berkeley, and a master's degree in biomedical engineering from the same university. He went to medical school at Case Western Reserve University in Cleveland, Ohio, after which he did two years of general surgical residency at Cleveland's Lutheran Medical Center, three years of general anesthesia residency at the Cleveland Clinic, and a year of postanesthesia fellowship in cardiothoracic anesthesia and pain management, also at Cleveland Clinic. He had been practicing in Reno since that time. He also had served as chair of the Department of Anesthesia at Washoe Medical Center from 1994 to 1996.

"Your Honor, I would offer Dr. Mailander as an expert in anesthesia," Hicks proclaimed.

The defense team stipulated and made no objection.

In response to a question from Hicks about the role of the anesthesiologist, Mailander explained that it was his job to take patients who are about to undergo surgery and render them comfortable and safe so that they could tolerate the stress and duress of surgery. Of course, he said, this was accomplished through the use of a variety of medications that place the patients in a hypnotic, or unconscious, state in which they would not be aware of what was happening to them. He said that the patients were carefully monitored during the surgery for any changes in their vital signs, and to ensure that they remained unconscious. When the procedure had been completed, he said, his job involved bringing them back to a conscious state and monitoring them through their recovery as they woke up.

"We have a variety of tools," Mailander explained, "but, basically, on any given general anesthetic, for example, where a patient is going to sleep, we use a rock-bottom minimum of about seven different medications. And that's for someone who is having a simple procedure, who is essentially healthy and doesn't have any outstanding medical conditions."

He said that an anesthesiologist will typically sedate patients preoperatively to alleviate any anxiety that they might be experiencing. To keep patients safe, their blood pressure is checked frequently, as is their pulse rate, oxygen saturation levels, and carbon dioxide levels. The patients' EKGs are monitored closely throughout their operations, and their motor responses are checked.

"Then we give them medications [that] will put the

patient into a state of what we call hypnosis," he said. "Most people . . . call it going to sleep. Most people are familiar with sodium pentothal . . . a sleeping medication that makes you basically fall into a state of unconsciousness."

Once a patient is asleep, he explained, the anesthetic needs to be maintained so that the patient will not wake up on the operating table. Sodium pentothal, which has no pain-relieving properties, works clinically for only approximately two to three minutes.

"We have to give the patient other medications to keep them comfortable for the duration of the procedure," he testified. "And, if needed, we give them medication to keep them immobile so they can't move. Surprisingly, if you're asleep, but not very deeply asleep, if someone does something painful to you, you're going to twitch or move. So by giving you some medications [that] either make you more comfortable, or in some case simply prevent you from moving, it makes things safer and faster for the surgeon and for the patient."

"Now, are one of those drugs that will prevent a patient from moving called succinylcholine?" Hicks asked.

"Yes," Mailander replied.

"If you would, please explain to the jury what, in a nutshell, succinylcholine is and what it is used for."

"It is a clear, colorless liquid that we inject almost exclusively intravenously into our patients," the doctor responded. "Virtually all of the anesthetic agents we use work on your nerves and your brain primarily. The muscle relaxants, including succinylcholine, work at the level of the muscle. It's the one medication, or one of very few, that actually works at the level of the muscle itself.

"Whenever you move a muscle purposefully," he continued, "making a fist, moving your hand . . . your brain sends a nerve impulse to your muscles, and there's a chemical released at the nerves on to the muscle [that] triggers the muscle to twitch. So I tell my hand to make a fist, the nerves stimulate the muscle fibers with chemical reaction, and I make a fist. . . . The muscle fibers all pull together.

"Succinylcholine is a medication [that] looks very much like the chemical that is the neurotransmitter, from the nerve to the muscle. And it is very avidly bound on to the receptors of the muscle. And by binding to the receptors of the muscle it blocks the neurotransmitter from working. As a result, the muscle fibers do not work. And that medication will stay in effect clinically on the muscle, making the muscle unable to respond to nerve stimulus until it is metabolized. And then it goes away and . . . regains normal function."

Mailander explained that succinylcholine is used in numerous types of surgery situations, and is commonly used in the intubation of a patient. He explained that succinylcholine wasn't the only medication used for that purpose, but that it was one of the earliest discovered. Because it has certain side effects that are not beneficial for the patient, its clinical use is avoided whenever possible.

"But in a circumstance where we need to place a breathing tube into a patient relatively quickly," Mailander explained, "succinylcholine is still the fastest-acting muscle relaxant that we use clinically. By giving it to the patient, they can be rendered motionless within about a minute of its injection, and then we can open their mouths and place a breathing tube basically into the top of their windpipe at that point."

"I just want to make sure I understand correctly," Hicks said. "If a person is administered succinylcholine, they are paralyzed, correct?"

"That is correct."

"Can they move anything?"

"Any muscle you can voluntarily control, your breathing, your eyelids, shrugging your shoulders, anything you voluntarily control, will be paralyzed and unable to move. Your heart will work. Your intestines will work. Other muscles that you don't normally control voluntarily will continue to work. But the skeletal muscles are what we call them, all will stop functioning, and the patient will be unable to move."

"So I assume your brain is not a voluntary muscle," Hicks said, generating mild laughter from the gallery. "It's always working. Is that right?"

"Well, your brain is not a muscle. In most cases."

"In some of us, it is," Hicks said, taking another stab at creating levity. "So it doesn't affect your brain?"

"No, it does not."

"And you said it doesn't affect your heart."

"No, it does not, either."

"So, if someone was administered solely succinylcholine, would they be totally awake during that state of paralysis?" Hicks asked.

"Yes, they would."

"Again, sir, assuming someone is administered succinylcholine . . . if there was no airway intervention, something to help them breathe, what would happen?"

"They basically would lose the capacity to breathe voluntarily, and it would be incumbent upon us to maintain an airway and either lift the patient's chin, make sure there's no obstruction, and then using a bag and a mask, which we use in surgery paramount to forcefully ventilate the patient for him or herself. So we would be driving oxygen and other anesthetic acid into the patient's lungs for their benefit and on their behalf until they can regain their own muscle tone."

"And if that didn't happen?"

"The patient would not breathe," Mailander responded. "And then it's a matter of how much oxygen they have in their system and how long a wait before they amass enough carbon dioxide. Their blood is still circulating, so there is CO_2, carbon dioxide, accumulation in the lungs as well during a period of paralysis. So it's a matter of how long you want to wait before the patient starts suffering the ill effects of too much carbon dioxide and too little oxygen."

"And if that happens?"

"You start basically having a condition that we call ischemia, which is a lack of oxygen, and you start suffering organ damage."

"To what organs?"

"Primarily to the most sensitive ones," Mailander responded. "And the nerves and the brain are the most sensitive organs to oxygen deprivation. They will be the first ones to suffer irreversible damage."

"After the nerves in the brain, are there any other organs that would suffer damage?"

"Well, all organs will eventually, but the actively metabolic organs. The liver, the kidneys are very sensitive as well. Not as sensitive as the nerves, but the kidneys and liver will start to show signs of ill effect. And eventually the muscles will, too."

He explained that the heart is a highly metabolic organ, a muscle that is constantly working, but that in the absence of oxygen and nutrition from the blood, it will start to suffer ill effects as well and will begin to fail.

"You had indicated that this particular drug is primarily administered intravenously," Hicks reminded the witness.

"Yes."

"Are you aware if it can be administered intramuscularly?"

"It can," Mailander affirmed. "And most of the anesthesia books [and] most . . . anesthesia instructors will tell you that in a pinch, if you have to get someone paralyzed and there is no intravenous access, you can give them a shot in a muscle.

It will take a little longer to act, but it will act, and the patient will be paralyzed, and you have to move accordingly."

Dr. Mailander said that he had not seen firsthand succinylcholine administered intramuscularly because, he explained, if a patient needed to be put to sleep emergently without an IV line, there were other anesthetic and sleeping medications, such as the hypnotics that he had discussed earlier, that could render the patient unconscious without paralyzing him or her. Paralyzing a patient without knowing that you can establish an airway is a major risk factor, he said. One of the circumstances in which a physician would not be able to administer succinylcholine intravenously would be when dealing with an uncooperative patient in an emergency situation.

"Now, if you were to administer succinylcholine intravenously, how quickly would it take effect?" Hicks asked.

"In a normal, healthy individual, normal circulation, in under a minute," Mailander responded.

"And intramuscularly?"

"About three minutes."

"Again, back to my hypothetical of a patient who is not being cooperative, and you have to administer it intramuscularly," Hicks said. "Would that three-to-five-minute window speed up if the person was still fighting?"

"Well, the faster someone moves, the faster their blood circulates, the faster the medication is picked up in the muscle and circulated through their system, yes," Mailander responded. "So, if someone is struggling, then medication takes effect faster."

"Are you familiar with a drug called etomidate?" Hicks asked.

"Yes."

"Is there any reason why a person would have etomidate at their home?"

"I can't think of a good therapeutic reason, no. I can't think of a reason."

"What is etomidate?" Hicks asked.

"It's a hypnotic medication," Mailander said. "Back to inducing an anesthetic, putting someone from essentially awake to asleep, etomidate is another medication we have, to inject in someone, which will put them into a state of sleep. It creates amnesia, which is a good thing. And anesthesia, which means you're unable to respond to stimulus. It does not . . . relieve any pain."

Mailander explained that etomidate, a controlled drug, is not commonly used because it has a side effect that affects the adrenal glands in that it interferes with normal adrenal gland hormone production, a complication that is potentially hazardous to patients. However, it has the benefit of maintaining normal cardiovascular stability when injected into patients to put them to sleep.

"(For) patients who have unstable cardiovascular systems," Mailander added, "whether they are anemic or have lost a lot of blood or simply have weak hearts, etomidate is a better choice than others because it maintains a normal blood pressure, normal pulse rate."

Hicks led the expert witness through a series of questions in which he confirmed through Mailander's answers that, among other things, etomidate is a drug that cannot be obtained through pharmacies because they don't stock it, and that etomidate, as well as succinylcholine, is under controls, with limited access in a hospital setting.

"Dr. Mailander, I want to digress for a second to intramuscular injections," Hicks said. "Again we'll go back to the uncooperative patient in which you need to get paralyzed, for lack of a better term, and you need to administer intramuscularly. Would the buttocks be an appropriate spot to do that?"

"Yes."

"And in your training and experience as an anesthesiologist, is there any pause you have as to say whether or not succinylcholine would work if administered in that manner?"

"It should work very well."

"And why would that be?"

"It's a large muscle. One of the reasons the buttocks is a general muscle of choice for shots is that it's a very large muscle mass, so the odds of hitting the muscle are very, very good without going too deep in the bone or going too superficially. And has a very, very good, strong blood supply for rapid uptake."

"And why is a strong blood supply important in a case of succinylcholine?" Hicks asked.

"Again, I don't inject succinylcholine intramuscularly if I can help it. . . . I have not done it myself. But the faster the medication gets to its target organs, which would be all of the muscles in the body, then the faster the patient is put into a condition where we can work with them more successfully."

"Dr. Mailander . . . again I am speaking to you hypothetically . . . if you were to . . . administer succinylcholine to a person in hopes that it would not be discovered by treating physicians or treating emergency personnel soon thereafter, where would you pick . . . ? Would the buttocks be an acceptable spot?"

"I think the buttocks are as good a choice as any," Mailander said. "I can't begin to imagine where a spot would be undetectable. But the buttocks, I presume, like the crease in the buttocks, might be a good choice because there's a natural body fold there. People might not look so carefully. I haven't got a great answer for that. Sorry."

"I understand," Hicks said. "Thank you very much. That's all I have, Your Honor."

Chapter 25

With Dr. Paul Mailander still on the witness stand, defense attorney David Houston fashioned much of his cross-examination in such a way that it was easy for everyone present to see that he was attempting to diminish at least some of what the state's expert witness had testified to in the presence of the jury during direct examination. It wouldn't be easy to change the image that had been presented to the jury, but it was his job to try. He had clearly done his homework, and he began after the usual greetings and introductions.

"Doctor, succinylcholine is primarily—and please excuse my vocabulary being not medical—designed to be administered IV, true?" Houston asked.

"Yes."

"And it's designed to be administered IV because you have better controls as far as time of onset and dosage, right?"

"That, and the fact that you don't want paralysis to onset slowly . . . if you can help it because it makes your patients a little unstable."

"And it could make your patient very aggravated if they were conscious to have that slow onset of paralysis," Houston said.

"Well, yeah, I suppose you could argue that," Mailander said. "As you get agitated, you get weaker."

"Sure. How many times have you injected a conscious patient with succinylcholine?"

"Never."

"And how many times have you injected a patient with succinylcholine in the adipose tissue, not the muscle?"

"Never."

"Would a reason not to inject in the adipose tissue be that we wouldn't know the time of onset or the dosage with any reliability?"

"I would say not a primary reason, but certainly a reason."

"Okay. And adipose tissue is fat, right?"

"Correct."

"Now, when we talk about the buttock area, there's a big muscle back there," Houston said. "That's the gluteus maximus?"

"Yes. And the medius and the minimus."

"And in some people, there may be a little bit more padding than others in reference to fat tissue, right?"

"Very much so."

"That's a delicate way to put it," Houston said. "So that being said, if you're injecting into the buttock area in order to get to the muscle, you'd have to have a needle long enough to do the job."

"Yes."

"Are you aware in this case that the autopsy had indicated what they thought might be this punctate-type area was only one point five or two centimeters deep?"

"I believe we discussed that in your office. Yes."

Houston was attempting to show the length of 1.5 to two centimeters, when Mailander explained that it was just under an inch. Houston also pointed out that the autopsy had shown how much fat existed from the surface of the skin on Kathy's buttocks to the point where it reached the muscle and characterized it as an important consideration in determining whether the injection dose had ever entered the muscle. Mailander expressed some concern over Houston's depiction of the fat and whether the dose had entered the muscle because, he pointed out, fat can be displaced if it is pushed upon with added force. Mailander also confirmed that succinylcholine is not a fat soluble drug.

Houston also questioned the state's expert witness whether he was aware of any scientific study or statistics that address dosage of succinylcholine in adipose tissue, and Mailander responded that he had found a study on the subcutaneous injection of the drug from the *Korean Journal of Anesthesia* that was done in 1995. It had been a controlled study, he said, in which they used identical doses of succinylcholine for IV versus intracutaneous or subcutaneous administration. The study, he said, had used patients who were asleep.

"If you inject succinylcholine in a subcutaneous way and the patient is awake, would it be fair to say it's going to burn or sting?" Houston asked.

"I would say it would probably hurt, yeah," Mailander responded. "I'm guessing. But . . . let's say yes."

"And then after that, we have the onset, which results in slowly depriving you of oxygen, true?" Houston asked.

"Well, you get weaker, yeah," Mailander said.

Mailander affirmed that a patient in pain and being deprived of oxygen would fight or thrash about. He also confirmed that there was no dosage specified in the medical literature for a subcutaneous injection of succinylcholine; however, he said, the standard accepted dose for the drug injected intramuscularly is typically three to four milligrams per kilogram of body weight, and that such dosage results in a one-to-four-minute onset before the drug takes effect.

"In this particular case," Houston said, "if Miss Augustine weighed one hundred eighty-nine pounds, that's approximately eighty-six point three kilograms, correct?"

"Approximately, yes."

"I'm not really that smart," Houston said. "I wrote it down."

"We knew that," Barb interjected.

"You didn't know that. You were amazed," Houston countered. "Again, using the charting, if we use three milliliters per kilogram, that appears to be a nine-point-five-cc dose."

"At twenty milligrams per cc. Yeah," Mailander responded.

"And the common . . . hospital vial . . . is twenty milligrams per cc, correct?"

"That's right."

"Now, if we factor in a twenty-five- or twenty-seven-gauge needle—I'm using that because of the depth—what amount of time do you think it would take to empty almost a ten-cc syringe into someone through a needle with that small a port?"

"It can be done relatively quickly," Mailander responded. "Within the course of about maybe ten seconds. I'm guessing."

"Okay," Houston said. "Your Honor, may I have an opportunity? I just happen to have a ten-cc syringe with a twenty-seven-gauge needle on it. I'd like to put some water in it, if I could."

"As long as you don't use it on me," responded Judge Kosach.

"That's a promise," Houston said.

Houston and his co-counsel, Alan Baum, approached the witness with the syringe and needle, and Mailander confirmed that it was a 10 cc syringe and what appeared to him to be a 27-gauge needle. He asked the anesthesiologist to fill up the syringe with water and to demonstrate how long it would take to empty it through the needle by squeezing the plunger.

"Doctor," Houston said during the demonstration, "if I were to put this in somebody . . . a live, conscious patient . . . injecting that succinylcholine into them in the left buttock, what do you think they're going to be doing while I'm doing that?"

"I—I imagine the patient would be moving around or trying to get away from it."

"Quite a bit probably, right?"

"Couldn't begin to tell you," Mailander responded.

"Doctor, would you anticipate if there were a needle mark—because I noted you said something on direct. You said, 'When something is done to you that is painful, you twitch.'"

"Yes. Absolutely."

"That's even when you're unconscious, right?"

"Yes. Absolutely."

In the courtroom with poor acoustics, nearly everyone sat perfectly still during this portion of Houston's cross-examination of the state's expert witness, anticipating the moment when it would become clear just where he was going with his line of inquiry.

"So if you're conscious," Houston continued, "or not rendered unconscious, but if you're conscious and somebody jabs you in the behind with a needle and starts pumping that drug into your skin, would you anticipate them to at least twitch?"

"Oh, yeah."

"Are you aware that when the autopsy was done in this case, this proposed punctate-type area did not show any tearing or anything that would suggest the needle was moved, if it is a needle mark?"

"No. I have no idea what the autopsy results are."

"But wouldn't you anticipate that if it was a needle mark—and somebody was injecting succinylcholine—that they're going to twitch or move?"

"I'd expect them to move, yeah."

"Okay. Doctor, that was at the base-minimum dosage for an IM (intramuscular) at three milliliters per kilogram," Houston said. "If we go to four milliliters per . . . kilogram, we've jumped up to seventeen point two-five cc's. . . . Now I need either a syringe that's twice that size or two syringes, right?"

"If you use that dose, yes," Mailander said.

"Now, just out of curiosity, each bottle that we note at the hospitals is two hundred milligrams, right?"

"Yes, that's correct."

"So, if I'm going to inject three hundred forty-five milligrams, now I've got to have two bottles, true?"

"Yes."

"If I were to inject five milliliters per kilogram, I'd require four hundred thirty-one milligrams, which is twenty-one point five-five cc's, true?"

"Yes."

"Now I need more than two syringes that size," Houston continued. "I need three. And that's only at five (milliliters per kilogram), correct?"

"That's correct."

"And if I'm to do four hundred thirty-one point eight milligrams, now I've got to have three bottles because I'm out, if I'm just using two, right?"

"Yes. Sure."

"Can you envision a situation where someone could inject that kind of quantity under the skin in somebody's left buttock without it not leaving some sort of welt or pronounced area?"

"Yes."

"And how much time do you think it would take for the introduced substance to . . . diffuse? Is that the word?"

"Diffuse, sure. Dissipate."

"How much time do you think?"

"Don't know because I'm not familiar with subcutaneous diffusion. We don't do subcutaneous injections."

"You think it might take more than thirty minutes?"

"I couldn't tell you."

"All right. Fair statement. And, of course, if we're talking about an intramuscular dosage, and the numbers just keep going up, then we're anticipating a much larger syringe, much more time to get it through the needle port, and you need more bottles to get the job done, correct?"

"If you do it that way, yes."

Mailander confirmed that he has frequently used succinylcholine as an anesthesiologist. When Houston asked him about its use with regard to intubation, he erroneously stated that the drug is used to prevent the gag reflex during the intubation procedure. Mailander corrected the defense attorney by explaining that the succinylcholine weakens the facial and neck muscles so that medical personnel can open the patient's mouth to insert the air tubing. The gag reflex goes away, along with the weakening of the facial and neck muscles.

"And when you have a patient in a surgical procedure, if you're going to airway them, and you've already kind of put them down a little with VERSED or something, do you still use something like succinylcholine to intubate them?"

"Every time."

"And so it doesn't matter really whether they're conscious or unconscious?"

"If they're conscious, they fight harder," Mailander responded.

"And if they're unconscious, you'd use it because you want to be able to weaken the facial muscles enough to where you can get that tube down their throat."

"Yes."

In finishing up his cross-examination, Houston asked Mailander if critical care nurses typically assisted in the administration of succinylcholine. However, Mailander said that he did not know the answer, and Hicks was left again, at center stage, with a brief redirect examination of the witness.

Hicks went through the intramuscular (IM) dosages that Houston had questioned the witness about previously, and he and Mailander agreed that it was three to four milligrams of the drug per kilo of body weight for an IM.

"Is that your therapeutic dose?" Hicks asked.

"That is a dose to create what we call intubating conditions," Mailander responded.

"And what . . . does that mean?"

"That means to make you weak enough, fast enough, that we can open your mouth, manipulate your neck, and gain access to your airway."

"Is that a requisite level for succinylcholine to have an effect on a person?"

"No."

"Would you like to expand on that?" Hicks invited.

According to Mailander's testimony, one milligram of the drug per kilogram on any one individual would be a typical intravenous dose. However, he said, the dose would vary for each individual depending upon his or her size, weight, age, and health. Less than a milligram per kilogram, say

.2 milligram—about one-fifth of that given intravenously—would weaken someone profoundly. He explained that such a small dose may not enable the medical practitioner to gain surgical control of the patient's airway, but that it would be sufficient to weaken the patient. He said that patients who had been accidentally injected with a small dose of succinylcholine during the course of having surgery have shown profound weakness with a fairly small dose.

"Enough to not even be able to breathe on their own?" Hicks asked.

"In many cases," Mailander said.

"So, assuming the hypothetical . . . one-hundred-eighty-nine-pound person, eighty-six point three kilos, you would not have to give that (previously described massive) dosage to get the effect that could cause them to stop breathing . . . ," Hicks said.

"That is correct."

". . . cause their heart to stop and suffer brain damage?"

"Does not cause the heart to stop."

"Their breathing—excuse me. Let me rephrase. Cause them to stop being able to breathe, and ultimately causing the damage to organs that you spoke of earlier."

"It's a graduated process," Mailander explained. "A little bit of paralytic medication weakens one to a degree. More weakens you more. So you reach a point where someone cannot exchange and ventilate, breathe, very successfully. But they don't have to be completely paralyzed."

"When you say it weakens the person, they might not be completely paralyzed. Would they be able to stand up and walk around?" Hicks asked.

"If they're not able to breathe, I sincerely doubt it."

"So they might just be able to . . . shrug a shoulder or blink an eye, or something like that?"

"They can try."

"You had indicated that the gluteus maximus and the tissue around it varies from person to person, obviously . . . and that fat can be displaced. Now, what did you mean by that exactly?"

Mailander explained that the reason the gluteus maximus muscle is used by medical personnel for most injections is because "it's a good recipient muscle for an injection." Because everybody has a fairly significant fat pad in the area of their buttocks, it isn't very difficult—with some pressure— to push a needle through the skin, through the subcutaneous fat and into the muscular tissue, he said. Because the fat is not a constant thickness, it compresses when pushed upon.

"So, if you take someone with an average fat pad and push really hard, you can compress the fat and get a needle through it," Mailander testified. "We do this all the time in putting in epidurals for pain control for labor and delivery. We have an enormous number of fairly hefty expectant moms, and we have to push on our needles substantially to get them into the target tissues."

"You had also indicated that for the most part the critical part of succinylcholine is getting it to work . . . its process in getting into the blood flow, is that correct?" Hicks asked.

"That's correct."

"Now, if you were to see a picture of a puncture wound on a buttock, and there was blood raised up to the level of the skin from the puncture, would that satisfy you that the succinylcholine had reached the blood system?"

"Not necessarily. Only because you can break a blood vessel going through the skin or into the fat. You can lacerate a capillary and have the needle point well beyond the level of laceration."

"You had indicated that you have never given a conscious patient succinylcholine," Hicks said.

"No."

"And why is that?"

"Well, for three reasons," Mailander explained. "Every anesthesia textbook advises against it except under emergency circumstances. Every anesthesia instructor I've ever had threatened to kill me if I did. And thirdly, it—to paralyze someone with no sedation is a terrifying experience."

Mailander explained that accounts of patients who were aroused or even awakened under anesthesia while undergoing surgery have been uniformly one of terror.

"Imagine how it would be for someone who has no anesthetics and no sedation," Mailander said, "being unable to breathe, being unable to open your eyes if they're closed, or close them if they're open, and being unable to do anything about that. It's reputedly one of the most horrifying experiences out there. At least, that's what they describe in the literature."

"Mr. Houston had also asked you about a conscious person being stuck with a needle, the amount of struggle that one might expect," Hicks said. "It sounds to me from what you're saying is that a conscious person administered succinylcholine unwillingly, if they fight, they're just making it worse. Is that right?"

"Well, if it's increasing their circulation, yes, it will help mobilize the medication faster."

"And the dosage in which he demonstrated for you and the jury is not what is required to affect somebody who has been administered succinylcholine, is that right?"

"Personally, I would think not," Mailander responded. "That would be, again, those doses—recommended doses are textbook numbers for intubating conditions . . . in a surgical setting."

With no further questions, Hicks handed the witness off to the defense for recross-examination.

"Doctor, this notion of struggle and fighting, we can't

put a time frame on that in reference to not knowing the time of onset of the amount [of drug] that may or may not have been introduced, correct?" Houston asked.

"If I may, discussing what we call a 'dose response reaction,'" Mailander clarified, "we don't know how much medication was injected, and we have no idea what the response was."

"And if you inject it IV, certainly you get a faster response regardless of the dosage, right?"

"That would be correct, yes."

"When you talk about displacing fat with the needle, then hitting a muscle, if we have an autopsy that demonstrates the track ceases, doesn't go as though somebody pushed it through, that kind of struggles against the notion that somebody pushed it all the way through the muscle, since there's no physical evidence of it, doesn't it? Or the fat," Hicks corrected himself. "I'm sorry."

"Again, I would have to study the mechanics of fat motion. That's a bachelor's degree in biological mechanics."

"That would be a guess, then?"

"I really don't have a good answer for that."

"Okay. In this particular case, if you want to use a needle to push through a large fat pad to get to a muscle, would you agree chances are therapeutically you're going to use a larger needle than a twenty-five- or twenty-seven-gauge needle?"

"Yes. Absolutely."

Chapter 26

Kathy Augustine's longtime ob-gyn, Dr. Jerry L. Jones, was sworn in as a witness for the state and took the stand in the courtroom that had poor acoustics. He was greeted by Tom Barb, Washoe County deputy district attorney, who took the witness through the formality of stating his full name and spelling his surname. Dr. Jones's obstetrics-gynecology practice was located in Las Vegas, and he had been seeing Kathy as a patient for fifteen years, from 1991 until the time of her death in July 2006. He had been involved in his medical practice for about five years at the time Kathy first came to him.

"During the course of her coming to you, was there ever any time when she complained of chest pains or shortness of breath, or anything like that?" Barb asked.

"No," Dr. Jones replied.

"What was her general physical condition during the course of your connection to her?" Barb asked.

"She was in good health," Dr. Jones said.

Barb elicited responses from the doctor that indicated that he had last seen Kathy as a patient on June 21, 2006. He reminded Dr. Jones of the poor acoustics in the courtroom and asked him to speak up "so that the lady in the back row at the far end can hear" his responses. Raising the level of his voice a little, Dr. Jones explained that Kathy had come in to his office on that date for her annual examination and a pap test. The examination, he said, indicated that she was in good health.

"Her blood pressure was normal," Dr. Jones said. "I listened to her heart and lungs. They were clear. Her heart rhythm was normal. And her female organs were all normal."

"So, generally, she was a fifty-year-old, healthy, happy human being?" Barb asked.

"Yes."

"Doctor, on the information that you provided, what was her blood pressure on June twenty-first?"

"Her blood pressure that day was one hundred ten over seventy-eight."

Dr. Jones explained in response to Barb's questions that there was not anything significant about Kathy's visit to his office on June 21, and that during the fifteen years that she had been his patient, there had not been any complaints or illnesses of a life-threatening nature to cause him any concern about her health.

"Did you ever prescribe her any medications?"

"Female medications, vaginal yeast, urinary tract infection antibiotics. That sort of thing."

"Is that all?" Barb asked.

"To the best of my knowledge," Dr. Jones responded. "I have reviewed all of my records. Yes."

"Thank you, Doctor. That's all I have."

One of Higgs's attorneys, California lawyer Alan Baum, gave his client a reassuring glance, stood up from the defense table, and approached the witness for his cross-examination.

Baum skipped the usual pleasantries and got right down to business.

"Dr. Jones, is it true that Kathy Augustine had some heart condition that caused you to actually make a referral to a cardiologist?" Baum asked. "Isn't that true?"

"I'm not sure that I referred her," Dr. Jones responded. "She may have gone on a self-referral. She did some years before. There's a referral from a Dr. Keith Boman. But that may have just been a note that he sent to us at her request."

Baum confirmed by verifying with the witness that Kathy's routine medical records from Dr. Jones's office had been submitted to the authorities, and referenced a report of her visit to Dr. Boman's office that was dated October 18, 1995. Baum asked the witness to read the first paragraph of the report to the jury, which prompted an objection from the state.

"Excuse me, Your Honor," Barb said. "What's the purpose of this? The doctor has said he has that report. He's not refreshing any recollection. Could he just ask a question?"

"The doctor testified that he wasn't certain whether he made a referral for cardiological examination, and this letter indicates that he did," countered Baum.

Judge Kosach agreed with the defense and overruled Barb's objection. Dr. Jones was instructed to read the first paragraph of the report aloud.

"Kathy Augustine is a thirty-nine-year-old white female referred by Dr. Jones for evaluation of mitral valve prolapse," Dr. Jones read.

"You're the Dr. Jones he was referring to?"

"I am. But he would have written [it] even if it was a self-referral by Kathy."

"Dr. Boman would write that she was referred to him by you even if that wasn't true?"

"As a reference to where he might send a report to, yes."

"Well, it doesn't say here that Miss Augustine is being seen by an ob-gyn by the name of Jerry Jones for the purposes of sending you a report. It says here she was referred by you."

"Okay."

Baum then took the witness through a series of questions regarding the report of the echocardiogram that was done by Dr. Boman in 1995, as well as its interpretation and the degree to which Dr. Jones had reviewed it.

"Have you reviewed the entire report?" Baum asked.

"It wouldn't mean anything to me," Dr. Jones replied. "I'm not a cardiologist."

"So if you read things about the results of an echocardiogram, you, as a licensed physician, wouldn't understand what that means?"

"I don't understand the number. I do read the interpretation . . . yes."

Baum confirmed with the witness that the report in question, slightly more than two pages long and without charts and graphs, consisted of narrative descriptions that even a layperson such as him would be able to understand. After determining that the witness wasn't sure whether he had read the report recently or not, the doctor was given a few minutes to read it at that time to refresh his memory of its contents. When he had finished reading, Baum took up the questioning again.

"You just testified that nothing in Kathy Augustine's medical history or any findings that you made in the entire fifteen years that you treated her ever gave you cause for concern," Baum stated.

"Correct."

"Is that still your opinion after reading this cardiological report . . . ?"

"Yes, it is. . . . To the best of my knowledge, that was Kathy's only visit to Dr. Boman."

"Yes, I understand that," Baum said somewhat testily. "But . . . you received this report shortly after it was written in October of 1995, did you?"

"Sometime in 1995, yes."

"And I think it's safe to assume that you read it."

"Correct."

"Okay. And this report indicates that 'the patient has been relatively asymptomatic.' What did that mean to you?"

"You know, to me, during the past eleven years, Kathy described no symptoms or pain."

"No, I'm talking about in 1995 when the report was written, after the paragraph that says that she was referred by you for echocardiogram."

"Right."

"And it says, 'For evaluation of mitral valve prolapse.'"

"Okay."

"So I assume that you knew or suspected that Kathy Augustine, when you made this referral, had mitral valve prolapse."

"I did not refer her for that reason," Dr. Jones responded. "I have no recollection that I referred her to Dr. Boman."

"So when Dr. Boman writes that . . . she was referred by Dr. Jones for evaluation of mitral valve prolapse—"

"Objection," Barb cut in. "Asked and answered."

"I'm sorry, Your Honor," Baum said. "This is very important."

"It's asked and answered," countered Barb. "He doesn't get to do it four times."

Judge Kosach sustained Barb's objection.

"And when you read in this report that 'she has been relatively asymptomatic,' what did that mean to you?" Baum asked again.

"You'd have to ask Dr. Boman," Dr. Jones replied. "I don't know what he meant by that."

"You don't have a common sense understanding of what the phrase 'relatively asymptomatic' means?"

"I'd be trying to read his mind [about] what he was saying."

"Well, no, he wrote it," Baum argued. "It's not a matter of reading his mind. My question is: don't you have a general understanding of what 'relatively symptomatic' means?"

"I do."

"And what would that understanding be?"

"That she came in with maybe some minimal complaints to Dr. Boman's office. Again, she may have been a self-referral. . . . So she might have even been referred by a friend . . . the way she reached my office."

"Notwithstanding what he said about your referring her?"

"True. Eleven years earlier."

"Okay," Baum said. "And when the cardiologist writes that 'she was known to have a heart murmur at an early age,' isn't a heart murmur some abnormality of the heart?"

"It is," replied Dr. Jones. "I have a heart murmur."

Dr. Jones went on to state that he obtains a checkup by a cardiologist every five years or so and that he has had echocardiograms in the past because cardiologists typically order that test on virtually each new patient that they see, and that such a test is ordered as often as the cardiologists think it needs to be done. It seemed that the questions being asked of the state's witness by Baum were being aimed at unraveling the doctor's earlier testimony that Kathy Augustine had been in good health. Dr. Jones seemed unshakeable, however.

Baum again read from Dr. Boman's report: *"Recently she had noticed some mild palpitations. Heart murmur was again confirmed by examination and was referred to this office for evaluation."*

"Heart palp and mild palpitations is not normal in a—" Baum said.

"I'm having those right now," Dr. Jones stated.

"All right. Listen, I don't want to be the cause of any event. If you need a break, let me know."

"No, I'm fine. . . . It's a common occurrence."

Dr. Jones testified that he had asked his cardiologist what he does when he has palpitations, and the cardiologist purportedly told him that he ignores them. Dr. Jones said that heart palpitations were a common occurrence in people with mitral valve prolapse, and he and Baum finally agreed that everybody handles their problems in their own way. Nonetheless, Baum persisted in his attempt to shake the doctor from his earlier testimony that his patient, Kathy Augustine, had been in good physical condition.

"When Dr. Boman writes . . . 'heart murmur was again confirmed by examination and was referred to this office for evaluation,' that sounds like someone who made the referral, confirmed a heart murmur, and thought it would be a good idea for her to have an echocardiogram," Baum said. "Is that a reasonable interpretation?"

"Well, not necessarily heard the heart murmur," Dr. Jones replied. "But if she had symptoms, [she] would have come in on referral. I did not refer to Dr. Boman as a practice, as a habit, in my practice in the past. So that's one reason I'm suspicious, sir, or reluctant to admit that I referred Kathy to him."

"But this report here was part of your medical records," Baum said.

"It's in the medical record from twelve years ago."

"Again, in connection with your opinion that nothing in the history of your professional relationship as the treating ob-gyn for Kathy Augustine gave you cause for concern— that was your testimony on direct examination?"

"To the best of my knowledge, that was the one and only time she ever described that symptom to anyone."

"Going on your evaluation or your opinion that nothing ever caused you concern, this echocardiogram report states [that] 'she notes only an occasional extra heartbeat.' Is an extra heartbeat normal, or is it kind of part of this heart murmur, mitral valve prolapse syndrome?"

"It's a common thing with mitral valve prolapse."

"Again, in connection with your opinion that nothing ever caused you concern, the report of the echocardiogram is that it confirmed late systolic mitral valve prolapse, which was definite. Do you understand what that means?"

"I do."

"And what does that mean?"

"It means that one of the leaflets of the heart valve flaps back into the opposite chamber from where the blood flows."

"And it was confirmed in the echocardiogram?"

"Dr. Boman described that. He is still alive and well and practicing, by the way."

"I'm glad to hear that," Baum replied with a hint of disdain in his voice. "Isn't an echocardiogram probably the best test or the most frequently recommended test for people that have mitral valve prolapse?"

"I think the invasive tests are more specific. The coronary catheterization tests are more specific," Dr. Jones stated.

"And when you say 'invasive,' that means that you actually have to go into the hospital . . . and then there's some kind of a surgical procedure?"

"Procedure, right. Put a line in."

"But in noninvasive, that is, electrical and photography-type tests, an echocardiogram is the recommended test for mitral valve prolapse?"

"The most common test, yes."

"In connection with the findings of the echocardiogram

here," Baum said, "this doctor also reports, 'Minimal mitral regurgitation was present.' Do you understand the difference between mitral valve prolapse and mitral regurgitation?"

"I have that also," Dr. Jones replied. "Yes, I understand."

"And what is that difference?"

"It means that some of the blood flows back from the ventricle into the atrium."

"Would you agree that . . . the regurgitation is somewhat more serious than the prolapse itself?"

"It's a common finding. You'd have to ask a cardiologist what they think about that."

"Well, since you have both conditions, hasn't your cardiologist told you that prolapse is fairly benign and hardly ever causes anything other than an occasional heart murmur or occasional extra heartbeat, that sort of thing, right?"

"Uh-huh."

"But regurgitation is a little more serious, isn't it, Doctor?"

"That's not what they tell me. He tells me I'm in good health."

"So, if we've had testimony from a cardiologist in this case that mitral valve prolapse, while in and of itself is not really dangerous, mitral regurgitation, where the blood flows back, can lead to arrhythmia, which can lead to fibrillation, which in some instances can lead to sudden cardiac death—would that cardiologist be wrong?"

"I don't know that," Dr. Jones replied. "I'm not a cardiologist."

"In the echocardiogram report that you considered, the doctor finds a mid-systolic click, with a very short systolic murmur heard in the left-lower sterna border and apex," Baum said. "Do you understand what that means?"

"I don't understand the clinical significance of that."

"Isn't it true that a click is an irregular heartbeat and something that when heard and detected is further assistance in diagnosis of heart problems?"

Baum was trying hard to get Kathy's ob-gyn to state in court that Kathy had a heart problem. However, Dr. Jones continued to stand his ground.

"Not that I'm aware of," Dr. Jones responded.

"In the portion of the report of this cardiologist for recommendations, you could perhaps take a look at page three of the report."

"I have that page."

"*Suggest yearly check, with possible echocardiogram every few years for further evaluation of the prolapse and the mild mitral regurgitation, which is clinically not significant at this time.* You understand that to mean that the cardiologist, in light of what he knew of the history and the findings that he made, recommended yearly checkups with possible echocardiogram every few years?"

"That would have been the advice he would have given Kathy, yes."

"Now, with that in mind, and being her regular doctor who she saw probably, what, three or four times a year?"

"Once a year."

"Once a year," Baum repeated. "Did you check with her to see if she was having what this doctor recommended—that is, these periodic echocardiograms?"

"Kathy had no physical symptoms or complaints that she described to me," Dr. Jones offered, instead of answering the question.

"Did you ask her if she was having regular echocardiograms as the cardiologist recommended?" Baum asked, persisting.

"No."

"And it was also recommended by the cardiologist here

in the report, *Also suggest a treadmill after her fortieth birthday to evaluate for any arrhythmias with exercise.* Did you check with Kathy Augustine to find out if she was having, as recommended by this cardiologist, a treadmill after her fortieth birthday?"

"No, I did not."

"Did you recommend that she do that after her fortieth birthday?"

"We discussed the report probably at the time it came back after her visit with Dr. Boman."

"And she was under forty at that time."

"She would have been under forty years old at that time."

Baum brought up the fact that Kathy was still a patient of Dr. Jones's after she turned forty, for approximately another nine or ten years.

"At any time, did you ask her, 'Listen, Kathy, that cardiologist recommended that you have a treadmill test after you were forty. I think it's a good idea that you do that'?" Baum asked.

"I hadn't discussed it with her," the doctor replied.

"And it says in here the reason the cardiologist wanted her to have a treadmill after age forty was to evaluate for any arrhythmias, doesn't it?"

"Yes, it says that . . . with exercise."

"And arrhythmias, as you've understood and agree, is one of the possible consequences of mitral regurgitation, which can lead to a more serious health problem," Baum stated. "An arrhythmia is a more serious health problem, isn't it?"

"Arrhythmias are common coincident findings with mitral valve prolapse."

"And arrhythmias can cause fibrillation?"

"I'm not a cardiologist. I can't answer that question."

Baum thanked Dr. Jones for his time and testimony, and told the court that he had no further questions. Deputy District Attorney Tom Barb, however, stepped forward and said that he had a few questions for the witness on his redirect examination.

Among the points he wanted to emphasize during his redirect was the fact that on page 3 of Dr. Boman's report—the one that Baum had been reading aloud from and had stated "with possible echocardiograms every few years"—Barb had wanted to make certain that everyone, particularly the jury, understand that the recommendation in the report had used the word "possible" with regard to getting the future echocardiogram tests.

"So that's not mandatory or doesn't put up any red flags for anybody, does it?" Barb asked.

"Correct."

"And in the next paragraph, *Suggest treadmill to evaluate for any arrhythmias with exercise.*"

Barb asked Dr. Jones whether he had Kathy Augustine's entire file with him. When Dr. Jones confirmed that he did, Barb asked him to hold it up so that the jury could see its size. It wasn't particularly thick.

"That's her entire file for fifteen-plus years?" Barb asked.

"Fifteen years, yes."

"Is that what you would call a file of a patient who has various and sundry acute illnesses?" Barb asked, attempting to accentuate the size of the file.

"No."

"It would be much thicker, wouldn't it?"

"Yes."

* * *

On recross-examination, defense attorney Alan Baum asked Dr. Jones if he could think of any reason "why a person presenting this entire history and evaluations that we have now considered should not have an echocardiogram or regularly monitor what could turn into a serious heart condition?"

"Are you asking what a reasonable person would do?" Dr. Jones asked. "I think that they would follow the recommendation of their physician."

"Thank you."

After Dr. Jones was excused, it still was unclear whether either side had proven the points that they had been trying to make. Had Kathy taken reasonable care of herself with regard to her health and the recommendations of her physicians? Had her physicians failed in their efforts to provide guidance to her, particularly regarding her heart issues? Or had Kathy failed by not heeding their recommendations? The only thing that seemed clear with regard to her heart's health was that it hadn't contributed to her death.

Chapter 27

As the murder trial continued, the jury heard testimony from Genevieve Reiff, a human resources representative for Carson-Tahoe Regional Health Care, the same hospital where Chaz Higgs had worked. Reiff testified that she had processed Chaz's paperwork at the time that he had been hired, including a direct deposit form. This had been done on June 12, 2006, she said, and had included the required blank voided check. It had the names Kathy Augustine and Chaz Higgs printed on it, showing that they apparently shared a joint account. However, Chaz had made a second request on July 7, 2006, the day prior to the emergency involving Kathy. For the new direct deposit request, Chaz had brought in a new blank and voided check. This one, however, did not have any names printed on it, she said. It was either a counter check, or was one that was associated with a brand-new account. Although the prosecution had been able to make the point that Chaz had opened a new bank account the day before he had allegedly injected Kathy with succinylcholine, Reiff had testified under cross-examination that there had been nothing unusual about his request. She confirmed that she processed a lot of paperwork, including that of people who got divorced and needed to switch bank accounts.

Later on during the afternoon of June 19, 2007, Madeline Montgomery took the witness stand to testify how she had determined that Kathy's urine had contained succinylcholine. After her qualifications were stated for the record, Tom Barb offered her as an expert witness in the area of toxicology and she began describing how the FBI crime lab came to be involved with the case and the bureaucratic process that the evidence went through before it reached her. Under questioning from Barb, Montgomery carefully described the process she used to detect the presence of the drug in the samples using liquid chromatography and mass spectrometry, as outlined in Jenkins's interrogation earlier.

"Would you ever expect succinylcholine in a live body or sample from a live body?" Barb asked.

"Not unless someone had been given succinylcholine in a medical situation," Montgomery replied.

"So it's not a natural thing that occurs in a live human being?"

"No."

"Did you test for succinylmonocholine in the samples you received?"

"Yes, I did."

"And did you find it?"

"I found succinylcholine and its breakdown product in the urine, yes."

Examples of the charts and graphs, the results, in other words, of the liquid chromatography and the mass spectrometry processes were discussed and explained in detail, and shown to the jury. Montgomery explained that the procedure she followed in looking for the succinylmonocholine was one that the FBI crime lab had validated and used for a number of years, and it looked for only the breakdown product.

"Because typically we are looking at autopsy samples," she explained, "and that's the only chemical we would expect to find present because the succinylcholine itself is so unstable. So I had to do a little bit of research in the lab in order to figure out what succinylcholine itself would look like if it was run through this method that we use for the succinylmonocholine."

Barb took Montgomery through a series of questions that led up to the procedures used in operating the machinery that does the analysis of the sample material being examined—in this case, urine. The first thing in the morning, she said, she ensures that the equipment is operating correctly by first using generic chemicals. If it is working as it should be, it will identify the test generic chemicals, the identification of which the lab technician is already aware. Afterward, she said, she then begins using the samples that she will be analyzing on any given day.

"Once I'm convinced it's running . . . correctly," she said, "we will do what we call shoot a blank through the instrument. I'll just take a blank water or a blank solvent and run it through the instrument and verify that nothing is going to pop up at that time of interest to indicate that there might be some kind of contamination in the system. We call that a blank. That's always run the first thing at the beginning of a run.

"Then I'll have all these concentrated extracts from the urine samples that I've worked on that day," Montgomery continued. "I will run . . . what we call a blank urine, urine from me or someone else in the lab who has not been exposed to succinylcholine that has been taken through the entire extraction procedure. I'll run that blank urine extract through the instrument to verify that there was no contamination or problems with the extraction method that I did in the laboratory. Then I'll either do another blank and then the urine from the patient, or I can do the patient's urine next. Doesn't matter since I've proven there is no contamination or no problems with the process so far. Then the final thing we do is we run a spiked sample, a urine sample that's been spiked with the drug of interest and taken through the entire process to demonstrate what a positive sample would look like."

Barb wanted to know how the lab technician could be sure that the patient's urine hadn't been contaminated during the process.

"Well, we—as I explained . . . run a negative urine sample right next to the patient's urine sample (inside the machine), to verify that there is no contamination throughout the whole process. And then we introduce that blank urine sample to the instrument before the patient's urine sample to indicate that there's no contamination there. And that's why . . . some may think it's overkill, but that's why we then go back to the sample again on a different day and rerun it just to make sure that nothing out of the ordinary occurred."

"How many times did you run this patient's urine?" Barb asked.

Montgomery responded that she ran the urine sample three times in her search for the presence of succinyl-choline.

"And did you get the same result every time you ran this patient's urine?"

"Yes. I found the drug there all three times."

She also explained how she had tested Kathy's blood plasma and tissue samples from the area of the alleged succinylcholine injection site, but had not found the drug in either, despite extensive testing.

* * *

During cross-examination, attorney David Houston began a line of questioning of which the answers, he hoped, would bring out any problems or mistakes that had occurred during the FBI's testing of Kathy's biological samples. It was his job to find a way, if possible, to cast doubt in the minds of the jurors on the FBI's handling and testing of those samples.

"Miss Montgomery," Houston said, "you would obviously never purposefully provide any kind of false or misleading result out of your lab, correct?"

"Absolutely," she responded.

"How long ago was it that your laboratory was indicating that you cannot find succinylmonocholine absent the introduction of succinylcholine?" Houston asked. "Was that 2000 or 2003?"

"I don't—I don't know what you're talking about."

"Okay. Do you know what the Sybers case is?"

"I'm familiar with the Sybers case."

"All right. In fact, Marc LeBeau is your supervisor, is he not?"

"Yes, he is."

"And were you aware that Mr. LeBeau testified in the Sybers case?"

"Yes."

"Were you aware that Mr. LeBeau had testified that succinylmonocholine does not exist in the body endogenously?"

"I wasn't at the hearing," Montgomery responded. "I did not witness the testimony, so I can't—can't answer that question."

"What does 'endogenously' mean?"

"Endogenous are chemicals that are naturally in our body."

"Did your laboratory receive any type of bulletin indicating to you that succinylmonocholine can exist in the body naturally?"

"Actually, our laboratory was the laboratory that reported that succinylmonocholine was found in autopsy samples from individuals who had not been exposed to the drug," Montgomery said.

She confirmed that prior to the aforementioned, the FBI crime lab, as well as other labs, had believed that succinylmonocholine would not be found in the human body unless succinylcholine had been introduced to the bloodstream. Because she agreed that the science surrounding succinylcholine is an ever-evolving science, she had conducted her own test in the lab to show that succinylmonocholine is not normally present in urine samples. To her knowledge, that had never been done before.

Montgomery confirmed that the FBI crime laboratory did not have a standard operating procedure for the detection of succinylcholine, but that it did have a standard operating procedure for succinylmonocholine. She also confirmed that they were two different chemicals but shared similar characteristics, and that she had utilized the standard operating procedure for succinylmonocholine in this case but had adapted the procedure to look for succinylcholine.

"Now, when you say 'adapted,' have there been any peer-review published studies of your adaption of the test?" Houston asked.

"No, we have not published this method," Montgomery responded. "I got permission from my supervisor after he reviewed the data that I had done on the succinylcholine itself before I ever looked at the urine in this case for succinylcholine. . . . He agreed that the testing I was doing was adequate and acceptable."

"Acceptance of testing procedures is sometimes actually accompanied by peer review and journals, studies, articles, correct?"

"It can be."

"Should be, shouldn't it?"

"Well, it depends," Montgomery answered. "The adaptations that were made to this method were not very different. And this method has never been published by us because we kind of borrowed it from another lab in the beginning, so it's not our property."

"Okay. So you're using a test that you didn't devise that's not your property that's never been peer reviewed or journaled, correct?"

"Our procedure has never been published, but it certainly has been peer reviewed within our laboratory."

Houston next began exploring Montgomery's qualifications in front of the jury, pointing out that she had been working in the field of forensic toxicology for eleven years and that her role in the field was that of a chemist. Although she explained that her title, the one that appeared on her paycheck, stated that she was a supervisor and a chemist, she pointed out that she was recognized by the FBI laboratory as a forensic examiner with an expertise in the area of forensic toxicology. Not yet satisfied, Houston wanted to know more about her title.

"What is the difference between an individual, for instance, like Dr. William Anderson or Chip Walls, that refers to themselves as a forensic toxicologist versus your title?" Houston asked.

"My title is just the title that the government gives me," she answered. "All of us in the FBI laboratory are typically biologists, chemists, or physical scientists, so that's . . . the area that my specialty fits into. I also manage the toxicology group within the . . . FBI laboratory. Right now, there's three other people who I supervise on a day-to-day basis specifically in toxicology."

Obviously having done his homework, Houston asked

Montgomery about interference studies and what they were designed to accomplish.

"The interference study is designed to show that the method is unique for that specific drug," Montgomery said.

"Okay. And you indicated that you used . . . 'John Doe' urine," Houston pointed out. "Meaning you got urine from folks in the lab, right?"

"Yes."

"And you got it from fifteen different people, true?"

"True."

"And how many of those fifteen people that you received urine from had epinephrine in their system?"

"I'd be surprised if any of them did."

"How about atropine?"

Houston was obviously going through the checklist of drugs that had been used on Kathy by paramedics and emergency department personnel at the hospital on the morning of July 8, 2007.

"I'd be surprised if any of them did as well."

"How about heparin?"

"Probably none."

"So the concept being the urine that you received was from fifteen very healthy drug-free individuals, correct?" Houston asked.

"Yes."

"And one of the purposes of an interference study is to make certain that there's no drug or other product in the urine, in this case, that could offer up a false positive by way of the testing, right?"

"Well, absolutely," Montgomery responded. "But we're also looking at natural components that we all have in our urine, things that we have from our diets. . . ."

"Sure. How many urines did you test as control samples that had as their characteristic epinephrine, atropine, heparin, and the people, say, have been in an emergency room, had died, and been resuscitated?"

"None met those criteria."

"In fact, though, Kathy Augustine's urine did possess all of those qualities. Were you aware of that?"

"I don't know if I was aware of all of those qualities, no."

Houston next went through the details of the process that Kathy Augustine's biological samples had gone through from the time they were collected, both before and after her death, until they were received by Madeline Montgomery. The package had left Washoe County, Nevada, on July 20, 2006, via Federal Express, he pointed out, and was received by the FBI laboratory the following day. He pointed out that the package, although received by the FBI lab on July 21, hadn't been received and inventoried by Montgomery until July 26. In the interim the package with frozen biological samples, he stressed, had gone into a refrigerator inside an FBI lab storage area. It was important, he said, for the samples to remain frozen, and Montgomery agreed.

"Well, if they're not frozen, they undergo certain biochemical changes, true?" Houston asked.

"If the samples aren't frozen, the drugs can break down and disappear over time," Montgomery stated.

"And different effects could occur between the different drugs in the urine, correct?"

"It depends what drugs you're talking about."

"Exactly. And you haven't done any studies on urine that has possessed epinephrine, atropine, heparin, that has come from a person who was dead for a bit of time and then revived, have you?"

"No, I have not."

"So you have no real knowledge on what those drugs may or may not accomplish in the urine as far as biochemical changes, true?"

"No. But they wouldn't make succinylcholine. I've analyzed enough urine to know that."

"Ms. Montgomery, you're a scientist . . . yet you're making a claim to something that you have no knowledge of by any sort of testing. That's not scientific purpose, is it?"

"Well, succinylcholine is a very unique molecule, and it's rather large when we are talking about chemicals. So it's not going to appear in a urine sample."

"Right. You don't know the chemical composition modifications that may occur by virtue of degradation of urine that contains the product of epinephrine, atropine, or heparin, correct?"

"I have not done that study, no."

Houston brought out the fact that when Montgomery received the samples for inventory purposes, they were not frozen—despite the fact that they had presumably been packed in dry ice. His inference, of course, was that with the passage of time, nearly a week in this case, the samples had become thawed. He elicited responses from the witness that indicated that she had frozen the samples after she had unpacked the box that they had arrived in to prevent further degradation or biochemical changes to them, particularly since succinylcholine has been shown to be a very unstable drug and that freezing is the best way to keep it.

Based on Montgomery's responses, Houston attempted to show the chain of custody of Kathy's biological samples and inferred that they had been out of Montgomery's control for a period of time. In response to his questions, she said that the samples had been kept frozen in the unit's evidence freezer until she was ready to do the initial screening for succinylmonocholine on August 16, 2006. His concern appeared to be centered on the fact that because there were approximately twenty people working in her unit at the time the samples were stored in the evidence freezer, they may have been accessed by others besides Montgomery. However, Montgomery testified that the materials are sealed prior to being placed inside the evidence freezer so that no one else can have access to them; if someone did get into the materials, she would be able to tell because her seal would be broken. In this case, it was not.

Houston next questioned the witness about the tissue sample that had been removed from the area of the suspected injection site. Montgomery had begun working on that sample on September 18, 2006. The first thing that she did, she said, was to get the sample "as close to liquid as possible" by placing it inside a blender to make it homogenous.

"When you say 'homogenous,' do you mean you literally take the tissue, kind of grind it up, blend it up to create a liquid so that you can actually test it?" Houston asked.

"Yes. It's . . . exactly like it sounds."

When all of the testing had been done on the tissue samples, including samples taken not only from the area of the suspected injection site but also from Kathy's right forearm and left wrist and forearm for use as control samples, all had turned up negative for the presence of succinylcholine. Similarly, Houston's questioning brought out the fact that Montgomery's testing of Kathy's blood plasma samples had also turned up negative for the presence of succinylcholine.

During Montgomery's lengthy testimony, Houston brought up the fact that there had been a power failure at the FBI lab during her testing of Kathy's samples. She explained that she had been working with positive and negative control samples, as well as Kathy's urine case samples, when the power failure had occurred on Friday, August 18, 2006. She had just finished the first, or screening test, and was working on the second test at the time of the power failure. Houston confirmed from questioning the witness that the negative control urine samples were those that hadn't been "spiked" with any succinylcholine and that the positive control samples had been spiked with the drug. He also wanted to know what happened to the samples and the equipment during and after the power failure, and whether the FBI lab used backup generators.

"We do have backup generators," Montgomery said. "But sometimes there's a power surge that will interfere with the computers and the computers that talk to the instruments. So it's not . . . a hundred percent foolproof."

He wanted to verify whether or not the machine that processes the samples was a computer as well.

"Well, it is a computer," she said. "And that's why with the power issues, I stopped and restarted."

"And, of course, you had the . . . tech come out and make sure the machine was okay, right?"

"I don't recall," she said. "I may have done the instrument checks myself."

In response to Houston's question regarding whether Montgomery was a liquid chromatography/mass spectrometry machine technician or not, she said that she was not, but she added that she was fully capable to operate the equipment.

"Well, I can drive my car, but I can't rebuild the engine," Houston retorted. "Are you a technician?"

"I'm not a technician, but I have a lot of training in liquid chromatography-mass spectrometry. We do have people in our laboratory that will help us service instruments, but I have as much experience as most of them with the equipment that we have, and am certainly qualified to fix the instruments," Montgomery said.

"Okay. And the short answer is you're not certified as a technician concerning that particular piece of equipment, correct?"

"No one in our lab is officially certified."

"That's why they have people that are, true?"

"Well, if there are big problems, we call someone from the instrument company, but that's very unusual."

"Well, sometimes you don't know there's a big problem until somebody points out a big mistake, correct?"

She explained that was why they performed quality assurance and quality control in the lab every day, ran known samples of drugs on the instruments, as well as the analytes of interest to prove that the instrument was working properly.

Houston went back to the power failure to drive home the point that the testing of the samples hadn't resumed until the following week, on Monday, August 21, 2006, after the samples had sat inside the machine all weekend.

"So during that three days, what do you do with all those positive, negative, and Miss Augustine's samples?" Houston asked.

"They would either be on the instrument or in a refrigerator."

"On the instrument? You wouldn't remove them and place them in a secure location?"

"Well, I don't recall if this was an incident that happened after I had already gone for the day. The instruments can work—their auto samplers can work way past five o'clock. So I don't know if I was there . . . or not when the power failure occurred."

"How long does it take to test the urine to determine whether or not it has succinylmonocholine or succinylcholine?"

"From beginning to end?"

"Well, once you stick it on the machine."

"The run itself is less than . . . half an hour for the monocholine. When we look for the succinylcholine, one run takes . . . about an hour. . . . We end up with a lot of samples . . . the blank urine sample, the patient's sample, and the control samples, so it very well can be several hours and go past the end of the workday," Montgomery said.

Before finishing up with the witness, Houston wanted to get across to the jury the fact that the succinylcholine used by the FBI lab to make their positive control samples was from a bag of a dry, powdered form of the drug that had sat on a shelf in Montgomery's unit since its purchase in the late 1990s. When asked about the documentation for the succinylcholine that Montgomery had used for the testing, she testified that all of the drugs that they purchased were certified by an outside company. They were again certified, she said, every time they were used by lab personnel who ran them through the testing process to ensure that they were what they were supposed to be.

It was difficult to tell whether or not Houston's chipping away at the FBI lab's testing methods had effectively shot any holes in the prosecution's case against Chaz Higgs in the eyes of the jury, but he had certainly made an exhaustive attempt at discrediting their efforts. No one, however, was ready to second-guess the jury at this point in the trial.

Chapter 28

The next witness called by the state was George Reade, the communications supervisor for REMSA that had taken the 911 call from Chaz Higgs early on the morning of July 8, 2006. In response to questions asked by Christopher Hicks, Reade explained his job duties and told of how in a typical day he might receive emergency calls involving traffic accidents, cardiac arrests, violent crimes, and people who are very sick and need help. He explained how he typically worked three days one week and then four days the next, in an alternating fashion, with overtime sometimes in between. He said that out of the thousands of telephone calls he had taken since working in that career field, the one from Chaz Higgs that morning in which he had exhibited such a high degree of calmness was the exception rather than the rule. He said that in his line of work, he had been able to get a feel for how people react in an emergency situation.

"Have you gotten a feel for what a person is like when they're making a call involving an emergency with a loved one?" Hicks asked, putting an edge of clarification on his question that he hoped would show in Reade's response.

"Yes, I have," Reade answered with emphasis.

"You seem to put an exclamation point on that answer," Hicks said. "Do you wish to expand on that?"

"There is typically a great sense of urgency," Reade said. "Pretty much a panic at different levels, depending on how certain people handle different situations. But usually, yeah, there's usually a great sense of urgency when a loved one is injured."

Reade described the phone call from Chaz to the jury in which he had reported that his wife was not breathing and that he was performing CPR on her. He explained that among the characteristics that he had observed over the years during such calls were pauses in between the conversation. Those pauses, he said, were present when the person giving CPR was giving breaths and chest compressions to the person who is down. Sometimes, he said, the person giving CPR can sound as if they are out of breath—depending upon how long they've been administering CPR.

"Is it common to be able to hear them doing CPR?" Hicks asked.

"Yes."

"In this particular call . . . did it sound like the person who had made that call was administering CPR as they claimed?"

"It did not sound so," Reade said.

"You also indicated that typically phone calls involving a loved one are accompanied by a great sense of urgency. . . . Did you sense that urgency in this particular call?"

"I did not," Reade said.

Hicks then played the 911 call for the jury to hear.

"Mr. Reade," Hicks asked a few minutes later after the tape had finished playing, "is it common in your experience for a person to—a loved one in an emergency situation to give specific directions to their house?"

"Usually, no. . . . I can't recall taking a call where they did," Reade said.

"Do paramedics have maps, GPS, and stuff like that to make sure they get to the right residence?"

"We have all of it," he said.

Hicks wanted to know if Chaz's demeanor that morning, while on the phone, was consistent with 911 calls that were made when a loved one was involved. Reade explained that Chaz was very calm during the situation when most other people would not be. He said that conversation with Chaz seemed "very lengthy"; normally, when someone is doing CPR, it is very brief because they are going back to the person who is down to continue the CPR on them.

During his cross-examination of Reade, David Houston confirmed that Reade did not know Chaz Higgs at all. Although Chaz had told him that he was a critical care nurse, Reade had no idea that Chaz had spent fifteen years in the military as a medic. Houston's line of questioning clearly was intended to show that people who work in emergency situations typically remain calm.

"Do you customarily break down or show emotion when you take calls?" Houston asked.

"No, I don't say that I do," Reade replied.

"And, in fact, your training is what causes you to be professional in your job, true?"

"That is correct."

"And do you think you rely on that training so that you remain calm?"

"Yes, I do."

"And most of the time you spend effort and words telling

people, 'Calm down. Calm down. Give me the address,' things like that, right?"

"That is correct."

Houston confirmed through Reade's testimony that it is more effective to be able to remain calm to provide the information to the dispatcher in order to get treatment for the person who needs it. He also effectively got the message across that if someone was trying to delay treatment for a loved one, he should simply not communicate well to the dispatcher. At one point, Houston elicited testimony from Reade that confirmed that the American Heart Association guidelines indicate that CPR should be administered for one to two minutes prior to making the emergency phone call.

Houston also elicited testimony from Reade that indicated that Chaz had repeatedly said, "I've got to stop and give CPR," and had placed the phone down several times so that he could presumably perform CPR on Kathy. Reade conceded that he did not know how Chaz would normally react in a crisis situation.

"As an ER ICU nurse, would you expect him to lose control in a crisis?" Houston asked.

"I would really expect anybody to, but—" Reade said.

"Okay. So the idea is you're not supposed to lose control in a crisis, right?"

"Ideally, yes."

"And if you have twenty years of training, ideally might actually manifest itself, wouldn't you agree?"

"That is a tough question," Reade responded. "When it comes to loved ones, it tends to be a little different."

"Sure, for some people. . . . Everybody is different."

"Yes, they are."

"You certainly wouldn't want to reach any judgments based upon somebody you don't even know, right?"

"Of course not," Reade said.

After a brief redirect from the prosecution and a just as brief recross-examination from the defense, in which little more than accentuating what had already been said was accomplished, Judge Kosach recessed the trial for the evening. He admonished the jury not to discuss the case among themselves or anyone else, and not to read, look at, or listen to any news media accounts of the case.

Chapter 29

The next morning, Wednesday, June 20, 2007, Christopher Hicks called REMSA paramedic Benjamin Pratt to the witness stand to provide testimony regarding the morning that he and his partner, Manuel "Manny" de Jesus Fuentes, responded to Kathy Augustine's residence on Otter Way after the dispatch center had received the 911 call from Chaz Higgs. After going through the formality of his qualifications, education, time on the job, and job duties, Pratt told the jury about his Code 3 lights and sirens call regarding the state controller being down with a cardiac arrest. He described how he had seen Chaz Higgs from a couple of blocks away, standing out in front of the house and waving them toward him. Upon their arrival, Pratt said, Chaz had seemed calm. He went through all of the steps that he, Manny, and the accompanying firefighters had gone through, including placing Kathy on the hard surface of the floor from her bed, to continue the CPR. They needed to do that, he said, to get better compression, which, in turn, would provide better blood circulation. He described how they had given her medication, including epinephrine and atropine because she had been a flatliner on the monitor, how they had gotten a

breathing tube into her and an IV started, all the while someone was performing CPR. It had taken two rounds of the
medications to get her heart beating again, he said.

In a lengthy question-and-answer session, Pratt explained how he and a firefighter had closely monitored
Kathy's vital signs on the way to the hospital. At one point,
he said, they had "shoved" another IV of normal saline
into her arm during the trip, but otherwise had managed to
keep her heart beating. Upon arrival at the hospital, she
was taken into the emergency department. His testimony
included the fact that Kathy hadn't remained at South
Meadows very long, perhaps forty-five minutes or so,
before doctors recommended that she be moved to the
main hospital because of a suspected heart condition.
Hicks took him through a lengthy process in which he
identified many of the items used that morning to treat
Kathy, including the drugs used, tubes and breathing de-
vices, tape to hold her head in place so that the intubation
remained intact, and so forth. He also testified that it had
been he and his partner who had transferred Kathy from
South Meadows to the main hospital.

During cross-examination, Houston seemed intent on
unraveling Pratt's testimony with regard to how calm Chaz
Higgs had appeared that morning, by using Pratt as an
example.

"Mr. Pratt . . . how much experience do you have on
the job?" Houston asked.

"About two-and-a-half years," Pratt responded.

"And do you think after you've had about twenty-two
years' experience, you might have a little bit different demeanor while you're on the job?"

"You could, but . . . with these calls—"

"—you don't know," Houston interrupted.

"—you don't know," Pratt agreed.

"But we do know certainly that you haven't had fifteen years as a medic in the military, part of that as a battlefield medic, correct?"

"No, sir."

"And you haven't had experience as a critical care nurse or an emergency room nurse for another five, six years after that, correct?"

"No, sir."

Houston switched his approach at that point to focus on how Pratt and his associates would normally gain entry into a residence upon their arrival. Pratt indicated that they would usually go in through a front door. If it was locked, they would check other doors. If they couldn't get inside, and no one answered the door, the fire department would bust it down for them.

"So to avoid getting the door broken down if it's locked, it's a wise idea of the occupant to at least let you in, right?"

"Sure."

"And if you're doing CPR and the ambulance is on the way and somebody hears a siren, a good idea would be to go to the door, let you in, let you know this is the house?"

"Could be."

"Okay. And that's what happened in this case, isn't it?"

"Yes."

Houston pointed out that the bedroom where Kathy had lain that morning was not that far from the front door, and Pratt agreed that it was about fifty feet. Houston ascertained that it might take five to ten seconds for someone in a hurry to traverse that distance. It seemed to be a defense move to diminish the impact in the jury's eyes of why Chaz had left Kathy to go outside and meet the paramedics. He also focused on how small the bedroom was—and with two paramedics and four firefighters in the room with Kathy, it had become crowded very fast. This was a reason why Chaz might have chosen to be in another area of the house, or outside, while emergency personnel had worked on Kathy.

"Did Mr. Higgs seem happy when you got a heartbeat?" Hicks asked Pratt upon redirect.

"You know, I don't recall," Pratt responded. "Like we just kind of—we put her on the gurney, we started wheeling her out, and he was just standing there."

"Same demeanor as—"

"Same demeanor as before," Pratt said.

"Mr. Houston had asked you . . . if you were administering CPR to someone at a residence, the importance of unlocking the door so that emergency personnel can get in. If you were administering CPR to a person, based on your training, and you had to unlock your front door so that emergency personnel could get in, would you then go out and wait on the street for them?"

"No, sir."

The next witness that day was Marlene Swanbeck, an emergency room nurse who had been on duty the morning that Kathy was brought into South Meadows. Swanbeck testified that Kathy had arrived in the ambulance with Pratt at 7:15 A.M., and that she had withdrawn a urine sample from her at 7:35 A.M. According to medical records, Swanbeck said, Kathy had been given heparin, a drug that is used to prevent blood clots, at 8:10 A.M., after the urine had been taken.

"Did anybody in that facility . . . administer succinylcholine to that patient?" Hicks asked.

"No."

"Would there be any reason to administer succinyl-choline to that patient?"

"No."

"And why not?"

"Because we give succs when a patient is intubated, and this patient arrived intubated," Swanbeck said.

"Were there any injections, new injections, administered to the patient when she was in the emergency room, aside from the IV she already had?" Hicks asked.

"No."

In response to questioning, Swanbeck said that she had discovered the identity of the patient when Chaz had come into the emergency room. She said that she had been surprised to see him there.

"Could you please explain the circumstances of him coming into the room?" Hicks asked.

She explained that as they had been treating the patient behind a closed curtain, Chaz had appeared from behind the curtain. When she had asked him what he was doing there, he had said that the person they were working on was his wife, Kathy.

"What was his demeanor?" Hicks asked.

"He acted like it was just another day," Swanbeck responded.

"Was he sobbing?"

"No."

"Was he excited?"

"No."

"Was he asking any questions about her well-being?"

"No."

Hicks wanted to know whether Chaz had explained anything to her and the others present about what had happened to Kathy, and Swanbeck said that he had gone into "great detail."

"And what was he explaining to you?"

"That he had been out in the garage earlier in the morning," Swanbeck said. "That Kathy had been under a lot of stress, so [he] was letting her sleep in. And he went into the bedroom after having made coffee and was bringing her coffee. And the room was dark, and he tried to rouse her, and she didn't rouse. So he opened up the curtains, checked for a carotid, and found that she had no pulse."

"Now, did he volunteer this information?"

"Yes."

"Did it seem odd to you?"

"Yes."

"And why was that?"

"Just his position, the way he was standing. That she had been healthy, and now she's suddenly down. He was removed from what was happening, it seemed."

Even though she said that he had indicated to her that he had been working on his car that morning, Swanbeck said that he didn't have any grease or oil on him. It was also clarified later that she didn't know whether he was working on the engine or other parts of the car that could have gotten him dirty, or whether he was working on something inside the passenger compartment.

After Kathy had been transferred to the main hospital, Swanbeck said, she hadn't seen Chaz again that day. She saw him the following day, however, when he returned to South Meadows to thank everyone for taking care of his wife. He had brought them doughnuts, and said that he wanted to pick up his paycheck. He had actually called Swanbeck and asked her to meet him in the parking lot to get the doughnuts, and to bring him his paycheck.

"To need your paycheck when your wife is ill and to bring us doughnuts," she said, "the timing didn't feel right to me."

She recalled telling a coworker that Chaz had asked her to meet him outside in ten minutes and had said, "You know where I am if I don't come back."

"What did you mean by that?" Hicks asked.

"I think that we were all sufficiently suspicious and we had been talking amongst ourselves that it didn't feel right to us, so it was just kind of—for me, it was just a smart-ass comment that if I don't come back, you know, maybe I was next," she said.

Swanbeck testified that she nearly always tried to avoid personal conversations with Chaz when he worked at South Meadows. She said that she always felt a little suspicious of him, that something wasn't quite right. She explained that she was never comfortable with the way in which he had talked about his wife, and being a mother, she said, she was never comfortable with the relationship that he had with his daughter. What bothered her, she said, is that he never seemed to have enough time to spend with his daughter, in part because Kathy purportedly hadn't allowed her to come to her house to see him. On one occasion, Chaz had said that his daughter was going to spend her summer vacation at his mother's home, and when he had been asked if he was going there to see her, he had indicated that he was not. She also said that she never heard him talk about his wife in a loving way, but instead had heard him refer to her as a "bitch." Sometimes when Kathy called him on the phone, he would become irritated and would let her sit on hold for a bit.

Swanbeck also described for the jury how the succinylcholine had been stored in the refrigerator in the emergency department, and took them through the process of how it is accessed—basically the same information that they had heard before from other witnesses. She confirmed that the rapid-sequence intubation kit kept on a shelf in the refrigerator contained succinylcholine, and that the drug was stored elsewhere in the refrigerator, "just sitting there."

"You had indicated that once you put in your . . . code, you get into the refrigerator storage area," Hicks said. "There are vials of succinylcholine stored right in the refrigerator, is that right?"

"That is correct."

"When you take a drug out of there as a nurse, do you have to write it down, or is there some way that . . . anybody can tell that you've taken it?"

"When we access the computer to get into the refrigerator, in theory, we do need to put in the drug that we're talking about," she said. "But because the refrigerator opens up and (there are) a whole host of medications, we can take what we want out of there."

"So, if I understand you correctly, a person could, we'll say—any nurse could type in their code, type in that they're going to take . . . tetanus. But then when they go in, they could take succinylcholine, for example, and that would not be tracked?"

"Exactly."

She also said that succinylcholine and other drugs were stored at other locations within the department and that they could be easily accessed by the nurses. Since Kathy Augustine's death, access to succinylcholine had been somewhat tightened.

Chapter 30

Dr. Stanley Thompson, a Reno cardiologist who began working in that medical specialty in 1970, was called to the witness stand by Tom Barb following a recess for lunch. Thompson explained that he came to be involved in Kathy Augustine's case when Dr. Arun Kolli had sent her from South Meadows to the Renown Regional Medical Center, as it is now known, for the heart catheterization procedure for an angiogram, which Thompson had been asked to perform. He described the procedure in detail, and discussed the compact disc that was made of the angiogram—in this instance, a cine angiogram. After resolving some technical difficulties regarding the operation of the equipment, the CD was played for the jury. Thompson explained what was happening as the jury viewed the cine angiogram.

"That's the catheter that goes up into the start of the left coronary artery," he said. "There we have the start of the dye that goes into the arteries, so the arteries are actually dark and black. Usually what you would expect if there was a problem causing a heart attack would be a blockage in there. And you see that the artery goes for a short distance and then bifurcates into two major branches. And one is called the left anterior descending, and one is called the circumflex. Both those arteries, even though they're kind of curlicue, have no blockage whatsoever."

He explained that the angiogram looks at the coronary arteries in multiple angles to ensure that any blockages present are not missed. He pointed out the left and the right coronary arteries, and demonstrated to the jury that there were no blockages.

"So, basically, these arteries were normal," Thompson said. "Everyone in this room would love to have those arteries."

While Thompson would not rule out the possibility that Kathy had suffered a heart attack—which are commonly caused by blocked coronary arteries—he did say that she did not suffer from any coronary artery disease and that this was not the type of angiogram one would expect if the patient had had a heart attack.

"You'd expect a blockage," he said, if Kathy had suffered a heart attack. "Or more likely, if someone had suffered a heart attack, a hundred percent occlusion. But an artery that goes a short distance and then is completely blocked off, and there's no blood flow getting to the heart muscle . . . that heart muscle would die and produce both symptoms and EKG changes of a heart attack . . . you can say that [Kathy's] arteries are perfectly normal."

Instead, the problem that Thompson had found, and that which he had explained to Detective Jenkins, was that Kathy's heart was not vigorous in its pumping action—it wasn't contracting as well as it should and therefore not pumping out the amount of blood that it should have been pumping.

"Normally, everyone should pump out at least fifty percent of the blood that is received inside the heart," Thompson said. "And usually closer to seventy or eighty percent. This heart was pumping out twenty-three percent."

Thompson's medical opinion as to why Kathy's heart was not "rigorous" and pumping out the blood in the volume that it should have been doing was that whatever she suffered from was not a typical heart attack or hardening of the arteries.

"Now, sometimes you see that when someone has not had any oxygen for a while," Thompson said. "I mean, that's basically almost a dead heart."

"When you say a 'dead heart,' you mean cells actually in the heart have died or are dying?" Barb asked.

"Well, they're at least stunned."

Barb asked Thompson if he was familiar with succinylcholine, and he responded that he had learned about it in pharmacology and medical school, but had never used it. He said that he knew enough about the drug to know that it was a paralytic.

"If a paralytic drug were given to a person and no assistance with breathing was done, would it show as this shows?" Barb asked.

"Yes," Thompson replied. "If someone were not breathing and became hypoxic, or lack of oxygen, after a while the heart would look like that."

"Okay. Dr. Thompson, did you have occasion to speak with Kathy Augustine's husband?"

"I met him. He accompanied her when she was brought to the cardiac cath lab from South Meadows."

"Did you speak to him at all?"

"Yes. And I stated that I thought the outlook was not good, considering her condition."

"What was his demeanor, if you recall?"

"Well, I was a little surprised in that he was unemotional, compared to what I would have guessed. In other words, generally, if a family member is—you know, has had an arrest (cardiac) and is in dire straits, you'd expect—I would expect more emotion. And there was not a lot of emotion."

"Does that go for medical personnel, Doctor?"

"It goes for any person."

"So the fact that he's allegedly in the navy for fifteen years and that he's a critical care nurse, does that change your opinion about emotional ties to what is going on?"

"No. I was in the navy for ten years. I have been very involved with medical situations. I will tell you if my wife were in that type of situation, I would be very emotional."

During cross-examination, Alan Baum wanted to know if Dr. Thompson, in his last response, had meant that he would expect every single person on earth who has a loved one going through a crisis to react exactly the same way.

"Surely, that's not what you meant," Baum said.

"No, it's not."

"And would you, therefore, allow for the possibility that certain people, whatever their background, might react different than other people, or even react different than what you would expect them or how you would expect them to react?"

"That's a possibility."

"Was the conversation that you had with Chaz Higgs the first time that you had ever met him?"

"Yes."

"Had you spoken to him on the phone?"

"No."

"So you have no idea as to what his general demeanor is—"

"No, I do not."

"—or was. This conversation is the sole basis for your opinion that he was not acting as you might have expected him to."

"That's correct."

Baum took the cardiologist through a number of questions and scenarios regarding Kathy's condition, particularly as it related to her heart. By the end of Baum's efforts, Thompson testified that he could not rule out sudden cardiac death as the cause of death in Kathy's case.

Toward the end of the day, Dr. Steve K. Mashour, a pulmonary and critical care physician, was called to testify. He said that he had examined Kathy Augustine when she came back from the cardiac catheterization lab to Washoe Medical Center's intensive care unit. He said that she had been intubated with an endotracheal tube in place and was on a mechanical ventilator. He explained how her pupils had been fixed and dilated by the time he had seen her, and how he had been told after speaking with one of the cardiologists how her cardiac catheterization—or angiogram—had essentially turned out negative. Similarly, he explained, he had not found any intercranial bleeding, which could have accounted for the pupils being fixed and dilated, and he had been able to rule out a pulmonary embolism, which is a blood clot in the lung that could be fatal because it can block oxygen from getting into the patient's bloodstream.

"Does one of the tests that you just told me about . . . measure the transfer of oxygen or test lung function?" Barb asked.

"No, it does not," Mashour said. "It's merely a qualitative test that looks to see if there's actual evidence of a blood clot there. It does not tell anything about lung function."

"Did you ever do any tests that would tell you about the

transfer of oxygen to the blood or carbon dioxide out of the lungs, or anything like that?" Barb asked.

"Indirectly," Mashour responded. "From the arterial blood gases you would get some idea of the amount of transfer of oxygen from the environment to the bloodstream."

"And the arterial blood gases were part of what test?"

"Part of the routine workup. As far as being on the respirator, you would get arterial blood gases to determine if the patient's carbon dioxide and oxygen levels and pH were—you know, where they were at and if you needed to adjust the respirator to adjust any of those parameters."

"Were Miss Augustine's lungs functioning properly with whatever breathing assistance she was having?"

"To the best of my knowledge, they were, yes."

"So we got no pulmonary embolism, we got no brain bleed, we got functioning lungs," Barb said. "Is there anything else that you can say about Miss Augustine?"

"Well, at that point . . . the usual differential of limitation would go down in an arrest such as she went down that— those are usually the first two or three that you would consider," Mashour said. "All of those being negative, then you would have to look at possibly a drug overdose of some kind, which is usually how these patients present."

"If succinylcholine had been administered in Miss Augustine and she wasn't properly ventilated, would the results that you saw be consistent with that situation?"

"Conceivably, yeah."

"Doctor," said David Houston upon beginning his cross-examination of the witness, "based upon what you saw, you can't, of course, rule out sudden cardiac death, correct?"

"Based on the information that I have, it's possible," Mashour responded.

"Now, Doctor, Mr. Barb asked you a moment ago about drug overdoses. And drug overdoses certainly can cause those types of conditions that you viewed, correct?"

"Sure."

"Now, Doctor, in reference to this particular case, you've also been advised that the alleged point of injection on Miss Augustine was in the fatty tissue on the left buttock, correct?"

"That's what I've been told. Yes."

"And you've also advised that you feel that would be highly unlikely to be the cause of death in this case. Haven't you said that?"

"Usually—I think it would. But based on the medication that is being suspected, that would be unlikely to be cause of death in my opinion."

"And the reason it would be highly unlikely that succinylcholine would be the cause of death is because you would have to administer so much, true?"

"Well, there's no data to support the administration of succinylcholine in subcutaneous tissue. I don't even know the data with regard to intramuscular injection. The only time I've ever given succinylcholine or have been involved with succinylcholine has always been intravenously."

"Didn't we actually discuss the notion that it could be as high as—what was it?—eight hundred milligrams in order to receive any effect whatsoever?" Houston asked.

"That's a very rough estimate," Mashour responded. "I mean, again, without knowing the pharmacodynamics in subcu tissue, which has not been studied, that's a ballpark guess at best."

"Okay. Now, Doctor, eight hundred milligrams would be forty cc's, correct?"

"That's correct."

"This is a ten-cc syringe?"

"That's correct."

"That would mean you'd have to inject four of these just to get the eight hundred milligrams, correct?"

"Correct."

"And you have a fellowship, or did your fellowship in critical care medicine, true?"

"That's correct."

"So, in your opinion, since succinylcholine is unlikely to be the cause of death in this particular case . . . does . . . sudden cardiac arrest seem . . . possibly more likely?"

"It seems more likely based on the information, yes."

"Thank you very much, Doctor."

"Doctor," asked Barb on redirect, "is it your opinion or Mr. Houston's opinion that succinylcholine isn't the cause of death in this case?"

"Well, I think it's less likely that—"

"Doctor," Barb interrupted, "has anybody told you that there was succinylcholine present in Ms. Augustine's urine after her death—or excuse me—when she first came to the hospital?"

"When she first came to the hospital, I was not aware of that," Mashour said.

"Okay. Does that change your opinion, if that was your opinion?"

"Well, it would change my opinion."

Chapter 31

The next day, Thursday, June 21, 2007, Dr. William Anderson, chief toxicologist for the Division of Forensic Science of the Washoe County Sheriff's Office, defined forensic toxicology as the study of poisons in a medical-legal context and provided testimony on how he became involved in the Kathy Augustine case. A qualified expert witness, Anderson had testified in more than one hundred cases over the course of his career and had become involved in this one, as with many of the others that he had provided testimony for, because of his position. His office had received all of the biological samples related to the case. After inventorying them, logging them into their computer system, and then storing them in either a freezer or refrigerator—depending upon what specimen was being stored—his division was responsible for sending them off to the FBI laboratory in Virginia, after learning that succinylcholine might have been involved. Succinylcholine testing, he said, is an assay that his lab does not perform.

At one point, he said, he had reviewed Kathy's medical records that stemmed from her emergency hospitalization to see whether she had been given any succinylcholine therapeutically, because if she had, it would negate their theories, as well as the need to look for the drug in her system. After completing his review of Kathy's medical records, and being unable to turn up any information that Kathy may have been given succinylcholine at the hospital in a therapeutic sense, he called the FBI's chemistry section leader and asked if they could do the testing.

"So we packaged it up and sent it to them," Anderson testified. "Then we began to do a series of analyses on the urine for common drugs of abuse and other things. The only assay we sent out was the succinylcholine, and the succinylmonocholine. . . . We did all the rest of them here in Reno."

"Let's talk first about what you did here," Barb said. "What did you test?"

"We tested the urine sample for the common drugs of abuse . . . didn't find any," Anderson said. "We did an acid neutral extraction for some other therapeutic drugs. And we looked for the organic base screen, which is a rather comprehensive screen that detects literally hundreds of compounds. And we didn't find any."

He said that because they had some interest in the drug etomidate, they repeated the base strain in the serum. However, they hadn't detected any. He explained that they had only looked at the blood plasma for the etomidate because it metabolizes fairly extensively and does not readily show up in the urine. Anderson said that his lab had also looked for the presence of barbiturates, but none were present. He also said that he didn't have any problems with the FBI tests and the manner in which they had determined that succinylcholine had been in Kathy's urine.

"The test appears to be conclusive to me that succinylcholine and succinylmonocholine were in the urine sample," Anderson said.

As the trial continued that morning, testimony was heard from a lab assistant who testified how specimens were labeled and received by the lab; a deputy coroner investigator who had made arrangements for Kathy's body to be transferred from the hospital to the coroner's office—he had also photographed the body; and another deputy coroner who testified about delivering Kathy Augustine's biological samples to the Washoe County Crime Lab. Their testimony, which had taken up most of the morning that remained, basically went through the motions of testifying about what they did as part of their job duties, with regard to the case. Although their testimony hadn't provided any earth-shattering new details about the case, it was, nonetheless, needed as part of the legal record.

Right after lunch recess, a defense witness, Dr. Anton Paul Sohn, was called out of turn, due to a scheduling conflict, even though the prosecution was still presenting its case. Everyone had agreed previously that Sohn, a medical doctor who was board-certified in pathology as a pathologist, forensic pathologist, and clinical and anatomical pathologist, would be taken out of order. Defense attorney Alan Baum asked him to tell the jury about each of the disciplines in which he had been board-certified.

Clinical pathology, he said, is the study of laboratory medicine and interpretation of laboratory results; anatomical pathology is the specialty that evaluates biopsies both from surgery and from the doctor's office to determine, for instance, whether a tumor is cancerous or not; forensic pathology, he explained, is the study of medical-legal medicine, including the cause and manner of death and toxicology related to death. He was currently on staff at Washoe Medical Center, now known as Renown. He was also on staff at Alturas Medical, at St. Mary's Hospital, and was active at the Veterans Administration Hospital. He also told the jury about his membership in a long string of professional societies, and the fact that he was presently the chairman of the Department of Pathology at the University of Nevada School of Medicine. He was proffered as an expert witness in this case by Baum.

Sohn explained to the jury that he had formed opinions about the case based upon his review of Kathy Augustine's autopsy, the circumstances surrounding her death, some, but not all, of the hospital records pertaining to this case, toxicology results, and Dr. Ellen Clark's testimony before the grand jury. He also had reviewed seven slides that Dr. Clark had taken of tissue from the autopsy. Spanning his forty-year career, Sohn said that he had conducted approximately three thousand autopsies—some were forensic cases, and some were not.

When Baum drew Sohn's attention to Dr. Clark's autopsy report, which appeared to have been divided into three categories—external examination, internal examination, and microscopic examination—Sohn testified that he had found no omissions or shortcomings associated with Dr. Clark's report on either external or internal findings, neither of which he'd had any comment upon, but had noted a condition of cardiac hypertrophy in her microscopic findings.

When asked to do so, Sohn described the condition of cardiac hypertrophy as an enlargement either of the heart or the muscle fibers of the heart, a condition that is sometimes seen in an athlete who lifts a lot of weights and his or her arms become larger because of the increased workload of the muscles. He said that a similar condition sometimes occurs with the heart under increased workload. In the tissues that Dr. Clark had examined, Sohn said, the muscle fibers and the nuclei in the fibers were larger than normal.

"What does that tell you about the health or lack of health of the heart from which those tissues were taken and microscopically examined?" Baum asked.

"Well, there are probably a hundred things that can cause cardiac hypertrophy," Sohn said, "all the way from congestive heart failure to hardening of the arteries of the heart to valvular problems to hypertension diseases involving other organs, such as the kidney, such as the adrenal gland. So this indicates to me that something is going wrong that's causing her heart to work harder than normal."

"Is this the kind of thing that a forensic pathologist conducting an autopsy to try to determine cause of death would consider important?" Baum asked.

"Yes, it is."

"Why is it important?"

"It's important because hypertrophy, just like using the example of the arm muscle, you may lift weights for weeks and your muscle [might] not get any bigger. So the heart may work harder, but it takes weeks to months for hypertrophy to set in. So this is something that just didn't happen overnight or over three or four or five days. This is something [where] her heart worked harder over a period of weeks to months."

"By the way, you discovered this condition by looking at the slides that Dr. Clark had produced as part of her microscopic examination in the autopsy, correct?"

"Yes. And she gave them to me."

"It was there in the slides for you to find?"

"Yes."

"Did Dr. Clark make any mention whatsoever in her autopsy of this cardiac hypertrophy?"

"No, she did not."

"Do you consider that an omission, a significant omission?"

"I do."

"For the reasons that you've indicated, that is a reflection of some abnormal heart functioning?"

"Yes," Sohn replied. "And I might emphasize to the jury that the muscle fiber enlarges before the heart enlarges. Most of the time, when we see cardiac hypertrophy, the heart is bigger than normal. For instance, you've heard of an athlete's heart, the bigger heart. And so what has happened here is this hypertrophy has occurred previous or before the muscle overall got significantly enlarged. And so I can understand why she wasn't thinking of that when she looked at the slides."

"Is that—in lay terms, is that condition that this is a reflection of a good thing or a bad thing for somebody to have in your heart?"

"It's a good thing."

"In your heart?"

"It's a good thing."

"The cardiac hypertrophy is a good thing?"

"It's a good thing."

"In what respect?"

"Because if the muscle does not enlarge, then the heart fails," Sohn said. "So this is a compensatory hypertrophy, if you will. In other words, she needed that in order to maintain her cardiac reserve."

Later, after testimony about mitral valve prolapse, or regurgitation, Baum asked: "I want to clarify my question, which was certainly framed as a layperson, and that is—the cardiac hypertrophy, I asked if that was a good thing or a bad thing, and you said it's a good thing. It's my understanding is the reason it's a good thing because—is because if the heart didn't respond that way, because it was working harder, it would fail."

"That is correct," Sohn said.

"So it's the heart's way of getting stronger to adjust for the defect, which in this case is mitral valve regurgitation."

"That is correct."

Also during Sohn's testimony, Baum posed questions to the witness regarding the alleged injection site on Kathy's left buttock. He showed Sohn a series of photographic exhibits of that area of her anatomy that had been taken at her autopsy, and he acknowledged that he could see the punctate area in the photos. However, he said, he had not based his opinion regarding the time frame of when he believed that the punctate marks appeared but rather had based it on the cut surface of the punctate area and other documentation that he had reviewed in this case. After examining tissue from the punctate area, medical records, and slides, Sohn said that it was "highly unlikely" that Kathy had been given an injection in that spot prior to being admitted to the hospital on July 8, 2006. Instead, he testified, he believed that the wound was no more than forty-eight hours old at the time of her death.

During his cross-examination of Sohn, Tom Barb wanted to know how the needle mark had come to appear on Kathy's buttocks during her hospitalization, since there was no record of hospital nursing staff having given her an injection in that area.

"Would it surprise you to know that there was no therapeutic care in the sense of a shot in the buttocks for any reason during her stay at the hospital?" Barb asked.

"No, it would not."

"Then the punctate wounds that you've described that

can only be at most forty-eight hours old would have had to have been caused by somebody other than the hospital personnel, medical personnel."

"Very often people do not chart things that happen," Sohn said in reference to hospital workers sometimes failing to notate each thing that they do when treating a patient. "She could have gotten a shot and it wouldn't have been charted. I've seen that a number of times."

Sohn said that it was highly unlikely that the puncture injury at the site of the alleged injection could have been made on July 8, 2006.

Later that afternoon, Detective David Jenkins was called to the witness stand. Jenkins, a solid man with a full head of hair and a mustache, faced the clerk and was sworn in as he had been many times before over the course of his thirty-year career. As he responded to Barb's questions, Jenkins explained to the jury how he had come to be involved in the case through the telephone call he had received from Kim Ramey.

Jenkins explained that after he had spoken with some of the nurses in the intensive care unit and had determined that Kim Ramey certainly seemed credible enough, he contacted the Washoe County Coroner's Office and requested that they consider doing an autopsy on Kathy Augustine's body. He said that he wanted to secure potential items of evidence in the event that the case turned into a criminal investigation, which it had. He said that he had also asked the nurses in the intensive care unit at Washoe Medical Center to confirm that the body fluids that had been collected would be retained and held as potential evidence. He told of attending the autopsy, after which he began drafting an affidavit in support of a search warrant.

He explained that he had obtained the search warrant for Kathy Augustine's home on Otter Way in Reno.

After confirming that Jenkins had executed the search warrant at Kathy's Reno home, Barb showed Jenkins an item that had been marked Exhibit 2.

"Would you tell us what that is, please?"

"This is a vial containing—or labeled to have contained drugs that I found inside the home on Otter Way," Jenkins replied.

"Would you open it, please? And what is that, sir?"

"It is a glass vial with a lid," Jenkins said. "It's labeled to contain twenty milligrams of etomidate."

"And where did you find this?"

"That was actually inside a pouch of a backpack that I found on the floor in the master bedroom that was next to the bed and between the master bath."

Jenkins described the backpack as newer condition, yellow and black in color, manufactured with a nylon-type material. It was filled at that time with several different items, including the etomidate. Jenkins explained that he hadn't taken the backpack at that time but had photographed it in place. He later collected it, he said, in Hampton, Virginia. Jenkins went over the items that were seized as evidence, both in Reno and in Hampton, Virginia. Among the items he mentioned was the bottle of etomidate, bedsheets and pillows from Kathy Augustine's bed, various types of medical literature that a nurse might possess, and so forth. Included in the items Jenkins testified about was the index card with succinylcholine information on it, as well as other cards with similar medical and pharmacological information on them. Other portions of his testimony pertained to procedural items, including evidence inventory and chain of custody. He pointed out that other than items used by REMSA personnel to treat

Kathy, investigators had not found any syringes at the Otter Way residence, nor had they found any succinylcholine on the premises or in Chaz's possession. They also hadn't found any of those items during the search of his car in Virginia.

During the course of Jenkins's testimony, it was brought out that a note had been found inside a black binder in the master bedroom of the Otter Way house that read: *Fly flag at half mast for Kathy,* and another that said: *Contact Dominic Gentile for protection.* Jenkins's testimony never provided any further information regarding those notes, nor did he speculate as to what they meant. Jenkins's testimony never really brought anything new or fresh to the table, and at times had seemed, correctly, like a formality that needed to be carried out.

When David Houston cross-examined Jenkins, he indicated that a skin assessment had been done on Kathy while she was in the ICU on July 8 that indicated that she had no wounds that anyone had notated.

"And as the case agent in this particular matter," Houston said, "you're aware there were a number of people interviewed that had direct contact with Kathy Augustine during the early-morning hours of July eighth while she was in the hospital, true?"

"Yes, sir," Jenkins responded.

"Not one of those people indicated ever having observed a punctate-type injury to the left buttock, did they?"

"No."

"When did that punctate-type injury occur, Detective?"

"Are you asking for my opinion?"

"No. I want your personal knowledge. I know what your opinion is."

"Prior to her death, sir."

"Would it surprise you to note that Dr. Sohn is a forensic pathologist, [and] testified that that punctate-type injury is acute and could not be any older than forty-eight hours, dating back?"

"That would surprise me."

"Well, if that's true, there was no injection port for the succinylcholine by Chaz Higgs, was there?"

"I'm sorry. What, sir?"

"There's no place for Chaz Higgs to have injected her with succinylcholine if this mark is acute, is there?"

"I'm sorry, sir," Jenkins said. "I didn't—I said I would be surprised if that was Dr. Sohn's testimony, but—"

"Well, it was. Do you know Dr. Sohn?"

"I do, sir."

"And you respect Dr. Sohn, don't you?"

"I haven't dealt with Dr. Sohn for a number of years. I don't believe he's been active recently."

"Well, he, as a matter of fact, used to work with you on homicide cases, didn't he?"

"Yes, sir."

"Did you respect him then?"

"I think he's a very nice man."

"Okay. All of the other injection sites according to your investigation on Kathy Augustine are therapeutic, save and except this one site on the left buttock, correct?"

"Correct."

"If this injection site on the left buttock was not there during the early-morning hours of July eighth, and there is succinylcholine in her system, it would have to come then from one of the medical therapeutic injection sites, wouldn't it?"

"Could you repeat that again, sir?"

"Sure. If there's succinylcholine in Kathy Augustine's

system, and if this mark on the left buttock is not there on the morning of July eighth, then the succinylcholine would have to have come from one of the therapeutic injection sites, correct?"

"No, sir."

"Well, how else would you think it got there?"

"Well, to my understanding—" Jenkins attempted to respond, but was cut off in midsentence by Houston.

"Do you know?"

"—there could have been other ways to administer succinylcholine."

"Oh, I see. You think it was atomized and sprayed in her mouth, or something?"

"Certainly, that would not be my first choice."

Chapter 32

During Dr. Ellen Clark's testimony on Friday, June 22, 2007, she told the Washoe County jury that a skilled nurse is capable of injecting a person without leaving a needle mark that can be detected during the autopsy. Clark, who performed the autopsy on Kathy Augustine's body, testified that the baffling puncture mark she found on Kathy's left buttock may not have even been a needle mark. It was possible, she said, that Kathy had been injected in a different area of her body in which no needle track had been left.

"A good nurse could have delivered it in a manner I did not detect," Clark said.

According to Clark, there was an approximate 50 percent chance that the suspect mark on her left buttock had been caused by a needle puncture. Nonetheless, using photographs that had been marked as exhibits, Clark pointed out an area where there was some blue-green and purple or red discoloration.

"There were actually two punctate areas of discoloration that are potentially significant," she said, "because they have an overall configuration in appearance that would be consistent with needle punctures or injection sites."

Clark explained how she had examined the punctate areas further by doing what is referred to as "cut-downs," which is simply making a straight surgical incision with a scalpel or other sharp cutting instrument to examine the skin and tissue underneath the exterior wound. She said that the procedure had established the presence of a thin path of bleeding into the tissue that was "directly beneath some of the punctate or very small injuries on the surface." She said that she had followed that same procedure for several of Kathy's punctate wounds, including those that "were obviously associated with therapeutic IV or intravenous tubing and such." She testified that the buttocks wound had not shown up anywhere in Kathy's medical records as having been a therapeutic injury. She also provided details of the internal examination of Kathy's body during autopsy.

"The internal exam particularly involving inspection of the brain showed that the brain was swollen," Clark said. "This is a nonspecific finding, but certainly a swollen brain can be associated with decreased blood flow or decreased oxygen to the brain, so that became a significant finding."

Because Kathy had been brought to the hospital with the presumption that she had suffered a heart attack, the internal examination of her heart was noted as being particularly significant. Clark said that she had found "no evidence of occlusion" or obstruction of the coronary arteries, but that the examination had shown some evidence of mild myxomatous degeneration, a deteriorative change within "one of the valves called the mitral valve." However, she said, the degeneration of the mitral valve had been minimal, and she had not found any evidence of significant scarring or "fixed injury of that valve." She had found, however, evidence of necrosis in the heart.

"I saw evidence under the microscope of rather extensive necrosis," she told the jury. "These were areas of very pinpoint degenerative changes or actually cell death in the heart muscle. And they were distributed widely all over the heart in virtually every section that I examined microscopically."

"Would it be fair for me to say that a global necrosis that you observed could be caused by lack of oxygen?" Barb asked.

"Yes."

"Would it always be caused by lack of oxygen?"

"No."

"What other reasons would there be of global necrosis?"

"Global necrosis in this case is different or contrasts with what we call localized or zonal necrosis," Clark said. "When a person typically suffers a heart attack, they experience an occlusion or a spasm in one of the main coronary arteries."

She explained that the coronary arteries carry blood and oxygen to specific areas of the heart. For example, she said, the left coronary artery that runs down the front of the heart brings oxygen and blood to the front and the left side of the heart. Similarly, the artery that runs to the right side in the back of the heart carries blood and oxygen to that area.

"So when we see a typical heart attack with an occluded artery," she continued, "we look for injury in that zone or that distribution of blood flow. In this case, that was not present. Rather, microscopically, there were very small pinpoint areas of heart cell death and inflammation. This characteristic or this distribution of the injury is highly characteristic of a global or a large and uniform insult to the heart, as we might see with shock, for example, or with something like an epinephrine surge. . . ."

"Did you also do a microscopic exam of the brain tissue?" Barb asked.

"Yes."

"Did you find the same necrosis there? I mean, differ-ent cell, the same kind of necrosis there?"

"I didn't find necrosis in the brain tissue," Clark said. "The brain tends to heal or respond to injury in a manner quite different than other tissues in the body. So in the brain, rather than necrosis, I saw evidence of swelling and leakage of fluid outside the normal blood vessel spaces around the cells themselves. I did see . . . what I would term degenerative changes of major nerve cells in the brain, but not, per se, necrosis like was in the heart."

"Was what you observed in the brain consistent with a lack of oxygen?"

"Yes."

"Did you see any brain bleeding, or brain bleed, as some people call it?"

"No."

"Any evidence that you can determine from that examination of a stroke?"

"No."

"Dr. Clark, Dr. Sohn testified . . . that the injection site was . . . at most forty-eight hours old," Barb said. "Do you agree with that?"

"No."

"Why not?"

"Because . . . Dr. Sohn kept referring to blood in the wound or the injection site," Clark testified. "Blood in the injection site has no relevance to aging. . . . We always see blood in—excuse me—I'm not going to refer to it as an injection site, but we always see blood in a bruise or a skin-break injury, provided that the heart is beating and blood is circulating after the injury occurs. The description of blood in a wound does not bear any relevance to dating that wound.

"He made reference to the color of the wound," Clark continued, "specifically regarding red-to-purple coloration. In fact, in Miss Augustine's intravenous lines, which were placed actually at the time she was partially resuscitated at

ier home, she had red and purple discoloration. We know
that those wounds predated death by at least seventy-two
hours. Actually, about three-and-a-half days. That's when
those IVs were placed. Also, as a course of my study, I have
done many, many autopsies, between four and five thousand
personally, and I have looked at bruises on many occasions,
both macroscopically or grossly and microscopically, and
found extreme variation in the rapidity of healing, the type
of healing, and the type of inflammation."

As an example regarding the differences in how people
heal, if a person bumped his knee and had a purple bruise
that took days to weeks to heal, and went through the usual
color change phases of blue to green to yellow, and eventually gone, the length of time for the healing depends
largely upon a person's complexion color, how healthy the
person is, and how rapidly a person heals, "based upon the
amount of bleeding into the injury," Clark explained.

"So in my experience, and also within the literature, it
is very precarious to date bruises specifically based upon
the coloration of the body," Clark said.

Clark described how she had performed the autopsy on
Kathy Augustine's body on July 12, 2006, but had not
signed the autopsy report until October 26, 2006, with a
cause of death because she had been waiting for the toxicology report from the FBI laboratory. In cases such as this
one, toxicology reports are crucial to determining the
cause of death because of the supposition or suspicion that
drugs may have been consumed or that poisoning may
have occurred. When she received those reports, she said,
she stated that her opinion was that Kathy had died from
succinylcholine toxicity, meaning that Kathy had been poisoned by the drug.

* * *

During cross-examination, Baum grilled Clark about the punctate wound, driving home the point that Clark had not called the injury in question a needle mark. She explained that she was not specifically identifying the injury as a needle puncture "to the exclusion of any other mechanism of trauma."

"You are not prepared to say to a reasonable medical certainty that it was a needle mark or an injection site?" Baum asked.

"If you can define reasonable degree of medical certainty," she replied. "If I'm fifty-one percent certain that that wound is a needle puncture mark, I would say yes, it is that characteristic or specific."

Clark and the defense attorney finally agreed that it was her opinion that there was a fifty-fifty chance that the injury was a needle mark.

"Prior to your getting back the report from the FBI, if there had been no report from the FBI, or if the report from the FBI had been negative for any drug or toxics, to what would you have attributed the cause of death in this case?" Baum asked.

"I would have attributed the cause of death to myocardial necrosis or heart muscle injury of undetermined etiology, because it did not have a classic distribution for anything that I could identify as directly having caused it at the autopsy examination."

Although Baum took the witness through a series of questions about mitral valve regurgitation and established through Dr. Clark's responses that, although rare, the condition can lead to sudden cardiac death, the subject, along with other considerations such as stress, being overweight, and so forth, was left open. It would be up to the jury to determine how they might view such a possibility. The one thing that was certain, however, was that the state's case against Chaz Higgs had clearly hinged upon the FBI laboratory's toxicological report. Without it, there would have been no case for the state to pursue against him.

Before he wrapped up his cross-examination of Dr. Clark, Baum hammered the possibility that, assuming that the FBI's toxicology report was correct and that Dr. Sohn's testimony about the timing of when the suspected injection injury to her buttocks occurred had also been correct, it was possible that Kathy had received the succinylcholine through a different entrance or portal into her body at a time that was possibly later than what the state had alleged.

"You're saying that this isn't the injection site where succinylcholine was delivered," Clark confirmed.

"But that they do find succinylcholine and succinyl-monocholine in her urine," Baum clarified. "There would have to be some other explanation for how it got there."

"That's correct," Clark agreed.

Clark agreed that she could not say with absolute certainty that the suspected injection was in fact an injection site, or that the suspected site had been the way that the succinylcholine had been delivered. On the other hand, she agreed with the prosecutor on redirect that succinylcholine poisoning can explain everything that she observed during the course of the autopsy.

Later in the day, the jury heard testimony from nurses Kathryn Almaraz and Tina Carbone, both of whom testified that Chaz had appeared to become increasingly harsh in his statements about Kathy because of the marital problems he allegedly had with her. Both women characterized Chaz as an excellent nurse who possessed good patient skills, but said that his marriage had seemed to deteriorate during the time of Kathy's impeachment proceedings.

They also testified to Kathy's jealousy and how she had harassed and threatened them, sometimes showing up unannounced at the hospital to demand his paycheck.

Almaraz recounted for the jury's benefit how Chaz had referred to his wife as a "bitch," and how on one occasion he had allegedly said, "If I didn't have a daughter in Las Vegas, I would kill my wife and throw her down a mine shaft." Almaraz also testified under cross-examination how, despite Chaz's purported comment about killing his wife, she hadn't told the police about the comment until Jenkins interviewed her on February 14, 2007.

"Ma'am, would it be a fair statement that at the time the statement was made you didn't take Mr. Higgs seriously?"

"It's not—it was not my decision if it was serious or not," Almaraz responded. "When a person is angry at their spouse, as I am with my husband sometimes, 'Oh, gosh, you know, he left the toilet seat up again. I'd like to kill him for that.' That seems normal to me. But to say something as calculated as strangling or hurting someone and wanting to throw them down a mine shaft, that seems a little bit excessive to me."

Although the state had planned to call Linda Ramirez to testify that afternoon regarding the flirtatious e-mail exchanges between her and Chaz Higgs, the judge decided to recess for the weekend early, thus ending the first week of the murder trial.

Chapter 33

On Monday, June 25, 2007, Linda Ramirez took the witness stand and gave her sworn testimony about the so-called flirtatious e-mails that she and Chaz Higgs had sent each other over varying periods of time. Over the course of the direct examination by the state in which Christopher Hicks questioned her, significant portions of her and Chaz's e-mails were read aloud, followed by specific questions, and made a part of the public record in this case. Linda described how she had met Chaz prior to her twenty-first birthday in July 2004, and how he had given her a rose for her birthday, how they had become friends despite Chaz's marriage to Kathy, and she told the jury some of the things that he had said about Kathy, such as how he hated her and called her a "controlling, manipulative bitch." The young admissions clerk also explained how she had been fired for sending personal e-mails to Chaz using the hospital's computers after Kathy had complained to hospital administrators about it and that how, after an absence, they had resumed contact via e-mail. Despite the flirtatious nature of the e-mails, Linda said that she and Chaz had never taken their relationship to the level of being physical.

* * *

Under cross-examination by Baum, Linda explained that between the rose incident near her birthday in July 2004 and up until January 2005, there had been no e-mails between them, only personal and friendly contact at work—but nothing inappropriate. The e-mails, she said, hadn't started until January 2005. It had been during that approximate six-month period that Chaz had begun to share personal information with Linda, such as that he was married but that he was planning to get a divorce. She indicated that she had no intention of dating or seeing him while he was married, and she had told him so.

Her testimony showed that there were only two occasions in which she had met with Chaz outside of work—once when they had taken an hour-long drive together to talk, and again when she saw his truck in traffic on the way to work in which she had followed him into a gas station, where they talked for a few minutes. Upon saying good-bye at the hospital, however, Linda said that she had kissed him. At one point, Linda told the jury that most of the e-mails between her and Chaz had been deleted, and that she had only printed out a portion of them to save.

When Chaz had told Linda that he was planning to leave Kathy, he had also told her that he was looking for a place to live. He also wrote: *I did what I did with us to protect you from her.*

"Didn't you understand that to mean that he stopped corresponding with you, that he stopped having this flirtatious relationship with you because of what Kathy Augustine had done to you, actually getting you fired?" Baum asked. "You understood that."

"Yes."

"So what he did was he broke it off with you to the

extent that you had a relationship with him because he didn't want to cause you any more problems, right?"

"Right."

A short time later, Baum brought up an e-mail in which Linda had said to Chaz: *I really, really want to see you. Maybe on one of your days off, you should rent a room at a hotel and let me know, and I could meet you there and we can do dirty things.*

"That was your e-mail to him," Baum said.

"Yes."

"It was flirtatious, wasn't it?"

"Yes."

"I mean, we know about the Internet and how people play roles and go into chat rooms and pretend they're something that they're not," Baum said. "Isn't that really what we're talking about here?"

"No, not really," Linda replied.

"Oh, you really wanted to meet with him?"

"Yes."

"Oh. Okay. But you never did."

"I didn't."

"Not because you didn't want to, but Mr. Higgs just simply didn't take you up on that."

"Uh-huh."

"Right?"

"Exactly. . . ."

". . . And you kind of moved on with your life," Baum said a few minutes later. "In fact . . . we now see you sort of referring to your relationship with Mr. Higgs as a friendship."

"Yes."

"Isn't that how you considered it at that point?"

"Yes."

"He never—Chaz never made a suggestion or an invitation to you, 'Let's meet. Meet me at this hotel, meet me at this weekend resort,' anything like that. He never did any of that, did he?"

"No."

"In fact," Baum said, "the only invitation was when you wrote him about him getting a room and the two of you could be together, to which he never pursued, correct?"

"Yes."

On redirect, Hicks asked Linda about a time when she and Chaz had made plans to meet. Linda had taken a day off from work, and Kathy had been planning a trip to Las Vegas. However, Chaz had backed out of the plan—Linda could not recall whether he had backed out because Kathy's plans had been canceled, or whether it was because Kathy had wanted him to accompany her. Hicks pointed out, however, how Linda had candidly responded to Chaz that she would have gone through with the idea of getting a room at a hotel.

"Did his e-mail . . . where he proclaimed his love to you and stated that he had made a pact with himself that he was going to live every day making . . . his wife's life a living hell, that he lived every day manipulating her and driving her crazy and that he hated her and wanted to make her break, and that he had nothing else to lose because you were everything he wanted and it was ripped away, so that it was his quest in life to drive that bitch crazy, did your inclination to go rent a room with him, did that e-mail have anything to do with that inclination?"

"Yes. . . ."

"Did you at that point feel that he was removed from his wife?"

"Yes."

"Did it sound to you that Mr. Higgs just wanted a friendship?" Hicks asked.

"No."

"When he wrote to you, *I can make you the happiest woman on this earth. . . . I know I can. I know me, and I know what I'm capable of and what I can do for you in every way. Again, I am not trying to freak you out here. I just love you, and that is a fact. You're all I wanted since I first saw you. I remember the rose I gave you. I wanted to give you a million roses because that's what I felt. I wanted to run away with you and never look back. I want to look in your beautiful eyes every day and tell you how much I love you. I do not want anything else in my life. It has been this way for two years. I want you with all my heart.* Did you perceive that as someone who wanted to continue a friendship?"

"No, not a friendship," Linda responded.

"More than a friendship?"

"Yes."

During his recross-examination, Baum pointed out that Linda Ramirez was not "engaged in a raging love affair with Chaz Higgs" in July 2006, the month that his wife had died. He reiterated that she and Chaz had kissed once, and that there had been major gaps in communication between the two of them. At that point, he stressed, the two of them had considered themselves just friends, and elicited a response from Linda indicating that there wasn't going to be a love affair between them, at least not as far as she had been concerned. Baum reminded the jury that Linda had provided Chaz an opportunity to meet with her and to engage in a more intimate relationship, but that had never happened.

Chaz, it was inferred, had remained faithful to his wife.

Chapter 34

Before the defense began presenting its witnesses, attorneys Alan Baum and David Houston filed two motions with the court—one for a direct acquittal of their client on the defense's contention that there "is no direct evidence of any crime in this case," and the other to throw out the testimony regarding the results of urine testing on the grounds that the state had failed to establish a reliable chain of custody for "whatever it was that the FBI tested in the way of urine." Judge Kosach denied both motions.

With regard to the motion for acquittal, Kosach said that there was sufficient evidence to "get to the jury in regard to succinylcholine in the victim's system.

"How did it get there?" Kosach asked. "And even though motive is not a legal element, it's certainly been shown. So the motion is denied. I'm not going to . . . direct the jury to a not guilty verdict."

As for the motion to throw out the scientific evidence that pertained to the urine testing, Kosach said that he didn't see a break in the chain of custody.

The defense, it was recalled, had already presented their first witness, Dr. Anton Sohn, out of turn. With everyone back inside the courtroom, the defense team called their next witness, William Michael Higgs, Chaz's twin brother.

In response to Houston's questions, William Higgs told the jury that he had first become aware of Chaz's marriage to Kathy Augustine when Chaz had called him in September 2003. Although he said that he had been surprised that they had gotten married, primarily because they hadn't been dating all that long, he said that he hadn't been particularly concerned because they had seemed like they were very happy to be together.

"They were bubbly," William said. "They were like schoolkids. They looked like they were in love. I figured they were two adults and they knew what they were doing."

William said that he had been living in North Carolina when Chaz told him about the marriage, and that he later came out to visit them in Nevada for about a week. He said that he didn't think that they'd had enough time to learn much about each other, and he said at the time of his visit he hadn't known what Kathy Augustine's position had been with the state of Nevada.

William testified that his brother and Kathy were still happy by the end of 2003 and the early part of 2004 when the two of them had traveled to Washington, D.C., when she was being considered for the position of the U.S. treasurer. He said that he hadn't seen them during 2004, due to serving in Iraq with the National Guard after his unit was placed on active-duty status, but that he had remained in contact with Chaz and Kathy throughout the year. He said that he began to notice that their relationship began going downhill shortly after commencement of the impeachment proceedings against Kathy.

"After that started," William said, "their relationship . . . just turned bad."

"Do you know why it turned bad?" Houston asked.

"Kathy was under a lot of stress, she was under a lot of pressure, and she took it out on Chaz."

William Higgs indicated that there were a number of e-mails between him and his sister-in-law due to the fact that Chaz had informed Kathy that he wanted out of the relationship. William said that he began playing the role of a marriage counselor of sorts, in part because he had been receiving requests from Kathy for advice on how to keep the marriage together. He said that he told her, "Just stick with it. It will all work out. You guys haven't been together that long." He said that Chaz hadn't made any secret out of the fact that he wanted out of the marriage. He said that the purpose of his e-mails was to encourage them to remain together.

"Why did you want to see them stay together?" Houston asked.

"Because I remembered how I saw them together the first time," William replied. "They were very much in love. And I thought they hadn't been married long enough to just give it up. I felt they should stick it out."

"What do you think about that advice today?" Houston asked.

"In hindsight, when things really got bad, I probably should have just told them to do the opposite. I probably should have just told them to split and get it over with."

The defense also called Dr. Earl Nielsen, a clinical psychologist with a specialty in life crisis, grief reaction, depression, and post-traumatic stress disorder, to testify about his evaluation of Chaz Higgs. Nielsen had been brought on board by the defense less than a week earlier, and hadn't had much time to fully study the case or to interview people associated with it, besides Chaz Higgs. He agreed early in his testimony with Houston that a person needs to know something about a person in order to decide the appropriateness of their response centered on a grief situation.

Nielsen said that some people experience grief with shock and panic initially, and others react with numbness and act as if they don't respond at all. Still, others react with denial and simply won't believe what they've been told, and the list, he said, goes on to include many possible responses to grief. It would be difficult, he indicated, to put a label on it, and he agreed that the calmness displayed by Chaz during the "crisis" (as opposed to grief) may have been appropriate considering his "exceptional training in repeated settings to deal with (the) most extreme kinds of crisis" and the years he spent serving in the military. Such a response wouldn't mean that he didn't care about his patient or what had happened, but instead would indicate that he had been taught to isolate his own feelings from what was happening at the moment.

Nielsen said that as he attempted to study Chaz Higgs a little further, he had concluded that he was a man who entered relationships with great romantic fantasy and great hope.

"He basically enters personal, intimate relationships wanting the perfect life," Nielsen testified. "I don't think that's real different from the way most people start out. But everybody wants to succeed, and I think he does, too. The weakness that I observed in Mr. Higgs is that he does, in fact, have some trouble with the concept of commitment with no back doors. And he's been married four times, he's been divorced three times and had intended to divorce a fourth. Each of those marriages were very short, really. I think the longest was six years, but they weren't together for six years."

Nielsen said that what he had observed from Chaz's descriptions of each of his marriages was that they were all different people, all different situations, but "the consistency is that he started out wanting it to be perfect." As he discovered that it wasn't going to be perfect, he looked for ways out, Nielsen said.

"He looked for an escape," Nielsen said. "That may also be part of his romantic fantasy. . . . I don't believe that he had a relationship with anyone that he left for someone else. Each of the relationships that he had before, he ended the relationship before he went on to another relationship. . . ."

With regard to Linda Ramirez, Chaz had begun another romantic fantasy, "a back door, a way out," because he had not yet resolved his conflict with Kathy, Nielsen said. He had not yet figured out a way to leave her, but he didn't want to leave her without an alternative, according to Nielsen. Nielsen testified that he had not seen anything in this case that would cause him to believe that Chaz Higgs would resort to murder.

"And when Mr. Higgs basically says, *I will live every day making her life a living hell. I live every day to manipulate her, driving her crazy. . . . I hate this woman, and I will make her break*," Houston said, "how is that consistent with a man who can still say, 'I care for Kathy Augustine'?"

"He has this conflict," Nielsen said. "He—on one level, he entered the relationship with Kathy Augustine with great excitement. This is going to save me. This is going to be the best thing I ever did. My life is finally going to change and be perfect. When he deduced that that was not necessarily true, he started to think about other ways to make his life necessarily perfect. And that meant some other object. But he can do both at once. We can have fantasies. We can have wishes. And sometimes that helps us go on with the thing that we struggle with."

* * *

"Dr. Nielsen, what's a sociopath?" Tom Barb asked during cross-examination.

"Well, it's a . . . term describing essentially a person without a conscience," Nielsen responded.

"And a person without a conscience does what?"

"Sociopaths tend to be cold, calculating, manipulative. They have their own best interests at heart. They can be very friendly and kind and cooperative and social, until that conflicts with their needs, and then they can be brutal and vicious and very deceitful."

"Sounds to me like you just described Mr. Higgs from what you've told us earlier," Barb said.

"I think that if you string all the pieces together, almost each of the things that I said could be attributed to Mr. Higgs," Nielsen said. "But it's . . . a bit out of context."

A short time later, Barb asked Nielsen if he thought that it was unusual that Chaz was reading the newspaper while riding in the ambulance with Kathy en route to the main hospital after being transferred from South Meadows.

"Well, again, I don't know how to use a statistic to measure unusual," Nielsen said.

"All right," Barb responded. "You don't think . . . we should think ill of him because he sat in an ambulance going lights and sirens from South Meadows to Washoe Main and read a newspaper?"

"No, I don't."

"What would it take for you to say to us, 'Yeah, you should feel ill of him'?"

"I don't know," Nielsen replied.

"You don't have any idea? Nothing in the world could make you feel ill of him?"

"Well, if someone in the ambulance had been able to observe him making some kind of overt comment or gesture that was derogatory—or demeaning—then certainly one would feel ill of him. . . . The problem I have with the newspaper is that we have to take that out of context and interpret what it meant, and its meaning can be many."

"Out of context."

"That's all I said."

"You're in the ambulance, your wife is in the back, she's near death, you are riding lights and sirens, and you read the newspaper. How can you take that out of context?"

"You can also read the newspaper, as I said, to avoid the grief, to avoid having to think about [it]. It's used as a distraction."

Nielsen had previously testified that grief usually sets in at the time of a loved one's death, and that in Chaz's case, he had been dealing with a "crisis" until Kathy actually passed away.

"But, Doc, she's not dead yet," Barb retorted. "There's no grief yet. You just said that."

"Well, okay. To avoid having to react to the fear or the anxiety of 'this is terrible [that] this is happening. I don't want to deal with it, and I don't want anybody else to confront me about it. I'm going to escape.'"

"Okay . . . she gets in the hospital Saturday morning. Sunday morning, he asks—calls a nurse and says, 'Will you bring my paycheck out . . . to the parking lot?'"

"Correct."

"And he brings her doughnuts for doing that."

"Yes."

"And now, again—is he ignoring everything that's going on just so he doesn't have to deal with his wife being in the hospital? Is that what that's about?"

"It may be. It may also be that he . . . has enough self-control and enough fear of being seen as weak that he focuses on getting the little daily things done that need to be done."

"Okay. Ms. Augustine died July eleventh in the afternoon, about four-thirty. July the tenth he goes to PERS, which is the state retirement system, and he signs up for her retirement, with him as the beneficiary, and if she dies, he gets it. And he signed up for the immediate payment of that. Does that change your opinion about Mr. Higgs?"

"It raises some questions," Nielsen said, somewhat taken aback. "That's a piece I didn't know."

"Oh. Well, let me show you," Barb said, grandstanding. "By the way, do you recognize his handwriting, or would you?"

"I would not."

"May I approach the witness?" Barb asked the judge.

"Yes," Kosach said.

"This says at the top, 'Public Employees Retirement System of Nevada.' It's dated July 10, 2006, and it says, 'Chaz Higgs.'"

"Uh-huh."

"All right? And he marked, 'Option 2.' What is Option 2?"

"This option provides an actuarially reduced allowance for lifetime of the retired employee," Nielsen responded. "After the retired employee's death, the allowance will continue in the same amount to the beneficiary for the remainder of the beneficiary's lifetime."

"Who is the beneficiary on the front page?" Barb asked.

"Chaz Higgs."

"Thank you, Doctor. Now, what does that do for your opinion of Mr. Higgs?"

A little later on, Barb again turned the subject toward Linda Ramirez and the e-mails between her and Chaz Higgs, and suggested that it was through those e-mails and his relationship with her that his sociopathic personality came to light.

"Would it be unreasonable for the rest of us to assume that he . . . found out he couldn't control Kathy Augustine, and he was searching for another person that he could control?" Barb asked.

"I don't know that that's unreasonable, no," Nielsen said.

"Okay. So we're back to the sociopath, aren't we? Could have been," Barb said. "Did he complete SEAL training?"

"No, he didn't."

"Then I'm not certain what all the hubbub has been about him being a Navy SEAL. So he wasn't one, was he?"

"No, he wasn't."

"He was a medic."

"He was a medic," agreed Nielsen. "He was not a Navy SEAL. He didn't complete the training."

"Right," Barb said. "He started, he stopped, he didn't make it."

Barb reminded Nielsen that he had testified that Chaz had not wanted to light the next romantic fantasy until the current one was finished. That had been his style in many of his relationships.

"What do you call what he's doing to Ms. Ramirez, a twenty-one-year-old, that he's starting these e-mails, and 'I love you,' and 'I wish I could give you a million roses,' and all that business? Isn't he starting that [next fantasy]?"

"Absolutely," agreed Nielsen. "He is starting—"

"Why did you say he didn't want to light the romantic fantasy until the other one was done?"

"I may have said it poorly," Nielsen said, now possibly beginning to feel a little beat up. "What I was trying to say was that he had [a] romantic fantasy in his head. He was, in fact, trying to engage her in the same fantasy. But he had not reached the point where, in his own mind, he could leave the relationship or have an open physical relationship with Ms. Ramirez that—"

"But that's not what I'm asking about," Barb interrupted. "You told us that he didn't want to light the next fantasy until the current relationship was over."

"Okay."

"But he did that."

"Okay. The dispute between us is about the word 'light.'"

"It was your word," Barb said. "I wrote it down. *Don't light the romantic fantasy.*"

"When I try to explain it, I'm not succeeding."

"Explain away, Doc. What does 'light' mean to you?"

"The way I meant it was that he—he had—at least what he told me and what Miss Ramirez's e-mails indicated—is that he had not crossed that boundary. He had not ignited the relationship to be an intimate relationship. He had only treated it as a fantasy. And then that's my understanding from both her e-mails and his."

"So unless it was actual physical relationship, it was just a fantasy," Barb said.

"I think that's the way he thought about it, is that it was innocuous and safe as long as he didn't make a final physical commitment."

"I see. Safe for whom?"

"Him."

"It's all about him, isn't it, Doc? Back to the sociopath?"

"That's true."

"Is it your testimony that after July eleventh when Kathy Augustine died that Mr. Higgs turned into a grieving husband?"

"It's my testimony that that's what he described," Nielsen said. "That he felt grief and that he responded with grief . . . after the death of Kathy Augustine."

"And how long did that grief last?"

"Well, again, it's tough to measure. I think there's probably still some grief. But I've also observed the e-mails in which he not long after her death made statements that would be inconsistent with deep psychological pain."

"Would be inconsistent with deep—so the August third e-mail to Ramirez and the August twenty-eighth e-mail to Ramirez . . ." Barb mentioned a third e-mail to another woman. "You didn't see that one?"

"I didn't see that one."

"I'll just ask you about the first two," Barb said. "Those would be inconsistent with grief?"

"They're inconsistent with a deep and persistent grief response, yes," Nielsen said.

"How about did they show you any pictures that Mr. Higgs received over his cell phone near the end of September 2006?"

"No." Nielsen must have sensed that another surprise was on its way.

"Did they tell you about a nurse that he was trying to kick off a relationship with in September? At least in September of 2006."

"Not that I know of."

"Well, either they did or they didn't?"

"I don't have all the dates and times and people nailed down, but I don't think they did."

"Okay. . . . May I approach, Your honor?"

"Yes," Kosach said.

"I'm going to show you some pictures," Barb told the witness. "This is a photograph that Mr. Higgs received from a nurse."

Barb flipped through a couple of photos, and each time, he said, "Same nurse, different outfit.

"Text message," Barb said. "That's the nurse's first name. The nurse is asking for his photos now. *Maybe we could try out the*—they didn't tell you about those?"

"No, I haven't seen those."

"Okay. Well, you've got pictures of a scantily cla
woman going to him. Two in just—I guess you'd call it 'th
bra and the cleavage' show. And one with the panties show
ing, and her hand right above the waistline. And the
you've got a text message about *Can I drive that cute littl*
Bug of yours sometime? Maybe we can try out the back
seat. This is in September 2006. Is he still grieving?"

"That's inconsistent with what I would call grief,'
Nielsen said.

"Okay. So now we've got what from your testimony'
From his words, and his words alone, he was grieving. Bu
from you getting all the information, or at least more infor
mation, he's inconsistent with grieving. Is that accurate?"

"Partly."

The defense made a gallant attempt at undoing the damag
that had been done by the prosecution's cross-examination o
the defense witness. His witness, under questioning by him
said that all of the psychological testing he had done on Cha
Higgs had not confirmed a diagnosis of sociopath or antiso
cial personality disorder. Going point by point through nearl
everything that Barb had questioned Nielsen about, Housto
called Barb's conclusions "half-baked truths" that had bee
chosen for the purpose of isolating certain facts "to mak
those facts stand for something out of context."

However, Barb's attempts at turning the defense witnes
to the prosecution's benefit had been skillful, and it woul
be difficult to erase the doubt that he had instilled in eac
juror's mind during the process.

Chapter 35

Chaz Higgs was scheduled as the defense's last witness, whereby he planned to testify in his own defense. Before allowing him to do so, however, Judge Kosach wanted to make sure that Chaz understood that he had the "absolute right" to testify in the case, and that if he did so, he would be cross-examined.

"And I will say vigorously cross-examined," Kosach added. "Do you understand that?"

"Yes, Your Honor," Chaz replied.

"Now you have the absolute right to not testify in this case," Kosach said. "Do you understand that?"

"Yes, Your Honor."

In his efforts to be fair, as well as prudent, Kosach also explained to Chaz that if he decided to not testify, the jury would be instructed to not form any adverse opinion about him because he did not testify. He also wanted to be certain that Chaz had consulted with his attorneys with regard to testifying.

When Higgs took the stand, Houston asked him why he had changed his name from William Charles Higgs to Chaz

Higgs. He responded that he had changed his name because there were four people named William Higgs in his family, and it had created a lot of problems over the years.

"So I dropped my first name, since everyone went by first and last name, and I shortened my middle name," he said.

In taking him through some of his past history, Houston enabled the jury to hear why Chaz, in his own words, had joined the U.S. Navy and that he chose the medical field because "I love helping people, and that was an avenue for me to be able to do that." He also testified that he had broken his arm during SEAL training, and that was why he had been unable to finish the program. He remained attached to the SEAL unit, however, as a medic for ten months.

Houston pointed out that Chaz had served in the Middle East, stationed in Bahrain in the Persian Gulf, an area that was designated a war zone. He had helped with the people injured in the June 25, 1996, terrorist attack of the Khobar Towers in Dhahran, Saudi Arabia.

"When you respond to an emergent situation or assist with a situation of emergency, Mr. Higgs, how do you personally react to that?"

"I have to—I have to focus," Chaz said. "I have to focus. And, I mean, I was trained to focus because you're ineffective, you can't function if you have all this chaos going on and you just lose it. So I have to focus on what I need to get done."

"Are you trying to explain to the jury why perhaps some of the folks that saw you the morning of July eighth might have misunderstood what they saw?"

"Yes. Exactly."

During his testimony, Chaz told about how he had decided to go to nursing school after leaving the navy and how, upon graduation from nursing school and passing the board exams, he had gone to work at Sunrise Hospital in

Las Vegas, where he met Kathy Augustine. He described his emotional involvement with Kathy at the beginning of their relationship. He explained how she had taken him out for coffee after forgetting to give him a thank-you card for the care that he had provided for her husband, Charles.

"It was almost instantaneous," Chaz testified. "I mean, we went out and—I guess the best way to describe it is, you know when you meet somebody you just feel—you feel chemistry. And that's what we had. We started talking while we were having coffee, and we just hit it off. We didn't talk about politics or nursing. We just talked about life. . . ."

At one point, Chaz provided details about how John Snow, who was Secretary of the Treasury in Washington, D.C., at the time, had invited Kathy to interview for the position of the next U.S. treasurer. After being told by Snow that she had the position, she had said that she could be back in D.C. within two weeks, according to Chaz. However, when they returned to Reno, the allegations that eventually led to her impeachment were being prepared by the state's attorney general's office, and an investigation was begun. He said that it hadn't taken long for word of the investigation to reach Washington, D.C., and they promptly told her that "we don't need you anymore" and that they were going to go in a different direction. Chaz said that the decision had devastated her, and had impacted her mood and her ability to communicate with him.

"Before that, she had been really loving and just open," Chaz said. "Like I said, we had this little world we had created, and it was fantastic. Then after that started, it was like she just closed off. She became very defensive. For obvious reasons. Very angry. And just, you know, trying to protect herself from all this."

He testified that he did not like politics and was not comfortable being in the political arena. Even though he had eventually told her that he couldn't take it anymore and was going to leave her, she repeatedly had asked him to stay to help her through the tough times of the impeachment, and he had done so. He hadn't abandoned her in the face of adversity. However, when he learned that she was planning to run for state treasurer, he decided that he'd had enough—that had been the straw that broke the camel's back.

After her impeachment trial and censure, he said, Kathy's career "had pretty much been decimated." Nonetheless, she kept trying to fix things to get her political life back on track, and in 2005, they had started going to political functions again.

"And it was sad," Chaz said, "because . . . nobody wanted to touch her now. She was damaged goods. We'd go to political functions, sit down at a table, and people would leave. People would get up from where we were sitting and just leave. . . . Every time we went to one of these things, we'd get back in the car and she'd be crying, she'd be hurt. She'd say, 'Oh, my God, I can't believe this is happening to me.' It was just sad."

Watching his wife's political life being destroyed had been devastating for him as well, Chaz said.

"I was a mess. . . . This was a woman I cared about . . . ," Chaz said. "I was stressed-out. I couldn't sleep. I was losing weight. I lost forty-five pounds in 2005 over this. . . ."

Even though he had wanted a divorce by this time, Chaz said, he was ashamed over the e-mails between himself and Linda Ramirez, and even though he was telling the jury how much he had loved Kathy, he explained that his mean comments about Kathy to Linda had been his way of venting his anger over the way that Kathy had been treating him and her refusal to leave politics, like she had previously promised she would.

"When it came time for you to make a decision on how

end the relationship with Kathy," Houston asked, "what
were you going to do as far as finalizing everything? How
re you going to end it?"

"I was going to divorce her."

"Did you plan to kill her?"

"No. No."

"You've been divorced before, haven't you, sir?"

"I have. Three times."

"Did you ever feel the need to kill any other wife?"

"No."

"Was there anything going on in this relationship with
Kathy that led you to the point of frustration or such extreme anger that you would have to murder her?"

"Never. Never. I never got to that point."

Houston turned the questioning toward Kathy's will, and
Chaz said that he had been aware of it. He had been aware of
the fact that many people had referred to him as "arm candy"
for Kathy, and he had encouraged her to make a will or a
trust and to list as a beneficiary anybody she wanted. Houston showed him the will, which had been marked as Exhibit
41, in which Kathy had left everything to her daughter,
Dallas. He said that he was never in the relationship with
Kathy for the money. What had kept him in the relationship,
he said, was what they'd had in the beginning because he
kept hoping that they would get that magic back.

Chaz said that he had made the decision to leave Kathy
in 2006 after she had made the decision to run for state
treasurer. He said that he had told her: "Kathy, I'm done.
I can't do this again. . . . I am really done this time." He
said that he had consulted a lawyer to draw up papers for
an uncontested divorce, began looking for an apartment
and had found one, and had opened his own bank account.

He said that he began to become concerned about her
health because he had been aware of the mitral valve

prolapse condition that she had. He said that he had urged her to see a cardiologist, and she always told him that she was taking care of it. Sometimes they'd go for walks together to try and work off the stress levels, but it became more difficult for her over time. She would get more tired, he said, and short of breath. She couldn't sleep, either, he said. He explained that she had tried to keep her health concerns to herself because she worried that the public might find out about her weaknesses, and was concerned that political opponents might take her health condition and use it against her. That was, after all, politics, he said.

In response to questions about fellow nurse Kim Ramey and what she said to the police, and subsequently had testified to, Chaz said that he hadn't remembered things the way she had portrayed them. He acknowledged having been in a somewhat heated telephone call with Kathy, but denied saying, "We'll talk when I fucking get home tonight," because he said that he would not have used the word "fucking" in another person's presence at work. It would have been unprofessional, he said. Instead, he charged that Ramey had been eavesdropping on him while he talked to Kathy. When Ramey had brought up the Darren Mack case, he said that he did not remember saying, "He did it all wrong. He should have just hit her with succs." He said that there were several things that he did not remember talking to Ramey about that day because he wasn't really paying attention to her. He said that he had been put off by the fact that she had just jumped into his conversation with Kathy. He also said that although he knew what the drug succinylcholine was, he hadn't known until this case that it could not be easily detected postmortem.

Chapter 36

The next morning, Tuesday, June 26, 2007, when prosecutor Tom Barb was supposed to begin his cross-examination of Chaz Higgs, Judge Steven Kosach suspended the trial for one day after it had been announced that Chaz had made another suicide attempt. According to the information that was being released, Chaz had been found with his wrists slit earlier that morning inside a Reno apartment that he had been sharing with his mother while he was out on bail. Kosach revoked Chaz's bail and ordered both sides to return to court the next day. Although Kosach had not declared a mistrial, he said that he would not rule out the possibility if it appeared that the defendant's recovery turned out to be lengthy. Higgs's attorney David Houston told the court, as well as reporters, that Chaz's injuries did not appear life-threatening.

According to published reports of the 911 call made by Higgs's mother, Chaz had used a knife to slash his wrists in the bathroom of the apartment they shared. She had found him on the floor, and the knife was in the sink. He had been taken to the Renown hospital, in Reno.

According to Houston, Chaz's latest suicide attempt hadn't been motivated by fear of cross-examination by the prosecution—instead, it had been because it had been difficult for him to relive his wife's death on the witness stand on Monday.

"His goal was to clear his name and then to join his wife," Houston said. "He felt he cleared his name yesterday."

The trial didn't resume until Thursday, June 28, 2007 when Chaz returned to the witness stand, wrists bandaged for his cross-examination from Barb. Barb asked him shortly after beginning if he understood that people might think his recent suicide attempt might been an effort to gain sympathy. He said that he understood, but that it didn't matter.

Early in his questioning, Barb pointed out to Chaz that his e-mailing hadn't been limited to Linda Ramirez and others that had previously been talked about. He showed Chaz, and the jury, a profile of Chaz's from an Internet Web site called Passion.com, an online chatting and dating service.

"Do you recall what your profile was?" Barb asked.

"I don't recall off the top of my head," Chaz responded.

Barb approached the witness, and asked Chaz to read his profile to the jury. He read the following:

"I would love to talk to you. I am a happy, healthy, forty-two-year-old male who likes to have fun doing almost anything. Laugh a lot and just enjoy life. Most say I look like I am [in] my late twenties. Blond-brown hair, blue eyes, very athletic, and an RN with a very good bedside manner in and out of bed. I am currently single, unattached, looking for fun or whatever else. And I am very good to whoever I am with. Their needs are very important. I am intelligent, mature and well traveled.

"As far as sex is concerned," he continued reading, *"I like*

to please my woman. I like to see her happy. I love giving oral sex. I love to do just about anything you can think of as far as sex. I have tried a lot and will try more. I am open to new ideas and completely adventurous."

"Now, you didn't mention in there how much you loved Kathy," Barb said. "Is there a reason?"

"Sir, at that time, I was in a fog. I was reaching out for somebody."

"When was this?"

"I don't remember, sir. It was after her death, sir."

"How do you know you were in a fog at that time?"

"I can't say I remember a lot of what was going on at that time."

"For the whole past year."

"A lot of the first few months."

"So you were in a fog, but every time you . . . come out of this fog, you remember you loved Kathy? Is that it?"

Barb was brutal in bringing out certain aspects of Chaz's character. He mentioned other e-mails that Chaz had sent shortly after Kathy's death. Some were to female nurses that he had also asked to run away with him. Barb asked him to read a couple of them to the jury. The first one that he had Higgs read was dated September 3, 2006, almost two months after Kathy died:

"Noodle, how are you—where are you?" Chaz read. *"If you are in Myrtle Beach, I'm only two hours away from you at the present. I am in North Carolina now.*

"And how about getting hitched, I think you should run away with me. What do you think? Sounds good to me. I will keep you in a manner to which you are used to. All right. At least run away with me for a little while. If it does not work, you can go back. Or if at any time you get hitched and it does not work, just remember I will always be there to run away with.

"Oh, by the way, did I tell you that I am single now . . . ? I think that you are totally hot, sexy, smart, nice, cool, caring. And did I say hot . . . ? I wish you the best. But if you change your mind I will be here. Keep in touch. I miss you.'

"You didn't mention . . . that your wife died," Barb said. "You just said, 'Oh, by the way, I'm single again.'"

"Yes, sir."

"Is that your idea of displaying love for Kathy?"

"No, sir."

The second e-mail that Barb asked Chaz to read was dated August 27, 2006, and it had been sent to a nurse that Chaz said he'd gone to school with:

"Oceanside is cool," Chaz read. *"I will only be less than an hour from there. . . . I love the video. I hope you do not mind me saying that you are hotter than you were before. Send some more. How about with a little less clothing on? You are damn beautiful. I look forward to seeing you. I did not want to leave North Carolina when I did because I wanted to spend more time with you. I was truly sad. You are a fantastic woman. I just think that you are with the wrong man. But we all do that, don't we? That's life. But just know that I am here for you."*

"'But we all do that, don't we?'" Barb repeated. "Isn't that your attempt to say, 'I was with the wrong woman'?"

"No, sir."

Much of Barb's cross-examination consisted of rehashing previous testimony of a number of witnesses by putting his own prosecutorial spin on things. Taken out of context or not, it was clear that it was having his desired effect on the jury. At one point, Barb zeroed in on the fact that Chaz had been assigned the duty of being a charge nurse during the course of his employment at South Meadows, and he, likewise, of course, reminded Chaz of testimony in which Marlene Swanbeck had said that the charge nurse could get inside the

:frigerator where the drugs were kept on a regular basis and
ould remove anything in the refrigerator without necessar-
y creating a record. Barb pointed out that Chaz could have
een a charge nurse as many as fifty times or more during
is employment, with the insinuation being that he would
ave had many opportunities to remove whatever drugs he
ked from the drug refrigerator.

After each side had rested its case, closing arguments
ook up much of the afternoon before the case was handed
ff to the jury to begin deliberating. The jury worked into
he night with their deliberations, but adjourned at about
en o'clock. They resumed their effort the following morn-
ng, Friday, June 29, 2007, at nine. Three hours later, the
our men and eight women returned and announced that
hey had reached a verdict: they had found Chaz Higgs
uilty of first-degree murder in the death of his wife,
Kathy Augustine.

Chaz stood at the defense table as the verdict was read.
His hands were clasped in front of him and he stared at the
loor. In keeping with his calm demeanor, he had shown
o emotion when the judge read the jury's verdict. Several
nembers of Kathy's family clapped their hands together
nce, but otherwise said nothing.

That afternoon, in what could almost be viewed as a
lam-dunk style of adjudication by those who regularly
ollow murder trials, the penalty hearing began. The jury
was told that they could sentence Chaz to life in prison
with no possibility of parole, life in prison with the possi-
ility of parole after serving twenty years, or to fifty years
n prison with a minimum sentence of twenty years.

Dr. Pamela Russell, an anesthesiologist, was called ; the first witness. She explained the characteristics of th drug succinylcholine, as well as its horrible and terrifyir effects if given to a person without a mechanism to assi him with his breathing.

The next witness was Dallas Augustine, Kathy's daugl ter. Christopher Hicks asked her to explain for the jury th impact that her mother's death had had on her life.

"First of all, to Chaz," Dallas said. "I just want to sa that I pity you. And after hearing your indifference towar my mother's suffering, I understand you could never kno what it's like to be a human being.

"My mother was the most influential person in m family," she continued. "She wasn't perfect, but sh worked very hard to truly make something special of he life. She could be here right now. And you in the span of morning took away not only her life, but everything I kne as family. She was my only family.

"Now, after a year of hell, I will finally be able to mov on with my life. And I hope you will spend the rest c yours in a cell. I miss her every day and will miss her th rest of my life. Nothing will ever take away the pain, but can find some solace in the fact that you will pay."

The state's next witness was Kathy's brother Ph Alfano. Hicks asked him the same question that he ha asked Dallas: "Sir, could you please explain the impac that this death has had on your life, and your family's life to the jury?"

"Well, I don't know where to begin," Phil Alfano saic "I've known two emotions for the past year, anger an sorrow, because of that man sitting right over there, Cha Higgs.

"When Kathy introduced Chaz to us," he continued "she talked about how he had swept her off her feet, hov he had been there for her and comforting her when her husband Chuck was dying. She referred to him as her angel. Fact is, he's an angel of death.

"You heard how Kathy suffered. We've lived with that memory every single day for the past year. It will be forever scarring our memories of our sister.

"His bogus suicide attempt robbed us of the opportunity to bury her in a dignified manner. I can think of no other individual more deserving of the maximum penalty in this case than Chaz Higgs. He took away my sister. He robbed my daughters of an aunt that they loved. And worst of all, my parents lost their first child and their only daughter. And I've seen this tear them apart for the past year. Words cannot express my feelings."

The state's final witness was Kay Alfano, Kathy's mother.

"Ma'am, what's your relationship to Kathy Augustine?" Hicks asked.

"Kathy was our firstborn and our daughter," she replied.

"Could you please explain the impact her death has had on you, and your family, to the jury?"

"It has been devastating," she said. "Chaz, you don't know, to take the life of another human being is just unheard of. But the way it has affected the whole family, friends, relatives, schoolmates that she went to elementary school with, high school, college, when she went after her master's, professors, her airline people that were her bosses—they called, they sent cards. They're all devastated.

"All you've heard from the defense over there is—'Oh, she was political and she was a terrible wife, and she was this and she was that.'

"She raised money for I don't know how many organizations. She—yes, she was political, but she was a wonderful human being. . . . She was very caring. She cared about everybody. She was always there to help. She never forgot anybody's birthday. If somebody needed something, she was there . . . for them. She'd drop everything.

"And I just also want to say I feel sorry for Chaz's mother and father and stepparents because what he has done to them is devastating, too.

"I—I hope he spends the rest of his natural life in prison. That's actually too good for him. He took our daughter. And to do that to another human being . . . If you had walked into the hospital room and saw her when we did—if you've got any compassion at all, you—you can't do that to a human being. She was just completely paralyzed. Her eyes wide open. Couldn't move, but she could hear. And as I said, life in prison is too good for him."

Tina Carbone testified for the defense during the penalty hearing and told the jury that Chaz Higgs was a good nurse, that patients liked him, and that he possessed a strong knowledge base of what was needed for emergency room patients. He had not had any human resources issues regarding his nursing abilities, and that during the course of his employment, he had saved lives.

The defense team also called Chaz's mother, Shirley Higgs, to testify during the penalty hearing. She described Chaz as having been a good kid who was very close to his brother. Neither of them ever got into any trouble. Chaz had been involved in sports, and had participated in the Cub Scouts and Little League baseball. Overall, she said, Chaz, as well as his brother, were just good kids who were well disciplined. She appealed to the jury to sentence Chaz to life in prison with the possibility of parole.

"Every person is entitled to hope," she said. "And I would like my son to have that hope while he's in prison."

Chaz's father, William "Bill" Higgs, in similar fashion, said that Chaz had been a good kid with no prior criminal record. Like Chaz's mother, he pleaded for the jury to sentence Chaz to prison with the possibility of parole. He also apologized to Kathy Augustine's family for what had happened, and said that he would say a rosary for her next time he went to mass.

Final arguments of the penalty phase were heard next, with coprosecutor Christopher Hicks summing up first.

"Ladies and gentlemen," Hicks said, "as I am sure you're feeling right now, this is an incredibly difficult phase of the proceeding. We have to hear the terrible things . . . how this has affected the Augustine and Alfano family, and also Mr. Higgs's family. And, sincerely, the state feels for both of them. It's a horrible situation. But we're all here, they're all here. Everybody who is suffering in this room is suffering because of this man, what he did.

"I want you all to understand right now the state is asking for the maximum penalty, life without the possibility of parole," Hicks continued. "It is the harshest penalty you can assess today. But that is precisely what this man deserves. Nothing else.

"What you're going to have to ask yourself when you go back to deliberate is—is this a person who deserves an opportunity to live in our society again someday? He is not that person. Does a person who would kill his wife because he hated her, because he wanted to go out and chase other women, does that person deserve to ever live in our society again?

"Does a person who will subject another human being to the type of death that was described to you by Dr. Russell . . . deserve to ever be in our society again? That death as explained, that scenario, is pure terror. You are paralyzed and yet you're totally awake. For six to ten minutes you lie there not being able to breathe. Mr. Higgs was there. He saw this happen. I wonder what he said to her . . . and then he has the audacity to come here under oath and swear to you that he loved her. That is not a man who ever deserves to be in our society again.

"Does a man who would call a grieving mother a day before her daughter's funeral and call her daughter two of the most offensive names for women deserve to ever be in our society again? No. And that man is Chaz Higgs. That is who he is. If a penalty ever fit a person, life in prison without the possibility of parole fits Chaz Higgs. He earned that. Give it to him."

Alan Baum, in his summation for the penalty hearing, told the jury that he would not plead for mercy for Chaz Higgs.

"I don't think anyone in this courtroom thinks that Chaz Higgs will live out whatever sentence you decide," Baum said, "whether it be by age or other circumstances. So what I'm asking you is to make a gesture of compassion, not for Chaz Higgs, but for his family. And that is no insult to the Augustine family, I hope. And I don't think that they would consider it such, because I know they also share the pain of the parents of Chaz Higgs.

"So I am not asking for compassion or leniency on behalf of Chaz Higgs. I'm asking for compassion and leniency for his parents. Whatever years they have left on earth should be lived with the hope in their heart that even after they're gone, their son may at some day be free. I think that they have one more tragedy to endure before they pass, and I think that tragedy will be seeing the death of their son. But let them have the remaining years they have with hope in their hearts, not for Chaz Higgs, but for them, please. Thank you."

The jury, having been charged with its duty and obligation to determine the sentencing for Chaz Higgs, was released to the custody of the bailiff so that they could begin their deliberations. The jury returned a short time later and announced that they had reached a verdict in the penalty phase, and Judge Kosach instructed the clerk to read it:

"We, the jury in the above-entitled action, having found the defendant, Chaz Higgs, guilty of murder in the first-degree, set the penalty to be imposed at life with the possibility of parole beginning when a minimum of twenty years has been served."

Neither the prosecution nor the defense cared to poll the jury, after which Judge Kosach confirmed the sentence. Chaz Higgs had nothing to say, and was taken from the courtroom to begin serving his sentence in the Nevada state prison system. An appeal likely will be filed in the case.

MORE SHOCKING TRUE CRIME
FROM PINNACLE